Richard III's Bodies from
Medieval England to Modernity

Jeffrey R. Wilson

RICHARD III'S BODIES
from Medieval England to Modernity

Shakespeare and Disability History

TEMPLE UNIVERSITY PRESS
Philadelphia • Rome • Tokyo

TEMPLE UNIVERSITY PRESS
Philadelphia, Pennsylvania 19122
tupress.temple.edu

Copyright © 2022 by Temple University—Of The Commonwealth System
   of Higher Education
All rights reserved
Published 2022

Library of Congress Cataloging-in-Publication Data

Names: Wilson, Jeffrey R. (Jeffrey Robert), 1982– author.
Title: Richard III's bodies from medieval England to modernity : Shakespeare
   and disability history / Jeffrey R. Wilson.
Description: Philadelphia : Temple University Press, 2022. | Includes
   bibliographical references and index. |
Identifiers: LCCN 2022006747 (print) | LCCN 2022006748 (ebook) | ISBN
   9781439922682 (pdf) | ISBN 9781439922668 (cloth) | ISBN 9781439922675
   (paperback)
Subjects: LCSH: Shakespeare, William, 1564–1616. King Richard III. |
   Shakespeare, William, 1564–1616—Characters—Richard III. | Disabilities
   in the theater. | Abnormalities, Human, in literature. | Stigma (Social
   psychology) in literature. | Sociology of disability—History.
Classification: LCC PR2821 (ebook) | LCC PR2821 .W57 2022 (print) | DDC
   822.3/3 23/eng/20220—dc25
LC record available at https://lccn.loc.gov/2022006747
LC ebook record available at https://lccn.loc.gov/2022006748

Printed in the United States of America

9 8 7 6 5 4 3 2 1

For Liam

Contents

	Acknowledgments	ix
	Introduction	1
1	Stigmatizing Richard III's Disability up to Shakespeare: The Figural Paradigm	25
2	The Models of Stigma in Shakespeare's First Tetralogy: Spirituality, Psychology, Sociology	49
3	The Reality of Physiognomy in *Richard III*	71
4	The Unnatural Age of Margaret: Antiquating the Spiritual Model of Stigma in *Richard III*	97
5	Richard III's Disability after Shakespeare: Discovering the Causal Paradigm	107
6	Richard III's Disability in Modern Performance: The Changing Bodies of Character and Actor	145
	Conclusion: The Anthropology of Audience: Historical Presentism in Shakespeare Studies	193
	Notes	209
	Index	249

Acknowledgments

Shakespeare's *Richard III* was written and revised over several years early in the author's career as he matured, finalized while theaters were closed during an epidemic. The same is true of this book, which—like Shakespeare's play—tells a complex story that clearly exceeds the author's capacity. My interest in Richard III began at the University of California, Irvine, in 2006 during a small-group study of Shakespeare led by Julia Reinhard Lupton, whose support and guidance kept this project going through several iterations. Also there were Robin Stewart, Sam Arkin, and Matt Seybold, who helped shape the argument at its inception. An independent study with Steven Mailloux provided a methodology. Victoria Silver was a steadfast mentor, reading, responding to, and challenging the many forms this argument has taken. At Irvine, Rebeca Helfer, Richard Kroll, Ian Munro, and Douglas Pfeiffer provided guidance on this argument and the larger project to which it belongs, *Stigma in Shakespeare*. Parts of *Richard III's Bodies* have been presented to audiences at Boston University (2010); San Diego State University (2010); the Rocky Mountain Modern Language Association (MLA) Convention (2010); the South Central Society for Eighteenth-Century Studies Conference (2010); the Pacific Ancient and Modern Language Association Conference (2011); UC Irvine (2011); the Renaissance Society of America Conference (2013); Harvard University (2014); the Moses Greeley Parker Lecture Series in Lowell, Massachusetts (2017); Lowell High School (2017); the MLA Annual Convention (2018); and the British Shakespeare Association (2018). I'm grateful to organizers, audiences, and interlocutors at these events for conversations and comments. I am also grateful to Sibylle Baumbach, Stanley Fish, Philippa Langley, and Philip Schwyzer for commenting on individual chapters from afar. As the project developed and was revised more times than I can count, it benefited from insights from Kendra Boileau, Sara Cohen, Mark Dudgeon, James Elliott, Marina Gerzić, Peter C. Herman, Michelle Houston, Bellee Jones-Pierce, Andy Kesson, Kathryn Vomero Santos, Emanuel Stelzer, Rebecca Totaro, Shaina Trapedo, Gerritt Vandermeer, Jackie Way, and Jim Zeigler, among many others. Pat Belanca, Karen Heath, and Tom Jehn provided opportunities to teach *Richard III*, and I learned a lot from students in our *Why Shakespeare?* course at Harvard University. The team at Temple University Press—Ann-Marie Anderson, Karen Baker, Aaron Javsicas, Gary Kramer, Irene Imperio Kull, Kate Nichols, Ashley Petrucci, Heather Wilcox, and especially Shaun Vigil—has been so warm and helpful. Thank you to the Harvard College Writing Program for help purchasing image permissions and to organizations that make images freely available for scholarly projects, such as the Folger Shakespeare Library and Houghton Library at Harvard University. My deepest thanks are to my wife, Allison Dolan-Wilson, who has had more conversations about Richard III than is fair to ask of anyone who isn't an early-modern scholar; to the Wilson family; to the Dolan family; and to our children, Liam and Queen Margaret, who have perplexed and intensified my understanding of human relationships in a way that has dramatically altered this project. The book is dedicated to Liam, one firstborn for another.

Richard III's Bodies from Medieval England to Modernity

Introduction

Shakespeare's *Richard III* was the first text to describe Richard as "hunch-backed," also the first instance of that word in English.[1] Earlier writers had addressed Richard's physical disability, but Shakespeare was the first to make him into an almost inhuman monster. The "hunch" belongs to Shakespeare more than Richard. But "hunch-backed" wasn't Shakespeare's word. It was a misprint in the second quarto of *Richard III* for Shakespeare's "bunch-backed," the common early-modern word in the first quarto and first folio.[2] The "hunch" belongs to us, not Shakespeare—his audience, not the author. It's our "hunch" that we see as his, interpretation incorporated into text, indicating the swirl of objective reality and subjective response that always attends Richard III's body.

This book shows Richard's disability traveling through time into and away from Shakespeare's hands, on down to today. While mired in details of medieval English history, *Richard III* and its configuration of disability, villainy, and tragedy still speak to us in the twenty-first century with a surprising urgency. "Foremost among the standard-bearers of Disability Studies is Shakespeare's Richard III," as Tobin Siebers noted just before his death in 2015.[3] Richard's body was international front-page news in 2012 when his skeleton was discovered.[4] He's in that echelon of Shakespearean characters—Shylock, Falstaff, Hamlet, Othello, Caliban—who have entire books written about them.[5] The four greatest Shakespearean actors of the past four centuries—Richard Burbage, David Garrick, Edmund Kean, Laurence

Olivier—all played Richard before Hamlet. The first Shakespeare play professionally staged in America? *Richard III*, in 1749.[6] The first play performed by an African American acting company? *Richard III*, in 1821.[7] Documentaries are made about the challenge and importance of *Richard III*.[8] It was Shakespeare's second-most popular play in quarto and the most performed history play in both the eighteenth and twenty-first centuries.[9] It inspired the recent Netflix hit *House of Cards* and drew comparisons to the rise of Donald Trump in the United States.[10]

James Siemon, a recent editor, says that *Richard III* is Janus-faced, pointing from the early-modern age back to its medieval past but also forward to a modern future, "socially topical both to Shakespeare's London, and, paradoxically, to subsequent social formations even today."[11] Katherine Schaap Williams similarly notes "Richard's double-facing presence in the narrative of disability theory," the character cited as evidence both for and against the presence of "disability" in the early-modern age.[12] Thus, both literary scholars looking at the play and disability scholars looking at the character sense a multi-temporality. How is Richard III always so historical and so current? Why are issues related to medieval disability so relevant to modern life? Why is Shakespeare's play so persistent? Why do we care so much about Richard III? What is the *significance* of his body—not only its *meaning* in Shakespeare's text (what it signifies) but also its *importance* as a cultural touchstone in England and beyond (why it is significant)?

This book connects the question about textual meaning to the one about cultural importance. I argue that Shakespeare's ironic representation of Richard's disability—which destabilizes meaning by dramatizing different meanings being made, deferring meaning to different audiences interpreting disability from different perspectives—creates a flexible conceptual space with a huge gravitational pull: some of our most consequential theories of modern aesthetics, theology, philosophy, ethics, psychology, sociology, historiography, science, medicine, and politics have been brought into attempts to understand Richard's body. In a quintessentially Shakespearean exchange, the playwright's dramatic mode, both tragic and ironic, calls upon some of life's biggest questions (because it is tragic) but defers answers to the audience (because it is ironic), leaving Richard's body open to interpretation in different ages embracing different attitudes toward stigma. The changing meaning of disability repeatedly recontextualized through shifting perspectives and circumstances in Shakespeare's first tetralogy has thus prompted and sustained more than four hundred years of changing interpretations of Richard, his body, his behavior, and his status as either the villain or the victim of Tudor history. Shakespeare's irony makes possible a cultural study using Richard's disability to tell the story of our encounter with tragedy in modernity. The conclusion to this book theorizes this multi-century story into a new approach to Shakespearean phenomena widely interpreted, debated, and adapted in modern culture, called the "anthropology of audience," which marries the historicism and presentism currently at odds in Shakespeare studies.

I. Disability, Monstrosity, and Meaning

Most start by interpreting Richard with their eyes. His body shows what we've been trained to see. Yet so much interpretation is already at work in him. The actor has decided how to embody the character. The director has amended the text. The editor has glossed Richard's opening soliloquy. The scholar has considered centuries of interpretation. Our first encounter with Richard's body is less about what we *think* than what we *perceive* based on what is shown to us. History does not display changing interpretations of Richard's body as much as it shows different bodies built by different historically situated people and placed in different dramatic contexts that create different meanings. So fundamentally visual, Richard's body is now an opportunity for what Alice Wong calls "disability visibility"—"creating, sharing, and amplifying disability media and culture"—in history.[13]

Everyone at the Elizabethan theater must've known when Richard (Burbage) first appeared on stage—*dressed how? walking how? "deformed" how?*—that his body called for interpretation. Disabled, alone, framed by the stage, on display, emblematic, Richard's first appearance invokes the posters announcing "monstrous" births in Elizabethan England—one term they used for physical disability.[14] There are usually four parts: a title advertising something as true and mysterious; a visual representation, not unlike a Shakespearean performance; a prose description of the facts, akin to Shakespeare's text; and a poetic interpretation of meaning, what audiences do when making sense of Shakespeare (see Figure I.1). Something is "monstrous, monstrous," according to two characters in *Richard III*, "when men are unprepared and look not for it" (3.2.62–63). From the Latin *monere*, "to warn," and *monstrare*, "to show," monstrosity is unexpected, difficult to classify, hyper-significant, and always a warning.[15] As Anna Dunthorne writes, "Monster literature was part of a culture of reading and looking."[16] Monstrosity activates hermeneutics—reflection on interpretation. The stakes were always high, Alan W. Bates explains: "The early modern reader was concerned not simply with the occurrence of monstrous births but with their significance, in how they fitted

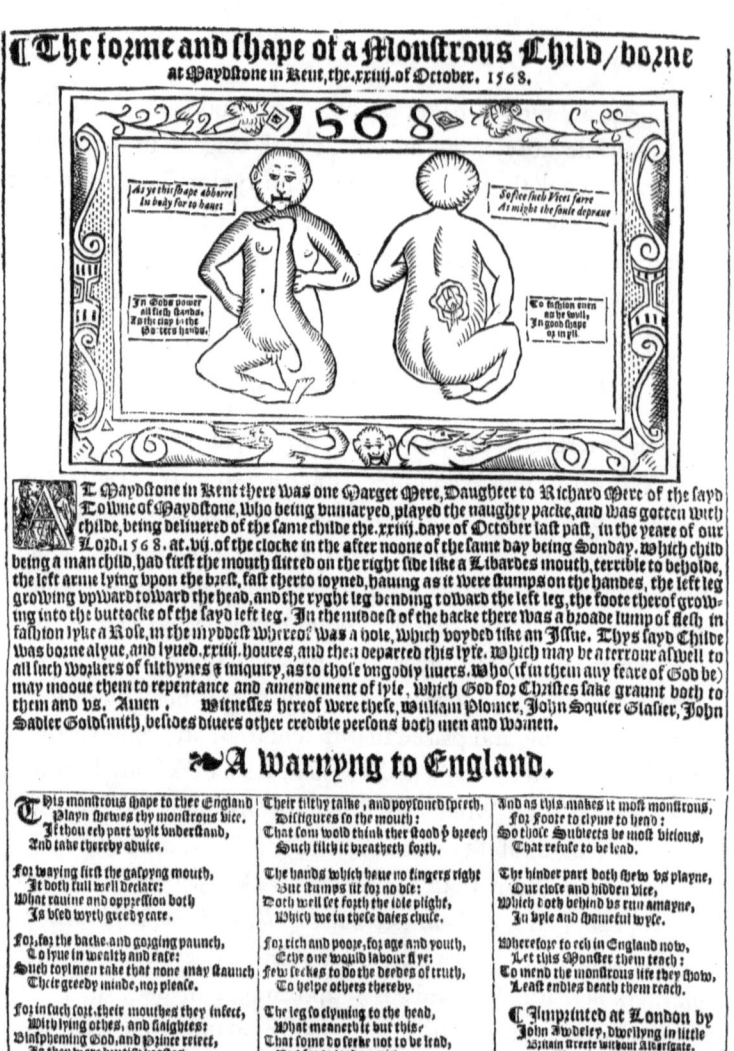

FIGURE I.1 *The Forme and Shape of a Monstrous Child*, Borne at Maydstone in Kent (London: John Awdeley, 1568). Image from Early English Books Online.

into the world."[17] Interpreting monstrosity revealed one's worldview, its assumptions and commitments—theological, scientific, philosophical, ethical. Monstrosity signals the need for interpretation and, to quote Lindsey Row-Heyveld, "disability in early modern England invited epistemological crisis."[18]

While "Renaissance writers frequently used monstrosity to imagine what we now call disability," Elizabeth B. Bearden cautions that the two discourses are not the same—"overlapping, but not coterminous," in the judgment of

Richard H. Godden and Asa Simon Mittman.[19] Monstrosity shows a culture looking at an individual; disability prioritizes the individual's experience with their body and cultural attitudes about it. As both man and myth—a disabled person of medieval England whose life as king was extensively recorded before, a century later, he was made into a monster by his nation's most important artist—Richard III will always be central to English disability history.

The play *Richard III* is no less "monstrous" than its title character. Both thematize the unexpected, the need for interpretation, multiple layers of meaning. The text revels in its own monstrosity from its opening lines. "Now is the winter of our discontent," Richard says (1.1.1), establishing discontent as England's current condition. But once our eyes scan down to the next line, or after a pause by the actor playing Richard, we learn that this winter is "Made glorious summer by this son of York" (1.1.2). Anticipating what David Houston Wood calls "the play's entwined representation of time, narrative, and disability," this elliptical opening needs an approach that experiences literature *in time*.[20] Consider the kind theorized by Stanley Fish as "reader response," which, though now out of fashion, is the origin of the audience-oriented approach to Shakespeare developed in this book, called the "anthropology of audience." Reader-response criticism works well for drama because performance moves at the speed of life: "The basis of the method is a consideration of the *temporal* flow of the reading experience, and it is assumed that the reader responds in terms of that flow and not to the whole utterance."[21] As we read or see a play, understanding is continually formed and reformed as additional information modifies the earlier sense of things, whether on the level of sentence or text as a whole. The first line of *Richard III* would have "is" be the intransitive main verb of the sentence, equating the subject ("now") and predicate ("winter"): "Now *is* the winter of our discontent." But the second line reveals that "is" is actually an auxiliary verb in the passive construction "is made," so the subject from the initial reading ("now") must be made into an adverb. Where we previously thought that "the winter of our discontent *is* now," we now understand that "the winter of our discontent is now *made* glorious summer." The climate in England is no longer winter; it's now summer. The current condition is not discontent; it's glory. With the opening of *Richard III*, Shakespeare pulled a Bill Clinton: "It depends upon what the meaning of the word 'is' is."[22]

That grammatical amorphousness is a warning of multiple meanings lurking in the play that follows. In the second line, it's the "son of York,"

Richard's brother, the newly crowned King Edward IV, who has shifted his family's fortunes, a pun on the "sun" that turns darkness to light, winter to summer. A pun is a mutation open to divination: "sun" means both "male child" and "shining star." And Richard says one thing but means another. He's claiming to have bid farewell to discontent; he hasn't. He's acutely disturbed, as he soon says. An amalgamation of multiple meanings, the second line of the play shows mutations that occur when translating words into ideas and considering meaning in context.

Richard's opening address has body imagery in fifteen of the next twenty-one lines. He inspects the "brows" of the Yorks (1.1.5) and their "bruisèd arms" (1.1.6), while Richard's lusty brother Edward now occupies "a lady's chamber" (1.1.12), where they enjoy the "pleasing of a lute" (1.1.13). I'm working toward a statement of the meaning of Richard's opening soliloquy—monstrosity calls for meaning-making—but let's start small with the meaning of "chamber" and "lute." Yes, "a room inside a building" and "a stringed instrument with a neck," but clearly "chamber" and "lute" signal sexual organs as well. Shakespeare used "chamber" and "lute" instead of anatomically explicit terms to offer audiences the not-unpleasant experience of making dirty little sense of the metaphors. These metaphors require an interpretive act, like monstrosity, and a statement of the meaning of "chamber" and "lute" must attend to that act of making sense.

I'm thinking about syntax ("is"), wordplay ("son"), and metaphor ("chamber" and "lute") in terms of monstrosity because Shakespeare made "deformity" the content that originates the dramatic action in *Richard III* and the form that organizes the language of the play. Richard's opening "descant on [his] own deformity" (1.1.27) begins with a series of ill-proportioned pentameter lines that resist any rhythm at all (try reading these lines without stumbling over your own breathlessness around the word "breathing"):

> But I, that am not shaped for sportive tricks,
> Nor made to court an amorous looking glass;
> I, that am rudely stamped and want love's majesty
> To strut before a wanton ambling nymph;
> I, that am curtailed of this fair proportion,
> Cheated of feature by dissembling nature,
> Deformed, unfinished, sent before my time
> Into this breathing world scarce half made up,
> And that so lamely and unfashionable
> That dogs bark at me as I halt by them (1.1.14–23)

In the final line, after the opening iamb ("That dogs"), the two trochees ("bark at me as") destroy any sense of rhythm, which is impossible to resume when the iambic meter returns in the final two feet ("I halt by them"). Richard's metrical feet "halt" like his actual feet. Deformity is both content and form: "deformed" might be two syllables, or three; "unfinished" two, or three, or four. Symbolizing ideas in language, Shakespeare raised monstrosity to the level of theme. The play runs everything through Richard's body via Shakespeare's obsessive imagery of deformity, even when not in reference to Richard. Not only the character Richard III but also the play *Richard III* is deformed: history told as tragedy, with chunks of comedy and romance. It's prodigiously long, with humps and bumps that fuse together disparate concepts—including a hero who is a villain—asking us to redefine our ideas of literary coherence and possibility. The play violates our expectations, calls for interpretation, and serves as a warning of dangerous things to come, epitomizing Bearden's argument that "experimental genres that diverge from neoclassical standards tend to make disabled figures central to their action."[23]

Encountering monstrosity always invites the same question: *What is the meaning?* Traditionally, *meaning* is understood as intent, as codified in "the intentionalist thesis": *a text means what its author intends it to mean*.[24] If so, what prodded Norman Rabkin to write *Shakespeare and the Problem of Meaning* in 1981? He worried that "a thesis about what the play means denies to Shakespeare's intention or the play's virtue what [it] actually *does* to us."[25] Rabkin articulated Shakespearean meaning in the exact terms of Fish's reader-response criticism: "What it *does* is what it *means*."[26] When we ask, *What does Richard's opening soliloquy mean?*, therefore, we must also ask, *What does it do?*

The intermingling of prologue and protagonist draws attention to the manifold orders of interpretation available in *Richard III*. Recognizing the audience and speaking directly to them acknowledges the theatrical event—thus, the inevitability of interpretation. Making the audience, not the author, the arbiter of meaning, *Richard III* is "predestined to contain the prolegomena of interpretation," said Walter Benjamin.[27] Imminent interpretation becoming a formal feature of the text changes the center of the dramatic event from the stage to the audience. Here, at last, is the meaning of Richard's opening address, understanding meaning as intent. Shakespeare intended not an idea but an experience—specifically, the pleasure of assuming the authority of interpretation conferred upon the audience at the start of this play. The text is monstrous because meaning resides in both the intent of the author and the experiences of its audiences. In every imaginable sense, authority is "deformed" in *Richard III*.

II. Disability, Tragedy, and Etiology

If the start of *Richard III* is a well-wrought monster, its prodigious head is the main clause of the long opening sentence, Richard's chilling "I am determinèd to prove a villain" (1.1.30). The meaning of Richard's entire address, arguably Shakespeare's entire play, hinges on this line—on who or what is the agent of determination. You might make God or nature or society the agent: *I was destined to be a villain.* Or you might make Richard himself the agent: *I have resolved to be a villain.* As Richard later gloats, in the second-most-important line of the play, he can "moralize two meanings in one word" (3.1.83). Richard "moraliz[ing]" meanings turns linguistic ambiguity into an ethical concern. The verbal phrase "I am determinèd" brings with it the imprecision inherent to the passive voice, giving audiences the responsibility of assigning grammatical agency, announcing a perennial problem of moral agency.

Entailed in this routine grammatical decision are competing modes of tragedy. Is the play governed by a fate that lords over the protagonist (*I was destined . . .*) or by the protagonist's desire for revenge (*I have resolved . . .*)? It would be reductive to say that Renaissance dramatists took the theme of fate from the Greeks and that of revenge from the Romans, but this formulation focuses the central concerns of the two classical traditions of tragedy. Are the bodies that pile up in *Richard III* the result of the title character's attempt to avoid his destiny (as symbolized by his body), or is he revenging the injustices committed against him (and his body) by nature and society? He may "moralize two meanings in one word," but Shakespeare upstaged Richard by moralizing two entire traditions of tragedy in the word "determinèd."

Shakespeare strung "I am determinèd" to the conditional "since I cannot prove a lover" (1.1.28), driving the core question of the play back to the cause of Richard's sexual frustration. Richard blames it on his body—in the words of another play published soon after *Richard III*, "Loue and deformitie cannot agree"[28]—but why would disability exclude one from the joys of love? By branding the most crucial question of the play onto Richard's body, Shakespeare created more problems than he solved: the play now requires a theory of disability. Our interpretation of the entire play follows from what we decide to do with Richard's body, which is why Shakespeare put it first. "Richard's body—and the various processes used to diagnose that body—always take center stage," Allison Hobgood observes.[29] And *Richard III* has remained central to modern culture because it presents the fragility of the human body as a starting point for reflection on the tragic—that in life which makes us sad—extending this consideration to a series of problems that cut to the core of modern thought, including the tension between appearance and reality, the conflict between individual will and external forces of nature and culture, the possibility of upward social mobility, and social interaction between self and other, including questions of stigma, discrimination, prejudice, hatred, oppression, power, and justice.

Encountering Richard's disability, audiences become literary detectives, seeking, like Polonius in *Hamlet*, to "find out the cause of this effect / Or rather say the cause of this defect, / For this effect defective comes by cause" (2.2.100–103). All Shakespearean tragedy asks audiences the same question. It's the question Benvolio asks about his cousin's melancholy at the start of *Romeo and Juliet*: "Do you know the cause?" (1.1.138). Shakespearean tragedy is fundamentally about etiology—the study of causes. It's about what determines the course of events, the circumstances that shape individuals and their decisions about meaning and action. And at the end of Shakespearean tragedy, audiences must say what one citizen says at the end of *Romeo and Juliet*: "We see the ground whereon these woes do lie, / But the true ground of all these piteous woes / We cannot without circumstance descry" (5.3.179–181). An ironic drama like Shakespeare's, moralizing many meanings at once, authorizing none, invites an audience to supply the "ground[s]" of interpretation, which are contingent upon the "circumstance[s]" of a given audience, predicated on its situation in time. Like its title character, the play *Richard III* is "unfinished" because its words only acquire meaning when placed in time. Like Richard, this play was "sent before [its] time . . . scarce half made up" because meaning, although it ought to reside in the author's intent and thus be stable, is flexible and does not come into existence until after the text enters the world. The notion of meaning based on authorial intent is not invalidated but is seriously complicated by an ironic author like Shakespeare, who intends for different audiences to have different experiences when responding to the same text.

Richard proceeds to murder his way through family, friends, and enemies. We know the outcome, but "do you know the cause"? As epitomized by the ambiguity in Richard's "I am determinèd," the origin of Richard's villainy is anything but determined. Yes, all literature is open to interpretation. Some texts embrace that openness, and some resist it. *Richard III* obsesses over it, thematizes it, and depends upon it for its artistic effect because Shakespeare paired the ambiguity in his representation of Richard's disability with a certain density of implications. I can think of no other moment in Renaissance literature that calls upon as many contexts of interpretation—artistic, historical, theological, philosophical, ethical, psychological, sociological, scientific—as Richard's body. Its contingency combined with a certain implicativity makes Richard's body simultaneously inscrutable, malleable, visceral, and consequential.

III. Disability, Philosophy, and History

Shakespeare's *Richard III* creates an interpretive space around disability, defining the contours of the questions to be asked, but not answering them apart from suggesting that responses are always conditioned by the context in which we come to Richard's body. In describing what is uniquely Shakespearean about Shakespeare's Richard III, this book highlights shifting circumstances of composition and interpretation and the implications of Shakespeare's decision to defer the meaning of Richard's body to different interpretive contexts. As the variously configured origin of the tragedy that occurs in *Richard III*, his disability is a way into intellectual history, allowing us to watch ourselves forming ideas, to see where they come from and how they work. Richard's body reveals histories of moral judgment on individual and cultural levels.

Consider a question commonly asked of Shakespeare's character—*Is Richard evil?*—which only becomes interesting when evil is historicized. In *Evil in Modern Thought* (2002), Susan Neiman argues that theologians and philosophers before the eighteenth century did not strongly separate natural evil from moral evil.[30] Saint Augustine developed these terms (*malum naturale* and *malum morale*) in his argument that evil is really only the absence of God's goodness. "Natural evil" is the absence of the natural order God established upon creation. It includes death, disease, and what insurance companies call natural disasters—disruptions of nature causing pain or suffering that exist independent of human agency. "Moral evil" is radical wrongdoing—sin— "the evil that men do" (*Julius Caesar*, 3.2.73), which Augustine saw as the absence of virtue, as defined by God's revealed law. Nieman argues that, while the distinction goes back to Augustine, modern philosophy only truly began when writers started treating natural and moral evil independently and disentangling them from a necessary connection—a conceptual uncoupling that came after the Lisbon earthquake of 1755.

Before Lisbon, most European philosophy and theology understood all manifestations of pain and suffering to have an active agent behind them. One version made God the agent, arguing that natural evil is deity punishing moral evil. The Book of Genesis describes how, displeased with iniquity, "the LORD rained upon Sodom and upon Gomorrah, brimstone and fire from the LORD out of heaven."[31] Augustine thought that it's not God but demonic forces and fallen angels who are responsible for such disasters. Here, natural evil is still the punishment for moral evil, not directly but because natural evil only exists due to the moral evil of humankind's original sin in the Garden of Eden, itself a product of temptation from the Devil. Augustine concluded that "the originall cause of euill or sinne" is "the reuolting will, first of angels, and afterwards of men."[32] Natural evil is here a catastrophic consequence of an ancient demonic moral evil. So, the premodern approach to the problem of evil saw any instance of horrific pain and suffering as a sign that signifies—somehow, someway, somewhere—some unethical action. Shakespeare's Cassius voices this attitude in *Julius Caesar*—"Of your philosophy you make no use, / If you give place to accidental evils" (4.3.144–145)—for all natural evil is connected to moral evil, no accidents, in this line of thought.

In contrast, Neiman's modern philosophers see natural evil as "sound and fury, / Signifying nothing" (*Macbeth*, 5.5.27–28). After Lisbon in 1755—when the fourth-largest city in Europe, not only a cultural and commercial center but also the capitol of a devout Catholic country, experienced ninety thousand of its citizens dying under the rubble of dozens of fallen churches—it became increasingly difficult for philosophers to justify natural evil as a sign of moral evil. In 1756, a young Immanuel Kant wrote three essays for the Konigsberg weekly newspaper, insisting that earthquakes are not supernaturally significant events.[33] In his "Poem on the Lisbon Disaster" (1756), Voltaire attacked the "whatever is, is right" axiom of Leibnizian optimism.[34] In response to the realization that "Lisbon ought not to have happened, but it did," modern thinkers in Neiman's argument came to a new understanding of evil: "Nature has no meaning; its events are not signs. We no longer expect natural objects to be objects of moral judgment, or even to reflect or harmonize with them" (267–268). Philosophers separated natural from moral evil and gradually stepped away from the former. Scientists became the authorities on natural disasters because philosophers no longer had purchase on the means to account for human pain and suffering with no agent behind it. Natural evil faded from philosophical conversations as unfortunate yet inevitable and philosophically inexplicable; empirically minded discussions turned to moral evil and the ethics governing it.

Historically, there are strong conceptual links between metaphysics and disability—between abstract theories of how and why the world works as it does and our all too particular bodies that often don't work as we want. That's why, writing in 1604, Joseph Hall cited sin in the Garden of Eden (moral deprivation) as the source of physical deformity in humans (natural deprivation): "At first, we were created vpright both in soule and body, but since through sinne, we are become deformed both in soule and bodye."[35] From the premodern perspective outlined by Neiman, the statement *Richard is evil* covers both his body (a natural evil) and his behavior (a moral evil). Consider Shakespeare's King Henry VI, just before Richard kills him:

> The owl shrieked at thy birth, an evil sign;
> The night-crow cried, aboding luckless time;
> Dogs howled and hideous tempest shook down trees;
> The raven rooked her on the chimney's top;
> And chatt'ring pies in dismal discords sung.
> Thy mother felt more than a mother's pain,
> And yet brought forth less than a mother's hope—
> To wit, an undigested and deformèd lump,
> Not like the fruit of such a goodly tree.
> Teeth hadst thou in thy head when thou wast born
> To signify thou cam'st to bite the world. (*3 Henry VI* [*3H6*],
>   5.6.44–54)

The convoluted logic of these claims surfaces in their convoluted language. Henry speaks not of "a sign of evil" but of "an evil sign": the sign itself, the natural evil, is just as "evil" as the moral evil it's supposed to signify. But is the "evil sign" the shrieking owl or the birth of Richard? Henry's grammar allows for either reading, but it might not matter, because Henry's point is that a piling up of signs attended Richard's birth. Among the eerie animal cries, the sign that stands out is that "tempests shook down trees." In the early modern age, physical deformity and natural disasters were grouped together in what Katharine Park and Lorraine Daston call "the canon of prodigious events": "comets and other celestial apparitions, floods, earthquakes, rains of blood or stones, and of course monstrous births."[36] While hugely different phenomena, these events were grouped because they were understood to be disturbances (per Augustine, privations) of the goodness of God's created order. They were natural evils and, as such, signified moral evil, just as Henry says that Richard's body "signif[ies]" his actions. Only as different signs of the same thing can Richard's deformity and villainy "signify" each other. The implication, from an Augustinian perspective, is that this symbolic connection of deformity and villainy—this "evil"—points both backward to the original moral evil of the devil who introduced natural evil into the world and forward to the eventual moral good of the God who will erase all evil upon the apocalypse.

Shakespeare called these superstitions "the excellent foppery of the world" in *King Lear*—"as if we were villains on necessity . . . and all that we are evil in by a divine thrusting-on" (1.2.107–114). It is a question of etiology—the study of causes—in *King John*:

> No natural exhalation in the sky,
> No scope of nature, no distempered day,
> No common wind, no customèd event,
> But they will pluck away his natural cause
> And call them meteors, prodigies, and signs,
> Abortives, presages, and tongues of heaven. (3.4.153–158)

Given the modernization of evil narrated by Neiman, one would expect (and would be right) that premodern (pre-Lisbon) principles and modern (post-Lisbon) principles bring very different responses to the question *Is Richard evil?* The conclusions might be the same—*Richard is evil*—but that statement has different meanings before and after Lisbon.

IV. From Reader's Response to the Anthropology of Audience

Making Richard alternately a villain and a victim, the stigmatization of his body has provoked more passion than any other event in England's political history. For centuries, professional historians have indignantly dismissed the image of an evil, deformed tyrant, while popular culture sheepishly preserves it. As Fish persistently asks in his reader-response criticism, "What if that controversy is itself regarded as evidence?"[37] What do the competing interpretations of Richard reveal about the original object itself—Shakespeare's text? Jean Howard points from the classic questions critics often ask about Richard toward answers:

> Is Richard's hunchback the cause of his villainy or merely its outward sign? Are his villainy and deformity unique or simply the most tangible manifestation of a social deformity that reaches far beyond this single character? Richard's hump invites such questions, but the answers must be sought by broadly surveying the dramatic world in which Richard is placed.[38]

The multi-temporality of the physical disability of Shakespeare's Richard III—a medieval king experiencing both ancient and modern forms of stigma over the course of three Shakespearean plays that have been wildly popular in theater and criticism in the early-modern, modern, and postmodern ages—highlights the extra-textuality of this literary figure. The circumstantial nature of Richard's disability, its unavoidable reference to "the dramatic world in which Richard is placed," prevents textual criticism from capturing its full meaning. Shakespeare's representation of Richard III's disability is a literary event that extends beyond a material text. It draws upon and captures the interplay among all elements of artistic meaning: the intent of the author, the experiences of audiences, and the worlds of author and audience. Because it demands attention in time, the meaning of Richard's body is experiential, only emerging, in Rabkin's words, "by watching one's own responses" (19). If so, experiential meaning also involves observing the responses of others. If, as Rabkin writes, "we are going to call the distillation of our experience of one of the plays its meaning" (23), our experience is not just personal but also cultural. Reception history is integral to the meaning of Richard's body insofar as Shakespeare made interpretive debate about disability a formal feature of his text. As Genevieve Love writes, "We are drawn to attend to Richard's locomotion, an understudied aspect of his disabled embodiment"—not only his movement within the play or on the stage but his "refracting oscillations" in culture.[39]

Because of its ability to draw out assumptions of audiences over time, a text like *Richard III* can be used to perform a reader-response criticism of culture. When Fish analyzes the series of meanings made in the course of interpretation, the record is always volatile, he theorizes, because the understanding formulated "when perceptual or interpretive closure is hazarded" gets revised upon the receipt of more information—when we read the next line.[40] Something similar happens in cultural history, the certainties of one age revised by the certainties of the next. We can shift the apostrophe (to *readers'*) in Fish's maxim that "it is the structure of the reader's experience rather than any structures available on the page that should be the object of description" (152). By treating a Shakespearean text like a perplexing line of poetry, and its reception history like the eyes of a reader scanning sequentially through it, making sense of the text and then remaking sense, cultural historians can discover not what a text *means* but what it *does*. This approach is "radically historical," as Fish would say, because "the critic has the responsibility of becoming not one but a number of informed readers, each of whom will be identified by a matrix of political, cultural, and literary determinants."[41]

These contextual "determinants" of audience interpretation are the real agent at work in Richard's "I am determinèd to prove a villain," for it is ultimately the structures of etiological thought in different ages that turn Richard's actions into evidence proving him evil, however conceived. The combination of Shakespeare's textual ambiguity and cultural popularity creates opportunities to use Shakespeare to do cultural studies—an anthropology of audience.

V. Richard III in Disability History

Siebers wanted a new literary icon: "When Disability Studies takes Richard III as its standard-bearer, it models itself after a murderer."[42] Seeking characters with disability knowledge rather than disability power, he offered Ophelia and Falstaff. Yet if Richard III is seen not as a dramatic character confined to Shakespeare's play but as a multi-temporal disabled man whose body has been defined, redefined, erased, recovered, repurposed, and reclaimed in successive eras from the Middle Ages to modernity, he represents knowledge of disability history.

Constructed, reconstructed, and deconstructed over centuries, Richard III's body is an opportunity for disability histories spanning the period categories that scholars construct—medieval, early-modern, modern, postmodern, whatever-we're-in-now. His is the story of a disabled individual's body that is often controlled by others and only recently reclaimed by the disability community. The central site of stigma in English history, Richard III reveals layers of disability experience—the individual's relationships with their body, with society, and with history. Richard ensures that complexity and openness of interpretation remain at the center of disability history. As a disability phenomenon that is both historical and well known today, Richard III can connect disability history to the activism essential to academic disability studies. "The reconstruction of a usable past can contribute to the building of an accessible future," as Paul K. Longmore put it.[43] But Richard III will remain central to the disability community only if scholars are able to recover the role of disability in this medieval king's biography and only if disabled individuals today find value in explorations of the disability experience made possible by Shakespeare's cultural prominence.

Identifying people with disabilities as "an oppressed group in society" in 1973, the Union of the Physically Impaired Against Segregation drew a distinction between *impairment* (a feature of the body) and *disability* (imposed by society) that guides all disability studies and disability history.[44] These fields attend to both the individual's experience and a culture's attitudes.

Thus, the emphasis on theorizing normality and ableism in early disability studies was matched by efforts to empower disabled voices in culture, scholarship, and legislation, epitomized in the rallying call of "Nothing about Us without Us."[45]

Similarly, disability history emphasizes the experience of individuals with disabilities rather than cultural biases, while remembering that encounters with ableism are part of the disability experience. To capture these layers, the first major disability historian, Henri-Jacques Stiker, influenced by Michel Foucault, employed a "historical anthropology" that sought to speak with disabled people of the past by detailing the structures of the societies they lived in: "To speak at all pertinently of disabled people discloses a society's depths."[46] In 2000, David Mitchell and Sharon Snyder similarly pursued "an anthropological unearthing of images that could help to reconstruct a period's point of view on human variation."[47] By one account, disability history moved from the margins to the mainstream in 2001.[48]

Early attempts to theorize disability history were explicitly intersectional, citing the feminist field of women's history and efforts to recover other historically stigmatized identities related to race, gender, sexuality, religion, and class.[49] Soon came Christopher Bell's critique that disability studies is not intersectional enough; indeed, the cultural history of Richard III's body is often a record of what White, able-bodied, English-speaking men have thought about it, with some important exceptions the closer we get to today.[50] As disability studies and disability history continue to become more intersectional in the coming years, Richard III will invite debate about how much of his experience is specific to a wealthy White straight male Christian in medieval England and how much transfers to other identity categories.

Like other oppressed identities, disability is often erased from the historical record—absent from the archive—leading to certain trends in early disability history: emphasis on institutional practices rather than individual lives, attention to the history of stigmatization over historical disability experiences, an orientation toward the modern age, a focus on England and the United States, and—because of all of this—recognition of the need to recover the lived realities of disabled people from the past.[51] Enter literary disability history, where texts by disabled authors and with disabled characters offer glimpses of historically situated disability experiences.[52]

Whereas in 2009 Hobgood and Wood could write that "minimal work has been undertaken on early modern disability," by 2019 Susan Anderson was able to register that "disability has now become one of the most exciting and lively areas of early modern scholarship."[53] Building from Greco-Roman,

Judeo-Christian, and medieval European disability histories, early-modern English disability history has identified several common cultural tropes—monstrosity, charity, medicine—plus a range of individual experiences as various as the impairments they involve, both physical and mental.[54] Historians have asked whether it makes sense to use the term "disability" in the middle and early-modern ages.[55] In Shakespeare studies, some have looked at disability before "disability," instances from the early-modern age that preceded the emergence of the discourse of "disability" in the eighteenth century.[56] Some have explored disability rhetoric that often strays far from physical impairment.[57] Some have argued for the presence of various models of disability—the religious model, the medical model, the social model, the cultural model—in different early-modern texts and traditions.[58] Some have used examples of early-modern disability to build new theories that can inform lived disability experiences today.[59] Some have considered disability in modern performances of early-modern texts.[60] Some have turned their attention to questions of pedagogy when bringing early-modern disability texts into twenty-first-century classrooms.[61]

These methodologies have generated new knowledge. To mention just some, Row-Heyveld has found a stunning number of counterfeit disabilities in early-modern English drama.[62] Love and Williams have shown that moments of disability in early-modern drama raise big theoretical questions about acting and audience in the theater and in everyday life.[63] Hobgood has identified several examples of "disability gain"—personal and social benefits of disability—in early-modern England.[64] Alice Equestri has explored understudied intellectual disabilities in early-modern literature.[65] Grace McCarthy has shown that filmmakers and their directorial decisions often mediate modern engagements with disability in Shakespearean stories.[66] And Sonya Freeman Loftis has redirected attention from Shakespeare's disabled characters to the lived experiences of present-day Shakespeareans with disabilities, from artists and actors to scholars and activists.[67]

"Concentrating on Richard gives too simplified a picture of disability on the early modern stage," as Anderson writes.[68] By the same token, restricting ourselves to early-modern drama gives too simple a picture of Richard III. Literary representations of disability—especially those that become canonical—create opportunities for disability histories that track audiences' responses over time. Deeply embedded in an early-modern age that saw the rebirth of ancient European culture, yet alive today all around the world in performance and adaptation, Shakespeare invites expansive disability histories that span centuries and continents. As the central author in the English language, and as the author of the most prominent representation of disability, *Richard III*, Shakespeare provides an opportunity to see disability through time. Richard III may be the main site of this methodology, but it could extend to Falstaff, Ophelia, Hamlet, Lear, Macbeth, Lady Macbeth, Othello, Caliban, and many others. Some might want Shakespeare to be cleanly either a friend or an enemy of people with disabilities. As someone who was skeptical of all meanings made of disabilities, yet nowhere interested in disability justice, Shakespeare is an uncomfortable ally at best. Yet because disabled Shakespearean characters are often overloaded with meaning in the plays and their afterlives, they allow for expansive cultural studies showing how disability acquires meaning when recontextualized. As someone who represented disability extensively (conveying and challenging the attitudes of his age in equal measure) and whose canonicity means that his disability representations have been interpreted and reinterpreted by centuries of increasingly global audiences, Shakespeare presents opportunities for disability histories.

VI. The Significance of Richard's Body

By the time he got to Shakespeare, Richard III already had what Linda Charnes calls a "notorious identity," where infamy becomes an opportunity for rethinking accepted narratives.[69] Why does Richard's body demand explanation in a series of increasingly global cultures with little in common outside a need to answer some basic questions about human being? Why is Richard's disability so significant—so full of significance, of signifying power, of the potential to mean very important and very different things to very different people?

Due to the size and difficulty of the task, commentators on Richard's body have read it in a limited way—picking and choosing from the *Henry VI* plays, making it little further through *Richard III* than the wooing of Anne, quoting characters out of context, missing allusions to Richard's disability unless it is explicitly stigmatized, or using Shakespeare's character for a thought experiment it might sustain but does not invite. Our general understanding of Richard's body is not wrong but disjointed, the outcome of a literary representation prodigious in size and monstrous in meaning. The perspectival quality of interpretations of Richard's disability is both called for by Shakespeare's text and an occasion for a more expansive consideration of it as a multi-temporal literary phenomenon.

A cultural history of Richard III's body is a long story with several twists and turns, not only because it addresses Shakespeare's first and most important depiction of stigma but also because it must attend to different worlds that create different Richards in different Shakespearean sources, traditions, texts, performances, adaptations, analogs, and criticism. The meaning of Richard's disability changes with time, not only in the course of Shakespeare's plays but also in the broader cultural history surrounding them. When reading or watching Shakespeare's first tetralogy in sequence, one is tossed between backward-looking and forward-thinking representations of stigma. This dialectic is not positively resolved in the text, leaving Shakespeare's representation of disability open for appropriation in different time periods that embrace different attitudes toward stigma.

An interpretation of Richard's body is never just an interpretation of Richard's body. It's a statement symbolic of one's core theological, philosophical, historical, and ethical habits and beliefs. Richard's disability as Shakespeare presents it has such massive implications because it exposes the assumptions, motives, and operations of thought. When we interpret Richard's disability, it interprets us in return. It brings us to declare our motives and commitments in our attempts to unfold, explain, condemn, justify, defend, and so forth. It catches something in our core and brings it to the surface through its configuration of abstract questions about reality and issues specific to our bodies. It brings us to consider how we would and should respond when, like Richard, we are born into a world that is totally confusing, deeply unsatisfying, or both.

Not all literary texts elicit such core elements of our existence. Something about the body of Shakespeare's Richard III makes for high-stakes literature. Something at the nexus of these two early-modern Englishmen, Richard III and William Shakespeare, speaks with urgency to something central in modern life. I believe that it is Richard's disability and Shakespeare's irony: Shakespeare's ironic representation of Richard's disability captures the problem of interpretation in an age obsessed with materiality. Like Shakespeare's Richard III, modern thought starts with embodiment and ends with ethics, making modern thought structurally analogous to the critical tradition devoted to the relationship between Richard's body and behavior. To interpret Richard's disability in Shakespeare's play is to confront, symbolically, the conditions and possibilities of ethical thought and action in the modern world.

Richard III connects four things—physical disability, moral depravity, political tyranny, and social tragedy—resulting in a character and a plot that have signified for audiences the epitome of evil. Audiences with local, specific concerns—physical, moral, political, social—find in *Richard III* a framework for thinking about the tension between the desirable and the undesirable. That tension manifests in any number of ways: beauty versus ugliness, ability versus disability, virtue versus vice, love versus hate, power versus weakness, freedom versus subjugation, and so forth. Ultimately, Shakespeare's *Richard III* is not about any one form of evil as much as it is about the mystery of tragedy understood as the invisible and inscrutable structure of relationships among those things—physical, mental, ethical, social, political—that evoke pity and fear. Disability isn't tragic, yet the interpretation of disability mirrors the interpretation of tragedy: accounts of causation and significance mustered in response to disability and tragedy closely resemble each other. To interpret Richard's disability is to interpret the problems that repeatedly present themselves in modern life. The range of possible responses to that which is not good in life—random accidents, romantic failures, financial hardships, social conflict, political corruption, crime, war, death, mourning, loneliness, uncertainty—is contained within the tradition dedicated to the interpretation of Richard's body. These problems' origination in disability in Shakespeare's text reveals the hidden centrality of disability to questions of modernity and transcends that context through conceptual affinities with other identities.

Interpreting disability in Shakespeare's first tetralogy is a lot like interpreting disability in life, not because the plays are an exact copy of nature, for they are the opposite—filled with artifice. In Shakespeare's plays, as in life, so many conflicting interpretations lie between us and disability, layers upon layers, each asking us to accept its claims, that we have no pure, unfiltered experience with the thing we seek to understand. Richard's disability—a physical thing visible in the character's body and the recipient of competing interpretations from other characters—reflects the status of Richard III himself as both a historical person (open to interpretation) and a literary character (already interpreted by Shakespeare). When making sense of Richard's disability, we are interpreting not only his physical body but also the meanings made of it dramatically and historically. The interpretation of Richard's disability is always an interpretation of interpretations and, as such, involves a second-order discourse about how interpretation works. This dynamic extends to Hamlet's madness and Falstaff's obesity: those famous Shakespearean creations have, like Richard's disability, marked physical conditions obsessively interpreted *in the plays*. That quality of being always already interpreted is what drives thought from interpretation to reflection upon the stakes and implications of interpretation, upon meaning and significance.

The emblem of this idea is Salvador Dalí's 1955 *Portrait of Laurence Olivier in the Role of Richard III* (see Figure I.2). While Dalí's image of Olivier's image of Shakespeare's image of Richard III includes the traditional deformities—humped left shoulder, withered left hand—the canvas is disrupted

FIGURE I.2 Salvador Dalí, *Portrait of Laurence Olivier in the Role of Richard III* (1955), oil on canvas, 73.5 × 63 cm, at the Dalí Theatre-Museum (Figueres, Spain).

---

on the left side, which depicts the fractured or split subjectivity associated with the modern age. Richard's face—prosthetic nose, wig, medieval hat—at three-quarters turn is overlain (awkwardly, unnaturally) on top of half of Olivier's unadorned face, which floats bodiless. It's not that actor blends into character; rather, the multiple personalities in play here—Richard, Olivier, Dalí—cannot be contained within one human body. The righthand side of Richard's body dissolves into a landscape of Bosworth field: what Richard does (his actions) becomes who he is (his body). The Richard III myth

FIGURE I.3 *Apr. 04, 1956 - Oliver - By Dalí*, photograph, from Keystone Pictures USA. Image from Alamy.

captured on the right side of Dalí's canvas points backward into a specific moment in medieval English history (Bosworth Field) and forward into generalizable aspects of modern subjectivity (Laurence Olivier). Additional layers of significance emerge in a photograph of Olivier sitting for Dalí (see Figure I.3). This image includes an overabundance of media—it is a photograph of a modern theatrical performance of an early-modern work of literature based on medieval history—gesturing to the refractions of Richard III over time and across cultures (just as Olivier appears three times in the photo: once in the chair, once in the mirror, and once on Dalí's canvas). As the viewer of this photograph, we consider one artist (Dalí) considering another artist (Olivier) considering another artist (Shakespeare) considering Richard III and his body.

Further recursions come in Peter Sellers's comic riffs—performing the Beatles song "A Hard Day's Night" as Olivier's Richard III in 1965 or "recit[ing] the soliloquy from Shakespeare's *Richard III* whilst, and at the same time, playing tuned chickens" on *The Muppet Show* in 1977.[70] The villain in the 2001 animated children's movie *Shrek*, Lord Farquaad, recalls Olivier's Richard III—the shoulder-length black hair, the bright red clothes, the campy tyranny—while reconstituting Richard's disability as dwarfism. Farquaad's size is both a frequent gag ("Men of his stature are in *short* supply") and the origin of his clownish ambition ("Do you think he's maybe compensating for something?").[71] Disability is especially used for glib comedy in the stage production of *Shrek the Musical* (2008), an adaptation of an adaptation of an adaptation: an able-bodied actor wearing fake legs moves around on his knees, to audience laughter.[72] While this recursion of Richard is obnoxiously ableist, it also shows a history of reconfiguration to be central to the prominence of Richard's body in the twenty-first century. The core of any modern encounter with Richard III is interpretation, not just in the context of other interpretations but in the context of interpretations of interpretations of interpretations of interpretations.

1

Stigmatizing Richard III's Disability up to Shakespeare

The Figural Paradigm

In Shakespeare's *Richard III*, the king's nephew, the young Duke of York, gossips about his uncle's allegedly unnatural body at birth, the legend that Richard was born with teeth.[1] "They say my uncle grew so fast," the youth whispers to Richard's mother, "that he could gnaw a crust at two hours old" (2.4.27–28). Shakespeare then satirized the Tudor historians who trumped up and transmitted the legend of Richard's prodigious birth:

> DUCHESS OF YORK I prithee, pretty York, who told thee this?
> YORK Grandam, his nurse.
> DUCHESS OF YORK His nurse? Why, she was dead ere thou wast born.
> (2.4.31–33)

The invention of Richard's deformity at birth is part and parcel of what E.M.W. Tillyard called "the Tudor myth," the organizing force of Shakespeare's history plays.[2] It suggests that Henry IV's 1399 usurpation of Richard II, an anointed king ruling by divine right, prompted almost a century of disorder that culminated in the Wars of the Roses and Richard III, evil incarnate, usurping the English throne in 1483; civil war plagued England until 1485, when Henry Tudor, the last Lancastrian and God's lieutenant here on Earth, cast Richard down at the Battle of Bosworth and, by marrying the heiress of the house of York, united the two rival dynasties. Historians have documented how this myth was invented by chroniclers commissioned by

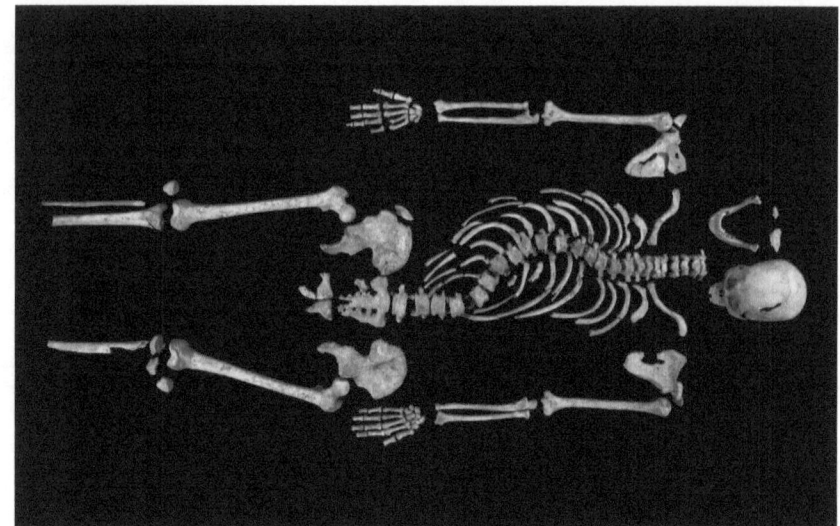

FIGURE 1.1 University of Leicester, "The Complete Skeleton," in *The Discovery of Richard III* (2012), photograph, http://www.le.ac.uk/richardiii/science/osteology-3-analysing.html.

the new king, Henry VII, and his son, Henry VIII, father of Elizabeth I, the queen of England when Shakespeare wrote *Richard III*. Historians have also shown how the myth stigmatized physical disability to demonize Richard III as the embodiment of evil.[3]

Upending many earlier historians, the 2012 discovery of Richard III's skeleton confirmed his physical disability as historical fact (see Figure 1.1).[4] The Tudors did not invent Richard's disability but did exaggerate it greatly: the exhumed skeleton shows signs of *scoliosis*, a sideways curvature of the spine, and perhaps uneven shoulders, but not *kyphosis*, the medical term for a hunchback. And the Tudors treated it as a congenital abnormality when, in all likelihood, Richard's scoliosis did not surface until his adolescence.[5] These findings carry the potential for authentic historical or artistic disability representation. With a little imagination, we can consider the experience of a privileged young Plantagenet noble becoming disabled and its impact on his mind, emotions, family, and society.

I. Reclaiming Richard's Disability

Because of Richard's nobility, many records of his life exist, including the prayer book dating his birth at Fotheringhay Castle to October 2, 1452.[6] Unlike five of his siblings, Richard survived infancy. War was all around, but he lived a comfortable childhood bouncing from one castle to another—private education from tutors, military training on horseback. At eight years old, he lost his father to the war. A year later, his brother became king, and Richard became Duke of Gloucester, aged nine.

If Richard developed scoliosis during his teenage years, whom did he tell when his body started changing?[7] His mother? His brothers? His friends? A doctor? Was he experiencing pain? Many with scoliosis don't during the early years. Did others at Middleham Castle in Yorkshire, where Richard spent his formative years, know about his condition? Did cruel kids tease him? Did he keep his emotions inside? Was there confusion, denial, and self-doubt from internalized ableism?[8] Did attempts to conceal disability isolate Richard from friends, family, and potential love interests? It didn't stop Richard from fathering two children out of wedlock, probably during his late teen years.

Did scoliosis affect nineteen-year-old Richard's mobility during his first combat experience at the Battles of Barnet and Tewkesbury in 1471? What conversations about his back did Richard have with his wife, Anne, whom he married in 1472? How did he experience the increase of his spine's curvature as he aged to adulthood? Did his lower back start hurting during travels across England on horseback? Did he pass as able-bodied? Did those who knew pity Richard? Pray for him? Whisper behind his back? Did they stare or look away? Richard would have had access to doctors that commoners did not. Did they try a brace? Or stretch his spine with ropes? How did Richard manage the pain of these medical procedures?[9]

As he gathered lands and alliances, building a stronghold of power in northern England during his twenties, did the adult Richard consider scoliosis to be a central feature of his identity, or was it no big deal? Did his impairment cause physical limitations—a disability? Did he encounter a society not built for people with lessened mobility—another level of disability? Did people who knew of his scoliosis mistreat him because of it—yet another layer? Would Anne massage his back? Was that a moment of intimacy that would have been missed if Richard hadn't been disabled?

Did his brothers and their wives make snide remarks during their frequent feuds? Did disability contribute to Richard's withdrawal from meetings at court, starting in 1478? As Richard became Lord Protector over his nephew, Edward V, how often did he think about his back—hardly ever, daily, once an hour, all the time? People with disabilities know that they're never far from your mind, even if you never talk about them. Did Richard dismiss concerns about his health when asked but manage the pain in private? Joke about his body to deflect attention? Adjust his saddle or combat style? Meet others with scoliosis? Did they form bonds? Did people read religious significance into his body? Did disability inform his religious piety, which is thought to have been genuine? Did he seek miraculous healing through the Church? Was charity offered where not wanted? Did he identify with physically disabled characters from the Bible (Mephibosheth, Herod, people healed in the Gospels)? Or from classical literature (Hephaestus, Thersites, Oedipus, Aesop)? Or English history and literature (from the Fisher King to the beggars in *Piers Plowman*)?[10]

There is no record of anyone during Richard's lifetime suggesting his disability was disqualifying. He became the richest and most powerful landowner in England, and king in 1483. Did those who knew that England had a disabled king think it remarkable? Did King Richard disrupt assumptions about disability? About royalty? Did people read Richard in light of the king's two bodies? Was he alone during the several changes of clothes on his coronation day, or were others around, with no one really caring about the shape of his spine? What did the archbishop of Canterbury think at the coronation, when Richard dropped his purple velvet gown to be anointed on the head, hands, and heart?

There was often music and dance in the York courts, and Richard joined in. During his twenty-six months on the throne, was he able to govern without people constantly thinking about his disability? Or was he questioned? Always wondering whether others were thinking about his body? How often did he see a doctor? Did his royal physician, William Hobbes, consult Avicenna's *Canon of Medicine*? Did it take Richard longer to dress, or travel, or catch his breath as he aged? Did he take days off work to rest? Would downtime have allowed Richard to think, read, talk with loved ones? His scoliosis seems to have borne no significant relationship to his political crimes against his family or his legislative accomplishments on behalf of people living in poverty. Richard's complexity of character, which historians have debated for centuries, is only deepened by the discovery of his scoliosis and questions about how or when it may have mattered in his daily life—or not. Richard III is a disability icon precisely because the fullness of his life is neither separable from nor reducible to disability.

Did Richard and Anne's son, Edward, who lived to be ten years old, ask him questions about his body? When Anne died less than a year later, was Richard's scoliosis one of the "tribulations, griefs and anguishes" he asked God to free him from in his prayer book? Did disability cause frustration?

Resentment? Limited breathing during extended physical exertion, like that experienced by Dominic Smee, a twenty-first-century person with a scoliosis similar to Richard's whom Channel 4 recruited to study Richard's physicality?[11] Did people doubt Richard's prowess on the battlefield, as they did Smee's? Did Richard find, like Smee, that his scoliosis wasn't really a hindrance on the battlefield?

Did Richard's ribs bulge up on one side of his back when, after his death in battle at thirty-two years old, he was stripped and tossed over a horse? As Richard's corpse was stabbed and desecrated, did people discover a disability they never knew about? Did they mock the body of their enemy? Stab around his spine on purpose? Express political hatred through violence upon disability?

II. The Figural Paradigm

Richard III is the central site of stigma in English literature. The Tudors turned him from a man with a disability into a monster in body and behavior. It's easy to see why: the Tudors mythologized their record for the sake of political legitimacy, and stigma was one way to demonize their enemy. This chapter shows *how*, rhetorically, Tudor writers discredited Richard III, how they made history into mythology. A rhetorical reading of Richard's body shows how stigma is made, how physical disability comes to acquire meaning, how the denigration of disability is mixed up with moral commitments, motives, and assumptions—with, in short, a constructed worldview. Historian of science Thomas Kuhn's constructivist reading of scientific knowledge helps us see how Tudor writers invented and sustained a reading of Richard's body that flew in the face of fact and reason.[12] Kuhn provides a vocabulary for addressing verifiable trends over time—"paradigms"—while avoiding totalizing grand narratives, thanks to the useful notions of "anomalies" and "suppression."

In *The Structure of Scientific Revolutions* (1962), Kuhn defines a "paradigm" as a pattern of scientific practice. This chapter shows that there was a paradigm for the representation of Richard III's body in sixteenth-century English literature. I call it the *figural paradigm* because Tudor writers treated the alleged deformity of Richard's body at birth as a figure for his villainous life and his tragic death—deformity figuring villainy and tragedy.

In Kuhn's account, a paradigm succeeds because it helps a group of practitioners solve a problem. Tudor chroniclers treated Richard's deformity as a

God-given sign of his evil mind, soul, or actions because this mystified metaphor helped them solve the political problem of the Tudor dynasty's dubious claim to divine-right monarchy in England. As Kuhn notes, however, the road to scientific consensus is often difficult. Kuhn's theory of paradigms helps us narrate the inconsistent treatment of Richard's body in a pre-paradigm period during the reign of Henry VII, the emergence of the figural paradigm in the age of Henry VIII, and the perpetuation of this paradigm by later Tudor writers, up to and including William Shakespeare.

III. The Pre-Paradigm Period

To see how Shakespeare was working with an established paradigm, we must trace the stigmatization of Richard's body beyond its roots in a civil war, a bloody battle, and a scramble for political authority, back to the rush to find the rhetoric for remembering Richard during what Kuhn calls a "pre-paradigm" period (17). During Richard's lifetime, several writers depicted him favorably, some mentioning a smallish size ("never before has nature dared to encase in a smaller body [*corpus exiguum*] such spirit and such strength"[13]), but none claiming deformity. The Warwick antiquary John Rous saw Richard firsthand. Two drawings in a document now known as the *Rous Roll* (1484) depict Richard with no discernable deformity (see Figure 1.2).[14] None appears in the image of Richard in the Salisbury Roll, dated to 1483–1485.[15] If Richard's scoliosis had produced not a hunchback but uneven shoulders, the right slightly higher than the left, it would have been concealed by the armor and regalia Richard wears in these images.

After the Battle of Bosworth in 1485, Rous needed to appease the newly crowned Henry VII, having previously praised Richard in the *Rous Roll*. Stigmatizing the disability of Henry's enemy, Rous's *History of the Kings of England* (1486) says that Richard was "retained within his mother's womb for two years, emerging with teeth and hair to his shoulders. . . . He was small of stature, with a short face and unequal shoulders, the right higher and the left lower [*Parvae staturae erat, curtam habens faciem, inaequales humeros, dexter superior sinisterque inferior*]."[16] Rous's Latin manuscript shows that the passage was originally written with blanks for the words indicating which shoulder was higher: "*inaequales humeros, _____ superior _____ inferior.*" Someone later filled in the blanks to make the "*dexter*," right, shoulder higher than the "*sinister*," left.[17] If Rous projected his newfound opposition to Richard back into an unnatural birth, he also threw his disgust with Richard's life

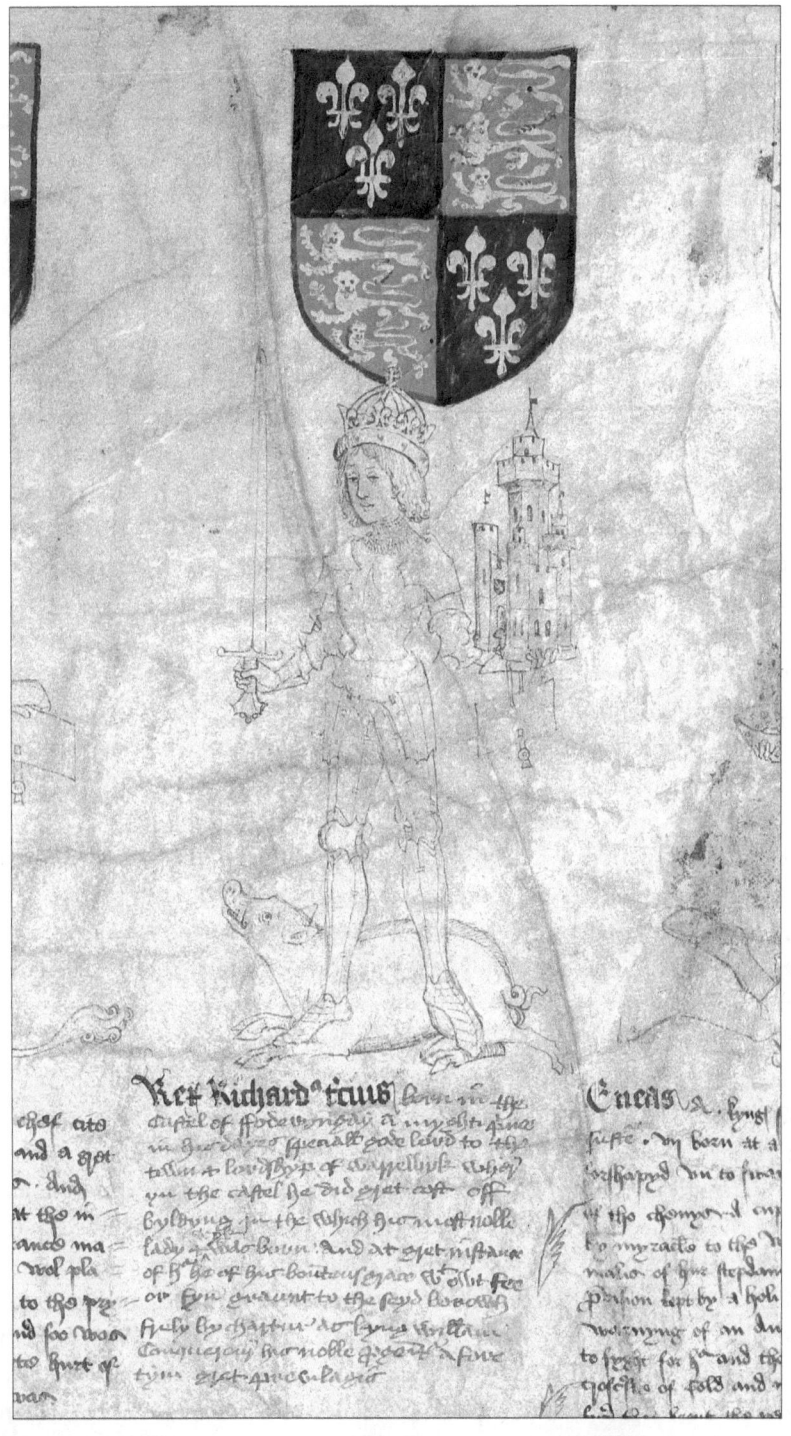

FIGURE 1.2 © The British Library Board. Richard III in *The Rous Roll* (ca. 1483), in the British Library (London, England), Add MS 48976, f. 2br.

forward into a mythologized death: "This King Richard, who was excessively cruel in his days, reigned for three years and a little more, in the way that the Antichrist is to reign. And like the Antichrist to come, he was confounded at his moment of greatest pride" (123). The first mention of Richard's disability is already mapped onto a mythological narrative of evil overcome by good.

From a Kuhnian perspective, Rous's versions of Richard were inconsistent because he was working "in the absence of a paradigm," which makes "early fact-gathering" a "nearly random activity" (15). For the same reason, other early chroniclers, even those hostile to Richard, did not mention any deformities.[18] There are competing facts—not interpretations, but facts—in the York civic record in 1491, which contains the second-known allusion to Richard's deformity. Accused of slandering a nobleman, one John Payntour denied the charge, claiming he heard another citizen, William Burton, "saye that Kyng Richard was an ypocryte, a crochebake and beried in a dike like a dogge, wherunto the said John Payntour answerd and said that he lied, for the Kynges good grace had beried hym like a noble gentilman."[19] Scooping Shakespeare by a century, Burton configured Richard's villainy ("ypocryte") with his deformity ("crochebake") and tragedy ("beried in a dike like a dogge"), while Payntour offered a competing interpretation of Richard's final resting place.

Early portraits of Richard III commemorate the instability of fact in this pre-paradigm period. The earliest surviving painting, the arched-top portrait now at the Society of Antiquaries in London, is estimated to have been painted in 1516, based on a lost prototype painted during Richard's reign (see Figure 1.3). There is no obvious physical deformity, though Richard's left shoulder protrudes out horizontally while his right slopes downward. In contrast, the Royal Collections portrait clearly shows an uneven shoulder line, right higher than left (see Figure 1.4). X-ray examination has revealed the portrait originally did not depict a noticeably deformed Richard. After its initial composition around 1520, someone modified the portrait later in the sixteenth century to include sneering eyes, a tight frown, and a hunchback: the jeweled chain hanging from Richard's shoulders was pulled to the left in the revision to suggest a massy shoulder.[20] As the Tudor myth grew and became codified, Richard's face became more villainous, his body more hideous. A 2007 restoration of the arched-top portrait at the Society of Antiquaries revealed that Richard's facial features were slightly modified after its original composition: the lips were thinned and pursed to make Richard seem more aggressive.

FIGURE 1.3 Richard III, Arched-Topped Portrait (ca. 1516, restored 2007), oil on panel, : © The Society of Antiquaries of London.

FIGURE 1.4 *Richard III* (ca. 1520), oil on canvas, 56.5 × 35.6 cm, Royal Collection Trust / © Her Majesty Queen Elizabeth II 2021.

IV. The Discovery of the Figural Paradigm

In Rous's *History*, Burton's comment, and the early portraits, the connection between deformity and villainy is only implicit. It was Polydore Vergil's *English History* (1512–1513), a text commissioned by Henry VII, that explicitly connected Richard's body and behavior for the first time:

> He was lyttle of stature [*habitu corporis exiguo*], deformyd of body [*corpore deformi*], thone showlder being higher than thither [*altero humero eminentiore*], a short and sowre cowntenance, which semyd to savor of mischief, and utter evydently craft and deceyt. The whyle he was thinking of any matter, he dyd contynually byte his nether lyppe, as thowgh that crewell nature of his did so rage agaynst yt self in that lyttle carkase. Also he was woont to be ever with his right hand pulling out of the sheath to the myddest, and putting in agane, the dagger which he did alway were.[21]

Rous gave Richard a toothed birth, but Vergil made those teeth meaningful: Richard "byte[s]" his lip while thinking unnatural thoughts, a conceit Shakespeare later referenced ("The king is angry, see, he gnaws his lip" [*R3*, 4.2.27]). Rous gave Richard a raised right shoulder, but Vergil made that deformity meaningful: Richard's right hand fidgets with his deadly dagger. The proximity of physical to moral descriptions in Vergil's account encourages a reader to see body as expression of character. Vergil posited an internal immorality as offensive to him as Richard's external appearance was, splitting mind and body only to parallel evil mind with evil body. Only by having an essential moral character sealed away behind his body could Richard have a "cowntenance" that "seemyd to . . . utter evydently" what existed underneath. Guided by a belief in changeless human character—and a desire (or obligation) to trumpet the Tudor myth—Vergil's research into Richard collected, in Kuhn's words, "more than 'mere facts'" (17).

Working either from Vergil's *History* or some common source, Thomas More wrote his *History of King Richard the Thirde* (1513) a short time later, including a similar passage that suggests the presence of a paradigm:

> Richarde the third sonne, of whom we now entreat, was in witte and courage egall with either of [his brothers], in bodye and prowesse farre vnder them bothe, little of stature, ill fetured of limes, croke backed [*extanti dorso*], his left shoulder much higher than his right

[*alteroque humero erectior*], hard fauoured of visage, and suche as in states called warlye, in other menne other wise. He was malicious, wrathful, enuious, and from afor his birth, euer frowarde. It is for trouth reported, that the Duches his mother had so muche a doe in her trauaile, that shee could not bee deliuered of hym vncutte: and that hee came into the worlde with the feete forwarde, as menne bee borne outwarde, and (as fame runneth) also not vntothed, whither men of hatred reporte aboue the trouthe, or elles that nature changed her course in hys beginninge, whiche in the course of his lyfe many thinges vnnaturallye committed.[22]

More contrasted Richard's mental and spiritual virtues ("in witte and courage") with his physical and moral vices ("in bodye and prowesse"). The isocolon polarizes aesthetics and ethics into categories of *the desirable* and *the undesirable* and then collapses the distinction between undesirable aesthetics and undesirable ethics, lumping ugliness and impudence into a single category—namely, *the undesirable*. More placed his physical description of Richard ("little of stature ... hard fauoured of visage") adjacent to his moral description ("He was malicious ... euer frowarde"), making deformity an avenue into villainy. The repetition of "forward" collapses the moral insolence of the "euer forward" Richard with the physical position of a fetus in breech position with "feete forwarde." Birth omens behavior, so More spoke about both with the same word, an instance of *antanaclasis*, repetition of a word in a different sense. Then, More described either a cesarean section or an episiotomy—"shee could not bee deliuered of hym vncutte"—making the infant Richard a violent slasher in his earliest moments. As the antimetabole in More's last line suggested ("nature changed ... vnnaturallye committed"), Richard's unnatural birth foreboded an unnatural life.

Between Rous and More, Richard's raised shoulder hopped from the right side to the left (Rous was right; More was wrong). More also wrote that Richard's left arm was a "wearish withered arme and small" (54). One higher shoulder in Rous evolved into one arm shorter than the other for More. Shakespeare only knew More's description of Richard in its English translation, but More's Latin text is even more unstable, making Richard's deformity variously greater and lesser. For "his left shoulder much higher than his right," the Latin text has "*alteroque humero erectior*," literally "his other shoulder higher," not specifying the side, while for "croke backed," the Latin has "*extanti dorso*," a "projecting back," the first description of Richard's deformity to suggest a hunchback, kyphosis as opposed to scoliosis.

This image of a hunchbacked Richard is captured in the broken sword portrait now housed at the Society of Antiquaries (see Figure 1.5). Around 1550, the painter closely followed More in showing Richard with a hump on his left shoulder and shortened left arm. But modern viewers only see this severely deformed Richard with the aid of X-ray technology (see Figure 1.6) because Richard's deformities had been repainted to be less severe by 1787 (the dark background was blended into Richard's dark vest, deemphasizing his raised shoulder, and the short arm painted out, though it retains a sense of disability in the crunched fingers). The broken sword in the portrait, symbolizing Richard's defeat at the battle of Bosworth, rests upon his raised shoulder, connecting deformity with tragedy.

More dutifully tempered his treatment of Richard's birth by acknowledging these slanders as the fabulous reports of inimical men: "it is for trouth reported," "as fame runneth," "whither men of hatred reporte aboue the trouthe."[23] In this regard, More anticipated Shakespeare, showing how a skeptical representation of a paradigm can still perpetuate the paradigm when that authorial strategy is missed by audiences trained up in the tradition. Moreover, as Phillipa Vincent Connolly writes, "Disabled people constituted a large part of society and were a visible part of everyday life of the peasantry, clergy, and nobility, where surprisingly, the Tudors were very adept at supporting those with disabilities."[24] Because the figural paradigm was a bottom-up custom of interpreting Richard III before it became a top-down theory of disability, aversion to Richard coexisted with the accommodation of disabled Tudor kings and courtiers, such as Henry VIII and Will Sommers. Paradigms precede theory, as Kuhn observes, and a paradigm suppresses anomalous ideas when they threaten its prominence.

Richard Grafton's *Continuacion of the Chronicle of England* (1543) was wary enough of More's passage to quote Vergil instead.[25] Edward Hall's *The Vnion of the Two Noble and Illustre Famelies of Lancastre Yorke* (1548) quoted More verbatim, but Richard Rainolde's *The Foundacion of Rhetorike* (1563) repeated More's rhetorical flourishes with none of the reservations:

> This kyng Richard was small of stature, deformed, and ill shaped, his shoulders beared not equalitie, a pulyng face, yet of countenaunce and looke cruell, malicious, deceiptfull, bityng and chawing his nether lippe: of minde vnquiet, pregnaunt of witte, quicke and liuely, a worde and a blowe, wilie, deceiptfull, proude, arrogant in life and cogitacion bloodie.[26]

FIGURE 1.5 *Richard III (Broken Sword)* (ca. 1516, rev. by 1787), oil on panel, 485 × 355 mm, : © The Society of Antiquaries of London.

FIGURE 1.6 X-Ray Photograph of *Richard III (Broken Sword)*: © The Society of Antiquaries of London.

Rainolde's moral judgments describe Richard's "countenaunce and looke" as if "cruell, malicious, deceiptfull" are categorically no different than physical descriptions like "bityng and chawing his nether lippe." Meanwhile, Rainolde's isocolon separates only to parallel qualities "of countenaunce" with those "of minde." His Richard is "of countenaunce . . . deceiptfull" and "of minde . . . deceiptfull," an identification of corporal and mental attributes.

The most significant suppression came from John Stow. After Stow's death in 1605, the seventeenth-century historian George Buck reported a conversation between his younger self (born around 1560) and an elderly Stow that, in turn, reported a conversation between Stow and some even older Englishmen: "Some peremtorily asserted [Richard III] was not deformed, of which opinion was *Iohn Stow* . . . who in all his inquiry could finde no such note of deformitie in this King: but hath acknowledged *viva voce*, that he had spoken with some ancient men, who from their owne sight and knowledge affirmed he was of bodily shape comely enough, onely of low stature, which is all the deformity they proportion so monstrously."[27] The belief that Richard III was not deformed survived as oral history, yet this anomaly was suppressed in print when Stow published his popular *Chronicles of England* (1580), quoting More's vignette of Richard without comment.[28]

When sixteenth-century historians said that Richard's body and behavior were similar, they meant that they had a similar emotional response to each. The disgust, fear, and aversion they felt for the way Richard looked and acted were confused for an actual connection between the two objects under consideration, which are quite different things. Perception was thrown out upon reality, aligning two isolated phenomena because the same judgment had been attributed to each. The conceptual force of similitude lured Tudor writers to draw their rhetoric for Richard's body from figures that encourage comparison or collapse the terms compared—such as isocolon, antanaclasis, and antimetabole.

Kuhn writes that "men whose research is based on shared paradigms are committed to the same rules and standards" (11). In the sixteenth century, the Tudor myth was the standard—probably the rule handed down from on high—and the analogy between Richard's body and behavior was the paradigm that followed. William Baldwin's verse collection *A Myrroure for Magistrates* (1559) avouched the providential historical narrative of the Tudor myth. George Ferrers's contribution, a ballad from the perspective of Richard's brother, the Duke of Clarence, glossed Richard's royal emblem thus:

> My brother was the Bore,
> Whose tuskes should teare my brothers boyes & me,
> And gave me warning therof long before.
> But wit nor warning can in no degree
> Let things to hap, which are ordained to bee.²⁹

Richard's "tuskes" are an omen, a "warning" of murderous ways "ordained" by God. For the first time, the providential political theology of the Tudor myth appears explicitly in a reading of Richard's deformities, insofar as the boar's tusks amplify the toothed birth described by Rous and More. Richard's tusks reappeared in the second edition of the *Myrroure* (1563), in John Dolman's ballad from the perspective of Lord Hastings, which gave a grotesque image of Richard:

> And lowryng on me with the google eye,
> The whetted tuske, and furrowed forehead hye,
> His Crooked shoulder bristellyke set vp,
> With frothy Iawes, whose foame he chawed and suppd.³⁰

By associating Richard's teeth with the tusks of the boar, the poets in the *Myrroure* were "achieving the anticipated in a new way," which is what Kuhn calls "normal research" (36). He compares paradigms to puzzles, normal research to puzzling out how to fit the pieces together to arrive at an image already known because it's printed on the box. The boar was a new piece to the Ricardian puzzle, but easily fit—was shaped to fit—into the paradigm the Tudor writers had been practicing for decades.

In sum, the comparative rhetoric Vergil and More used to align Richard's body and behavior produced what Kuhn calls "a synthesis able to attract most of the next generation's practitioners" (18)—namely, Grafton, Hall, Rainolde, Ferrers, and Dolman. Richard's troubled birth was made to signify the evils of his adulthood because these two events, although totally discrete historical phenomena separated by decades, elicited similar emotions in the Tudor historians: disgust, fear, aversion, and the like. The analogy of Richard's body and behavior was then attached to an additional event, the establishment of the Tudor monarchy, which assuaged the weary historian by eliciting emotions opposite to Richard: comfort, security, relief, and so forth. By connecting the figural reading of Richard's body and behavior to the Tudor myth, sixteenth-century prose and verse writers were, to quote Kuhn, "extending the knowledge of those facts that the paradigm displays" (24).

V. Normal Science

This paradigm received two additional extensions—"monstrosity" and "physiognomy"—in Shakespeare's most revered source, Raphael Holinshed's *Chronicles of England, Scotland and Ireland*, which connected Richard's body and behavior in two places. The first edition (1577) included only one short statement on "this monster of nature & cruell tyrant Richard the third."[31] Deformity ("monster") is so close to villainy ("tyrant") that body and behavior effectively signify each other. That construction was by this point conventional, but (you may have noticed) Holinshed's *Chronicles* was the first to refer to Richard as a "monster," at least in print.[32]

The word came from the flurry of early Elizabethan broadsides reporting monstrous births. They differed from previous monster literature through their proto-scientific attempt to interpret what modern physicians call congenital malformations, as opposed to preternatural "prodigies," such as a woman giving birth to a dog with a snake's head. But the "monstrosities" were not just biological abnormalities: "They ar lessons & scholynges for vs all (as the word *monster* shewith)."[33] From the Latin *monere*, "to warn," monsters were admonitions that an iniquitous England must mend its ways or face the wrath of an angry God. These births could be human or animal. The most common animals were swine, recalling Richard's royal emblem. In the *Myrrour*, the boar's "tuskes" were a "warning" of an "ordained" evil; the monstrous pigs on the broadsides were "wonderful tokens, wherby we ought to be warned."[34] With human monsters, it was usually unmarried or incestuous parents whose sins were shaped out in physical form, but often it was the entire nation: "This monstrous shape to thee England / Playn shewes thy monstrous vice."[35] The discourse of "monstrosity" gave Tudor writers a way to extend the immorality of Richard III to his family, the Yorks, and then to his entire society, Plantagenet England, including the Lancastrians. As A. P. Rossiter writes of Shakespeare's *Richard III*—the language of vision is important—"Look, then, with a believing Tudor eye, and ought you not to approve Richard's doings? *Per se*, they are the judgments of God on the wicked."[36]

The broadsides said that the life of a monster is but short, as is the time remaining for the sinners and Sodoms they signify. Like the prodigies and portents in the Biblical book of Revelation, English monsters were eschatological, foreboding the end of an age, if not all time: "These be tokens now sent foorth / To preache the later daye."[37] Monstrosity gave Tudor writers a system for connecting the metaphorical reading of Richard's deformities with the teleological account of an English *eschaton*. The God punishing sinful parents and iniquitous societies by sending a sign of his anger in the form of physical deformity is the same God who guided England out of the Wars of the Roses and into the holy hands of Henry Tudor.

The sixteenth century brought major advances in medical treatments for people with physical disabilities, most notably from French surgeon Ambroise Paré, but they never came into readings of Richard III.[38] The figural paradigm did not expect or need that knowledge, ignored it, suppressed it. Consider that when the wickedness that deformity signifies belongs to the child's parents or their society, the infant himself is innocent: "Beholde a guiltlesse babe / Reft of his limmes."[39] This observation endangers the very foundation of the Tudor Richard, the analogy between innate deformity and innate villainy. With no need for coherence, Tudor writers took what worked from the discourse of monstrosity and left what didn't. The figural paradigm suppressed the anomalous novelty encountered. As Kuhn writes, normal research is "an attempt to force nature into the preformed and relatively inflexible box that the paradigm supplies"; the paradigm influences the phenomena we perceive, and "those that will not fit the box are often not seen at all" (24). *Look with a believing Tudor eye.* At the same time—looking forward—the idea that deformed children are born with a mental and moral *table rasa* (to use John Locke's term) eventually powered Shakespeare's production of an anomalous interpretation of Richard, one suppressed for centuries until it effected a paradigm shift in the eighteenth century.

Written in the generation before Shakespeare, Thomas Legge's university play *Richardus Tertius* (ca. 1580) treated the Tudor Richard with the language of monstrosity (in Latin). Richard's body and behavior merge as an "abominable monstrosity [*monstrum nefandum*]," a "monstrous . . . depravity [*immane portentum*]," and a "monstrous villainy [*immane . . . scelus*]."[40] Nouns and adjectives fall into each other. Legge's England was "torn by the impious teeth [*dente lacerata impio*] of the raging boar" (444). Legge alluded to Richard's teeth about a dozen times, while another play, *The True Tragedie of Richard the Third* (ca. 1590), included another conceit already noted. Richard's deformed arm takes on a bloodthirsty life of its own: "I hope with this lame hand of mine, to rake out that hateful heart of Richmond, and when I have it, to eate it panting hote with salt."[41] With each iteration of the paradigm, Richard's tyranny was more deeply written into his deformity, and this analogy of body and behavior was more clearly connected to the Tudor myth that managed—invented and vanquished—the Ricardian evil. Thus, the allegorical induction to the *True Tragedie* has Truth tell Poetry that Richard is

"A man ill shaped, crooked backed, lame armed, withal, / Valiantly minded, but tyrannous in authoritie" (57–58), while the play's conclusion breaks actors out of character to trumpet the Tudor myth by detailing the genealogical descent from Henry VII to Elizabeth I.

Anomalies do exist. Giles Fletcher, writing about Richard at the same time as Shakespeare, said nothing about Richard's body in *The Rising to the Crowne of Richard the Third* (1593).[42] But it was much more common for someone like Anthony Chute (also in 1593) to call Richard "a true-borne-infant-bloud-spilling murtherer: / Vsurping monster."[43] The assonance of *m*, *o*, *t*, and *r* sounds encourages readers to overlap the two epithets, "murtherer" and "monster." Another anomaly confirms the presence of a paradigm: the 1585 image of Richard by the Dutch engraver Hendrick Goltzius shows no deformity because Goltzius, working outside England, was outside the paradigm.[44]

The second new piece Holinshed's *Chronicles* added to the Ricardian puzzle came in the second edition (1587). It quotes More's vignette verbatim but then adds a coda: "The full confluence of these qualities, with the defects of fauour and amiable proportion, gaue proofe to this rule of physiognomie: *Distor tum vultum sequitur distorsio morum* [A deformity in appearance follows a deformity in character]" (3.712). From the Greek *physis*, "nature," and *gnomon*, "interpreter," physiognomy is the art or science of interpreting the nature of an individual, implying that humans have a distinct and definite nature at birth that stays with us. Physiognomy started in ancient Greece with some scattered suggestions in Hippocrates's medical tracts, but it gained philosophical authority in the myth of Er that concludes Plato's *Republic*.[45] Socrates described the souls of famous Greek men going into the afterlife, each assuming the shape of the animal whose nature he shares: the warrior Ajax becomes a lion, and the unintelligent Thersites—also the first physically deformed man in European literature—an ape. Two points. First, like humans, animals were thought to have natures, and physiognomy asked which animal you look like to attribute the manners of that creature to your nature. The Tudor Richard looks and acts like the animal on his emblem, the boar. Second, to function, physiognomy needs spirituality, the belief that—somehow, somewhere—humans have souls stashed away inside our bodies and that these souls are permanent and real in a way that our bodies are not. With extreme caution, Aristotle entertained the possibility that we can interpret souls from bodies, "if there is a single sign for a single thing."[46] That's a big *if*. Overlooking this provision, Aristotle's students systematized physiognomy in a treatise often mistaken as one of his. They made a manual sorting bodies and behaviors into schematic categories and then connecting those categories on the basis of "congruity," as in this reading of a man looking like the Tudor Richard: "An ill-proportioned body indicates a rogue, the argument being partly from congruity and partly from the female sex. But, if bad proportions mean villainy, a well-proportioned frame must be characteristic of upright men and brave."[47] Blatant misogyny only exacerbates the ruthless categorical thinking: well-proportioned means bravery, and ill-proportioned means villainy, just as men are good and women bad. "There never was an animal with the form of one kind and the mental character of another," they wrote (805a). "Permanent bodily signs will indicate permanent mental qualities" (806a).

Physiognomy gained an air of dignity when Galen used it to describe the four temperaments in his humoral medicine, and when the fifth-century philosopher Adamantius the Sophist wrote his own *Physiognomonica*, insisting "he who has a hunchback and whose shoulders are bent in the direction of his breast is malicious and a sorcerer."[48] In the words of Martin Henry Porter, there was "a persistent fisnomical consciousness" in Europe from 400 B.C.E. to the fifteenth century.[49] Variously Hippocratic, Socratic, Aristotelian, pseudo-Aristotelian, Galenic, and Adamantine, physiognomy came into Renaissance culture in two ways, one popular and one professional. First, as a social convention, European aristocrats abided by the Greek ethical ideal of *kalokagathia*, "the beautiful in the good," with its concomitant antipathy to ugliness and deformity. As Baldassarre Castiglione's book of *The Courtyer* (1528) said, "The foule therfore for the most part be also yuell & the beawtifull, good" because the body is "a marke of the soule, whereby [one] is outwardlye knowen."[50] Wildly popular in Tudor England, Castiglione's book promoted the amateur physiognomy that produced the Tudor Richard: "A man hath that default or blemishe (as it were) for a patent and token of his ill inclination" (N.n.iiii).

Physiognomy survived in a second way, as a practical science with a litter of textbooks. The 1504 Italian physiognomy of Bartolomeo della Rocca (called Cocles) was translated into English by Thomas Hill in 1556; the 1522 German physiognomy of Johannes Indagine by Fabian Withers in 1558; and the 1542 French physiognomy of Richard Roussat (called Arcandam) by William Warde in 1564.[51] The reading of physical deformity in these tracts was ruthless. Someone shaped like the Tudor Richard III was every bad thing one could be. For Cocles, "the necke croked . . . argueth hym to be deceatfull, a wary talker, and vnfaythfull" (E.i); "the shoulder poyntes crokyng inwarde: declare that man to be wary, slouthfull, secrete, ingeniouse, and a surmise" (E.ii); "the shoulder poyntes vnequall, as the one greater then the other, declare that man to be slouthful, of a dul vnderstandig, of a grosse wit & feadyng, sipie, of a dul capacitie, faithful, bold, a niggard or one hard to be moued, and somtymes an vtterer of secretes, false, and not credityng one" (E.ii); "the crokednes of the backe, declareth the maliciousnesse of condicious, and ouerthwartnesse in maners" (E.vii); "the legges croked, and hollow or bending in the nether part of the legges: declare those men, to be euil" (F.v). Indagine associates spinal deformity with envy: "A croked backe is token of a nigarde, and couetous persone" (H.viii). The judgments of Roussat were as unqualified ("all lame men are wicked") as they were perplexing ("the most wicked of al other, are ye croke backed men seing the faulte of them is neare vnto the hart whych is the prince of all ye body" [S.iii]).

Elizabethan England's most prolific physiognomer, Thomas Hill, wrote his own text in 1571.[52] The dedicatory epistle of *The Contemplation of Mankinde* commends Aristotle's prohibition against government positions for people with disabilities; affirms that "an euill fauoured and crabbed countenance, doth euermore yeelde vntoward condicions"; translates some verses from the Roman poet Martial about how disabled people are better off dead ("Thy fete be short, / purblinde to ... A good deede do (the Prouerbe sayth) / and then cut of thy headde" [¶¶.i]); and translates some verses from the Greek poet Agathyllus ("Why doste thou limpe and halt, / thy minde is lame I see, / These outward signes are tokens plain / of secrete yll in thee" [¶¶.i]). *The Contemplation of Mankinde* includes a woodcut image of a hunchbacked man, saying that it is "impossible after nature, that such deformed persons shoulde possesse in them laudable actions. . . . Out of an euill shaped bodie, can no lawdable actions procéede" (161). Hill made the spirituality of physiognomy specifically Christian: "This Phisiognomie is a knowledge which leadeth a man to the vnderstanding and knowing both of the naturall motions, and conditions of the spirit: and the good or euill fortune, by the outwarde notes and lines of the face and body" (★iiii). There's something new here, in the phrase "and the good or euill fortune." It's the same innovation added by Shakespeare's Italian contemporary, Giambattista della Porta, when he wrote *On Human Physiognomy* (1586): "Everyone knows that amongst the Philosophers it is a commonplace that the monster in the body is a monster in the soul, and being a monster in the soul, what can be expected of such a person, what should become of him, if not evils and misfortune."[53] For Hill and Porta, deformity signified more than villainy; it signified tragedy as well. Ancient Greek physiognomy linked body to soul, but Renaissance physiognomy added a temporal dimension. Physiognomy provided Tudor courtiers with the image of a universe where deformity is congruent with villainy—this is the "rule of physiognomie" cited in Holinshed's *Chronicles*—and an account of time and history in which deformity and villainy are congruent with tragedy, allowing the beautiful and the good (the Tudors) to establish their messianic state by conquering the deformed and vile Richard.

In sum, "monstrosity" gave Tudor writers a way to ascribe Richard's evil nature to his family and society and then to imagine an angry God ending this age of iniquity, while "physiognomy" explained how Richard's body signified his evil nature, prophesied his criminal behavior, and certified his death at the hands of England's savior. This was "normal science," not only in Kuhn's sense of a repeated paradigm of research that suppresses anomalies and expands outward into theory but also by being research conducted by those the sociologist Erving Goffman calls "the normals": those who "believe the person with a stigma is not quite human," who "exercise varieties of discrimination," who "reduce his life chances," who "construct a stigma-theory, an ideology to explain his inferiority and account for the danger he represents," who "use specific stigma terms such as cripple, bastard, moron in our daily discourse as a source of metaphor and imagery," who "impute a wide range of imperfections on the basis of the original one."[54]

Physiognomy was extremely popular in the sixteenth century, yet it took Tudor writers decades to invoke the "rule of physiognomie" in their readings of Richard III, illustrating Kuhn's point that "rules . . . derive from paradigms, but paradigms can guide research even in the absence of rules" (42). Physiognomy was not the philosophical principal or methodical set of rules followed to read villainy and tragedy from Richard's deformity. Instead, physiognomy explained and justified what the Tudors had been doing all along. By simply interpreting Richard, rather than formulating rules for interpreting him, the Tudors displayed what Kuhn calls "tacit knowledge" (44n1), a term he takes from Michael Polanyi's *Personal Knowledge* (1958):

> The premises of a skill cannot be discovered focally prior to its performance, nor even understood if explicitly stated by others, before we ourselves have experienced its performance, whether by watching it or by engaging in it ourselves. In performing a skill we are therefore acting on certain premises of which we are focally ignorant, but which we know subsidiarily as part of our mastery of that skill.[55]

Rather than being an explicit scientific theory, the constellation of assumptions, values, commitments, and practices surrounding the representation of Richard III in the sixteenth century amounts to what Kuhn calls a "disciplinary matrix" (182). This matrix includes the metaphorical treatment of Richard's deformities as a paradigmatic model, the figure of the boar as an additional example, comparative rhetoric as a technique for normal research, Tudor historians as a professional community, the Tudor myth as its standard, Christian spirituality as a shared belief, monstrosity as an assimilated discourse, and physiognomy as a recognized "rule."

VI. Stigma as Figura

Modern historians of Richard III have a different disciplinary matrix. They write history that is analytical, not political, and the Tudor myth is seen as myth. The rhetoric Tudors used to connect Richard's body and behavior is seen as either naivety or propaganda, surpassed by the modern historiography explaining events in terms of material causes and effects, called realism, naturalism, materialism, historicism, or historism. If realism is the mimesis of modernity, as Erich Auerbach outlines in *Mimesis: The Representation of Reality in Western Literature* (1946), the mimesis of antiquity was "figuralism."[56] The philology in Auerbach's essay "Figura" (1938) and the literary history in *Mimesis* addressed much more than the Pauline typological exegesis that explains events of the Old Testament through those in the New.[57] To differentiate that Biblical exegesis from a general way of reading and representing the world, Auerbach coined the term "figural realism."

Figural realism builds a horizontal bridge between two historical events, connecting this bridge vertically with a mystical and felicitous view of time. If something happened, the reason it happened is that God made it happen, but this greater meaning is obtained without trivializing the concrete historical event that did happen. A figure and its fulfillment have the same meaning, as it were, but different registers of significance. Figural realism preserves the historical particularity of the events it connects but uses this connection to glimpse an understanding of truth in its final form. This theory of history sees God shaping time through a system of figures and their fulfillments, events joined by a perceived similitude in a way that illuminates the rational organization of the world.

The historical imagination that Auerbach called figural realism was put into words by the comparative rhetorical devices that Tudor writers used to represent the body and behavior of Richard III.[58] His invented deformities at birth were made to prefigure his villainies later in life. The murders he committed were seen as fulfilling the prophecy of his prodigious birth. Tudor chroniclers placed the horizontal connection between figure and fulfillment in a vertical relationship with a divinely governed narrative of their nation's history—namely, the Tudor myth. Richard's deformity was usually not a spatial metaphor (aligning inside and outside, soul and body) but a temporal metaphor (aligning the birth of a man and his behavior in adulthood). This connection of Richard's body and behavior may have been a facile analogy at the start of the sixteenth century but, by the end of the century, this figure was the centerpiece of a systematic strategy for English history. A way of writing about Richard became a way to read the world: rhetoric became history, then theology and philosophy, and in effect reality.

During the sixteenth century, the figural representation of Richard crossed the borders of artistic medium and literary kind, from visual arts to written word in prose, verse, and drama. It can be said, along with Kuhn, that Tudor historians "achieved a paradigm that proved able to guide the whole group's research" (22), including the "research" of William Shakespeare. Scholars have recently emphasized the collaborative aspects of the plays called "Shakespeare's first tetralogy," but the scenes where stigma is central to the character of Richard III were all written by Shakespeare.[59] The figural representation of Richard's deformity is already in play at the end of *2 Henry VI* (ca. 1590) in the scene, likely by Shakespeare, where "crookback Richard" first appears (5.1.89sd in Quarto). When some of Richard's first words offend Lord Clifford, this Lancastrian lashes out with two figural epithets and a memorable simile: "Heap of wrath, foul indigested lump, / As crooked in thy manners as thy shape" (5.1.157–158). The simile associates Richard's body ("shape") and behavior ("manners"), while the epithets use the physical ("heap" and "lump") to bracket the moral ("wrath" and "foul"). According to Lord Clifford's son in the next scene, again by Shakespeare, Richard is a "crookback villain" (5.2.57 in Quarto), adjective and noun falling into each other: deformity points forward to villainy, villainy backward to deformity. Adjective and noun again form a figural relationship when Young Clifford calls Richard a "foul stigmatic" (5.1.215), one of the first instances of the word *stigma* or its cognates (*stigmatic, stigmatize, stigmatized*) in English.[60] The history of this term, from the Greek *stigma*, "brand," indicates the vertical connection in the figural reading of Richard's body. In ancient Greece, a stigma was a tattoo or brand given to a criminal or slave by someone who wanted others to be cautious.[61] Even though the Tudor Richard's deformity is congenital, Young Clifford sees it as "stigma," as a mark made by God at the time of Richard's birth to warn the English of crimes not yet committed, crimes to be committed, but crimes to be overcome and punished by God's white knight, Henry Tudor.

2

The Models of Stigma in Shakespeare's First Tetralogy

Spirituality, Psychology, Sociology

By calling Richard a "stigmatic" at the end of *2 Henry VI* (5.1.215), Shakespeare represented the idea that Richard's body at birth in 1452 was somehow a sign of three things: (1) the essential and changeless moral character of a villain, (2) this character's expression in a series of murders while usurping the English throne in the 1470s and 1480s, and (3) the rational universal order whereby divinity not only gives deformity to villains to warn the virtuous but also steers history so that virtue conquers vice at the Battle of Bosworth in 1485. "Shakespeare was applying medieval notions of disability," as Abigail Comber has argued, and his "original audience would have viewed Richard's impairment as a marker of his evil because that is what lingering medieval perceptions of disability had trained them to do."[1] Looking at sixteenth-century monster literature, such as Pierre Boaistuau's *Histoiries Prodigieuses* (1561) and Ambroise Paré's *Des Monstres et Prodiges* (1575), Geoffrey Johns has illustrated that "the popularity and ubiquity of monstrous birth ephemera throughout the sixteenth century is a key factor in the literary genealogy and cultural significance of Shakespeare's *Richard III*."[2] But did Shakespeare endorse the figural interpretation of Richard's disability? What did Shakespeare believe about Richard's body? What did he believe about physical disability in general? Can those beliefs be culled from a close reading of his plays about Richard?

Given the dominance of the figural paradigm in sixteenth-century depictions of Richard's disability, there was a remarkable anomaly in *3 Henry*

VI when Shakespeare suggested, for the first time ever, that Richard's body was not the sign but the cause of his behavior—a causal interpretation opposed to the figural interpretation of disability. But Shakespeare went even further, inventing a new way of thinking about stigma that informs sociology to this day. He represented the figural interpretation of disability found in his sources but ascribed it to Richard's enemies, making it a position taken by characters in a narrative, not by the author of the narrative. Contrast a source like *The True Tragedie of Richard the Third* (ca. 1590), in which the figural interpretation comes in an allegorical conversation between Truth and Poetry. If, on the order of *The True Tragedie*, Shakespeare had brought Truth out on stage to say, *Actually, Richard's deformity is the cause, not the sign, of his villainy*, that would have been a step forward in the history of stigma. Or if Shakespeare had written an essay outlining the causal interpretation, as Francis Bacon did some twenty years later in "Of Deformity," that, too, would have been a step forward. But Shakespeare took the additional step of attributing the causal interpretation of disability to Richard himself. By ascribing figural and causal interpretations of disability to different characters, each beholden to their own biases and desires, Shakespeare dramatized the contest to make sense of and control the meaning of disability, which had never been done before, illustrating Allison Hobgood's point that "early modern literary representations seemingly beholden to ability logics often cultivated oppositional worldviews."[3] For Shakespeare, stigma was a social and rhetorical phenomenon, situated and perspectival, emerging from hostile social interaction and compromised thought. With Shakespeare's Richard, the representation of stigma took two steps forward—first from a spiritual to a psychological model and then into a sociological model of stigma.

I. Margaret and the Spiritual Model of Stigma

The spiritual model of stigma appears early in *3 Henry VI* in scenes written by Shakespeare. Queen Margaret voices it twice. First, outside Sandal Castle, Margaret captures Richard's father, the Duke of York, and asks, "Where's that valiant crookback prodigy, / Dickie, your boy?" (1.3.75–76). A "prodig[ious]" body is more than just a body—it's a sign. Formed from the Latin *aio*, "I say," and the prefix *pro*, "forth," a *prodigy* is an opening to speak on meanings behind the materials of our world.[4] Prodigies imply spirituality, the belief that humans have souls behind our bodies, that the world is a playground for spirits benevolent and malignant. As corridors from the material to the spiritual, prodigies are located in an aesthetically clean universe where divinity reveals essential truths and forebodes future events with eerie signs. In the Renaissance, prodigies were often geological or meteorological—earthquakes or comets—but could be biological, as when physical deformity was conceived as a disturbance interrupting the regular course of nature. Thus, Adam Cohen reads Shakespeare's *Richard III* as a "prodigy play, which highlights a prodigious birth come to maturity whose political rise and fall signals a significant political upheaval—the final battles of the War of the Roses and the establishment of the Tudor dynasty under the Earl of Richmond."[5]

Margaret's second statement envisions divinity stigmatizing Richard for crimes not yet committed, calling Richard "a foul misshapen stigmatic, / Marked by the Destinies to be avoided" (2.2.135–137). If "foul" describes Richard's character and "misshapen" his body, "stigmatic" collapses character and body into a marked criminal and then mystifies this mark, with Margaret crediting it to a providential history warning of villainy through deformity. She says that "the Destinies" have marked Richard because, for Margaret, the physical "mark[ing]" of Richard is both ethical and temporal: he is marked as a villain to be avoided and marked for tragedy by destiny.

In one of Shakespeare's later scenes in *3 Henry VI*, Margaret further mythologizes the "mark" on Richard's body, calling him "that devil's butcher, Richard / Hard-favored Richard" (5.5.77–78). Turning to *Richard III*, it is no longer the destinies but now, Margaret says, "Sin, death, and hell have set their marks on him / And all their ministers attend on him" (1.3.292–293). Here Richard was "mark[ed]," or targeted, by the evil forces of "sin, death, and hell," and his involvement in this enterprise of evil is "mark[ed]," or indicated, by his deformity. Even little elves mark Margaret's Richard:

> Thou elvish-marked, abortive, rooting hog,
> Thou that wast sealed in thy nativity
> The slave of nature and the son of hell;
> Thou slander of thy heavy mother's womb,
> Thou loathèd issue of thy father's loins,
> Thou rag of honor, thou detested— (1.3.227–232)

Before Richard cuts her off, Margaret backdates his villainy to his mother's womb, even to his father's seed. Upon Richard's conception, the evil in this deformed little homunculus was fully formed or "seal'd," a word with moral and physical meanings. His villainy was fastened, bound, "seal'd" inside, his body becoming a hermetic container of character. And deformity is the "seal," or emblem, visibly identifying villainous contents contained within. In calling

Richard a "rooting hog," Margaret alludes to his royal seal, the boar, its arched back resembling Richard's "lump[y]" and "heap[ed]" back (*2H6*, 5.1.157), its bloody tusks aligned with Richard's toothed birth. Margaret sees Richard as other animals as well, a "bottled spider" (*R3*, 1.3.241) and a "poisonous bunch-backed toad" (1.3.245), bridging discourses of animality and monstrosity, as John W. Ellis-Etchison argues.[6] Because Richard's hunchback looks like a beast's, Margaret associates him with the aggression of a boar, the frenzy of a spider, the venom of a toad, and the bite of a dog: "Look when he fawns, he bites" (1.3.289).

Margaret's final figural reading of Richard, screamed at his mother shortly after his coronation, reads his body through several mythical dogs and monsters, but the basis is the legend that Richard was born with teeth:

> From forth the kennel of thy womb hath crept
> A hellhound that doth hunt us all to death.
> That dog that had his teeth before his eyes,
> To worry lambs and lap their gentle blood;
> That foul defacer of God's handiwork,
> That reigns in gallèd eyes of weeping souls;
> That excellent grand tyrant of the earth
> Thy womb let loose to chase us to our graves.
> O upright, just, and true-disposing God,
> How do I thank Thee that this carnal cur
> Preys on the issue of his mother's body. (4.4.47–57)

John Milton probably had this passage in mind in *Paradise Lost* when describing Sin, whose lower body is composed of "Hell Hounds" who creep "into her woomb, / And kennel there."[7] Milton then mentions Scylla, whose "hinder-loynes" were changed into snarling dogs in Ovid's account: "In seeking where her loynes, and thyghes, and feet and ancles were, / Chappes like the chappes of *Cerberus* in stead of them shee found."[8] Scylla's "hell-hound" also invites comparison to Cerberus, whom Milton mentions. This three-headed hellhound was a source for Dante's Lucifer, frozen in the depths of hell, gnawing sinners in his three jaws, blood and tears mixed in his drool.[9] Rather than sinners, Margaret's Richard laps up the blood of lambs, a reference to the blood of Christ and Christians, making Richard the Satan of the Bible. Identified in Christian theology with the serpent in the Book of Genesis, Satan is, like Richard, "that foul defacer of God's handiwork," thrown down to Earth in the book of Revelation (12.9), just as Richard is, to Margaret, "that excellent grand tyrant of the earth." This last line could be an allusion to the Titans, offspring of Gaia, or "Earth," perhaps specifically Typhon, father of all monsters, including Scylla and Cerberus. These analogues—Greek myth, Ovid's *Metamorphoses*, the Book of Revelation, Dante's *Comedy*, Milton's *Paradise Lost*—all exploit the symbolic power of monstrosity in the representation of a reality that looks nothing like the world we experience from day to day. In these heightened realities, monsters and the death, destruction, and disorder they signify are conquered and constrained by, in Margaret's words, an "upright, just, and true-disposing God," a mythic narrative she redistributes to Richard, whom she calls "hell's black intelligencer" (4.4.71), by stigmatizing his disability.

II. Stigma as Magic

Like all figural interpretation, Margaret's treatment of Richard as a "prodigy" and "stigmatic" who is "marked" and "sealed" depends on the structure of consciousness that social anthropologists call "magical thinking." E. B. Tylor and James Frazer use this term to study people who believe they have access to and control over a spiritual realm that exists behind the material world.[10] Sigmund Freud's *Totem and Taboo* (1913) brings psychology to anthropology, and we can do the same to unpack the mental and cultural qualities underwriting the magical thinking of Margaret and Shakespeare's other Lancastrians.

Freud emphasizes Tylor's definition of magical thinking, "mistaking an ideal connection for a real one," which is what Margaret does when reading disability as a sign of villainy and tragedy.[11] It is an "ideal connection" because it exists only in the world of ideas. In an ideal world, danger would be self-evident, "mark'd by the destinies to be avoided." There would be a transparent identity between what something is and what it seems to be. Magical thinking posits a real and permanent world of spirit behind the illusive and transitory world of matter only to claim some correspondence between these two worlds in an attempt to stabilize otherwise limited and unreliable interpretations. By making the world as humans see it from our limited perspective into the world as it truly and incontrovertibly is, magical thinking tries to evade the fallibility of interpretation, claiming a God's-eye view of existence.

As Freud writes, the connection between the apparent and the real does not occur out in the world; it occurs in the mind of the person interpreting that world, a confusion of belief and reality called the "omnipotence of thoughts" (107). Two things that would go together in an ideal world are brought together in the actual world by being brought together in a mind that mistakes thought for reality. Once this ideal connection is presumed to be real, it conditions perception to confirm expectation rather than experience. Thus, Margaret sees evil in Richard, eliding a material world in which disability has other meanings, or no meaning at all, in favor of the world of spirit and myth.

Insofar as Margaret's account of Richard is shared by her son Edward, her husband Henry, her daughter-in-law Anne, Old Clifford, and Young Clifford, Lancastrian England in Shakespeare's first tetralogy is one of Freud's "primitive races" (95). From a Freudian perspective, their magical thinking stems from the problem of death: they are in the midst of a horrible civil war. The pain and suffering of war clash with the human desire to amass pleasure and comfort. Shakespeare's Lancastrian England starts thinking magically because the belief that their destiny is happy and secure, despite the evident sense of things, is a salve to their anxious family. As the House of York gains more and more footing on the English throne, Margaret increasingly believes herself to have been wronged by a disruption to the proper course of history, where her son receives the crown. She makes sense of injustice by mapping her story of Lancastrians versus Yorks onto the spiritual world in which good is always at war with evil, God versus Devil. The enemy in her war here on Earth is matched up with the enemy in that otherworldly war, so Richard is understood to be evil, his deformity the sign of his evil nature. The defeat of evil that is never in doubt in the cosmic war of any mythology allows Margaret to envision a similar outcome in her war against Richard. Calling Richard a "devil" (*R3*, 1.3.117) uses the inevitable damnation of devils to prognosticate an end to the evil Margaret thinks that Richard embodies: "Hie thee to hell for shame, and leave this world, / Thou cacodemon! There thy kingdom is" (1.3.142–143). Margaret extrapolates Richard's actions (murder) to his character (villainy) and soul (evil) and then to a supernatural monster (devil) whose metaphysical location (hell) and eschatological destiny (damnation) are read back into Richard's earthly plight as far back as his birth and as far forward as his death. His deformed birth may be an omen of the danger he poses to Lancastrian England, but the defeat of evil in the spiritual realm of magical thinking certifies the same fate for Richard during the Wars of the Roses.

Were Margaret to explain this to Freud, he would diagnose her as "neurotic," as someone who has retreated from the material world as it is experienced because of the unpleasant truths of that experience. Insofar as Lancastrian England is all together on our couch here, it is a neurotic culture.

When Lancastrian England posits a cosmic justice gone awry, it creates the conditions of its own suffering, turning misfortune into tragedy.

III. Richard and the Psychological Model of Stigma

With Margaret's figural interpretations, Richard's disability in the *Henry VI* plays begins as a conventional Tudor treatment, but halfway through *3 Henry VI*, Shakespeare swerved to consider the emotional life of a man subjected to stigma. Imagine someone saying to you the horrible things Richard's enemies say to him: "Heap of wrath," "foul indigested lump," "foul stigmatic," "crookback prodigy," "abortive," "bunch-backed toad." That's what Shakespeare did, asking how a disabled man would experience those insults. In act 3, scene 2 (written by Shakespeare), Richard starts talking to the audience in soliloquies and asides, giving voice to his inner life, his torment, his anger, his ambition, his irreverence, and his plans to deceive, betray, and kill his family. Prompted by his brother Edward's sexual bravado, Richard begins his first soliloquy by lamenting the discrepancy "between my soul's desire and me" (3.2.128). He imagines himself atop a cliff, gazing out across an ocean, seeing in the distance a future where he is king of England. But too many heirs separate him from the crown, so "there is no kingdom then for Richard" (3.2.146). Longing for a better life, Richard asks, "What other pleasure can the world afford?" (3.2.147). He considers emulating his lascivious brother, Edward, but quickly abandons the possibility of love. His improbable success in wooing Lady Anne in *Richard III* (after earlier killing her husband) shows Richard to be perfectly capable of courtly romance. In *3 Henry VI*, however, he does not believe himself to be:

> Why, Love forswore me in my mother's womb
> And, for I should not deal in her soft laws,
> She did corrupt frail Nature with some bribe
> To shrink mine arm up like a withered shrub,
> To make an envious mountain on my back,
> Where sits deformity to mock my body;
> To shape my legs of an unequal size,
> To disproportion me in every part
> Like to a chaos or an unlicked bear whelp
> That carries no impression like the dam—
> And am I then a man to be beloved?
> O monstrous fault, to harbor such a thought! (3.2.153–164)

Where his enemies call him a "stigmatic" and a "prodigy," Richard speaks of his "deformity," and of specific deformities in a way that distinguishes his identity from his body. It's a Richard of "person-first language": not a disabled man but a man with a disability. It's also a moment of what Ato Quayson calls "aesthetic nervousness," "when the dominant protocols of representation within the literary text are short-circuited in relation to disability."[12] It's a more naturalistic, humane account of disability than Richard ever received before Shakespeare, which is partly why the subsequent logic in Shakespeare's play has made sense to many modern readers:

> Then, since this earth affords no joy to me
> But to command, to check, to o'erbear such
> As are of better person than myself,
> I'll make my heaven to dream upon the crown
> And, whiles I live, t'account this world but hell
> Until my misshaped trunk that bears this head
> Be round impalèd with a glorious crown. (3.2.165–171)

As the first time anyone had suggested that someone treated as Richard is treated in the Tudor chronicles would suffer anguish and have his own opinions about his body, Richard's soliloquy in act 3 of *3 Henry VI* is the first modern representation of physical disability. In the premodern figural interpretation of disability, to quote Erich Auerbach's *Mimesis*, "The horizontal, that is the temporal and causal, connection of occurrences is dissolved; the here and now is no longer a mere link in an earthly chain of events, it is simultaneously something which has always been, and which will be fulfilled in the future; and strictly, in the eyes of God, it is something eternal, something omni-temporal, something already consummated in the realm of fragmentary earthly event."[13] In contrast, Auerbach writes, modernity seeks "to explain to a certain extent every single historical fact by its immediate causes and to foresee to a certain extent its immediate consequences, moving so to speak on a horizontal plane."[14] From Bacon to Freud, modern essayists have read deformity as Richard does here—as a link in a chain of causes and effects. In Bacon's essay "Of Deformity" (1613), he wrote, "It is good to consider of *Deformity*, not as a Signe . . . but as a Cause, which seldome faileth of the Effect."[15] Freud used a more clinical terminology.

His "libido theory" posits a social economy of loving and being loved.[16] Like all humans in Freud's scheme, Richard has instincts to love those who care for and protect him, especially his mother. As revealed in *Richard III*,

Richard's mother does not love him back ("I see my shame in him" [2.2.54]) because she, like Margaret, thinks magically about deformity. "O my accursèd womb, the bed of death," his mother laments, "a cockatrice hast thou hatched to the world" (4.1.53–54). Richard's mother is borrowing the language of his mortal enemy, Queen Margaret. Margaret called Richard the "slander of [his] mother's heavy womb," while Richard's mother enchants her own womb with evil, calling it "accursed." Margaret called Richard a "cacodemon," an evil spirit, from the Greek *kakos*, "bad," and *daimon*, "spirit," while Richard's mother outdoes her with "cockatrice," a mythical rooster-headed dragon often identified as a basilisk, the king of serpents who can kill with a single glance. Margaret saw Richard as a "poisonous bunch-backed toad," which Richard's mother echoes when chiding him, "Thou toad, thou toad" (4.4.145). Margaret called Richard "abortive," and Richard's mother says that she should have had an abortion: "Oh, she that might have intercepted thee, / By strangling thee in her accursèd womb, / From all the slaughters, wretch, that thou hast done" (4.4.137–139). In the biography of Richard that follows, his mother transfers the myth of hell to her experience on Earth, her surprising rhyming granting her figural reading more authority than we might like:

> By the holy rood, thou know'st it well,
> Thou cam'st on earth to make the earth my hell.
> A grievous burden was thy birth to me;
> Tetchy and wayward was thy infancy;
> Thy school days frightful, desperate, wild, and furious;
> Thy prime of manhood daring, bold, and venturous;
> Thy age confirmed proud, subtle, sly, and bloody,
> More mild, but yet more harmful, kind in hatred. (4.4.166–173)

The figural reading that uses Richard's troubled birth to comprehend and articulate his villainous life is epitomized in these isocolons, different life stages curving off the pronoun "thy"—"birth," "infancy," "school days," "prime," "age." But this figural reading plays a role in the causal reading of Richard's deformity: it is not only his deformity (a physical phenomenon) but also the stigmatization of his deformity by his enemies and his family (a social phenomenon) that make Richard distressed, depressed, and ultimately devious and diabolical.

For Freud, when Richard loves others, it depletes the quantifiable amount of love he has, and, when the love he gives away is not returned, Richard shores up his sense of self-worth by repressing his instinct to love others. He saves all his love for himself, which Freud would see as his patient holding two contradictory images of himself: the surge of love Richard sends himself creates a sense of superiority over others, yet it only exists because an intense inferiority was felt in the first place. Richard views himself as both much worse and much better than others. The narcissistic Richard who turns his deformity into an object of affection does not emerge until *Richard III*. Freud's term for this inflated regard for things loved is *idealization*, as opposed to *sublimation*, which redirects love to something other than sexual fulfillment. Sublimation is what happens in Richard's first soliloquy in *3 Henry VI*, when he swears off sex for politics. His inferiority complex culminates in a later scene, by Shakespeare, in a form of compensation replacing failure in love with success in hate:

> I have no brother, I am like no brother;
> And this word "love," which greybeards call divine,
> Be resident in men like one another
> And not in me. I am myself alone. . . .
> Counting myself but bad till I be best. (5.6.80–91)

Robert Watson and Linda Charnes argue that Richard wants to replace his deformed body with the ideal body of the king, as envisioned in the medieval political theology of "the king's two bodies."[17] Stigmatized, alienated, and alone because his physical body is "bad," Richard's political body, once achieved, would be "best," these polarized values reflecting warring feelings of inferiority and superiority.

But this reading only applies to *3 Henry VI*. In *Richard III*, Richard does not say that he will pursue the crown because he is upset about his deformity. He devotes himself not to politics but to villainy: "And therefore, since I cannot prove a lover, / . . . I am determinèd to prove a villain / And hate the idle pleasures of these days" (1.1.28–31). He now sees himself as what Freud would later call, with reference to Richard, an "exception," someone who has been slighted by nature, has suffered an unfair congenital disadvantage, something he does not deserve and will use to excuse himself from the laws and morals that govern civil society:

> What the soliloquy thus means is: "Nature has done me a grievous wrong in denying me the beauty of form which wins human love. Life owes me reparation for this, and I will see that I get it. I have a right to be an exception, to disregard the scruples by which others

let themselves be held back. I may do wrong myself, since wrong has been done to me."[18]

He has suffered enough, Richard reasons, and will not submit himself to restrictions usually placed on social life, such as "thou shalt not kill."

The opening of *Richard III* adds only one more idea to Richard's soliloquies from *3 Henry VI*. It comes in a new source of "delight":

> Why, I, in this weak piping time of peace,
> Have no delight to pass away the time,
> Unless to see my shadow in the sun
> And descant on mine own deformity. (1.1.24–27)

Richard describes his deformity as an object that exists out in the world, a "shadow," rather than an organic element of his self. A shadow is an outline, a negation of light, a darkness with no detail or dimension. Richard delights in descanting not on his deformity *per se* but on the crude image of his deformity cast by some source of illumination. If the "sun" in these lines is the same "sun" from the opening sentence of *Richard III*—the "son of York," his hypersexual brother Edward—it is the iridescent beauty attributed to royalty in Plantagenet England that creates the shadowy image of Richard in the shape of deformity. His only joy, he says, is to stare at that shadow and "descant" upon it. A musical term from the Latin *canto*, "I sing," with the negative prefix *de-*, to *descant* is to sing a tune set apart from the main melody of a song. With the same prefix, to be *deformed* is to bear a body set apart from the usual human body. To descant on deformity is to voice an interpretation different from the usual interpretation of the body different from the usual body. Doing so gives Richard joy. He replaced love with hate in *3 Henry VI*, but in *Richard III*, he takes pleasure from gazing upon, commenting upon, and changing the meaning of his deformity.

Richard's physiognomic revisionism is coupled with his narcissism. He ends his opening address in *Richard III* by bristling, "Plots have I laid" (1.1.32), asserting authorship of the play's political conspiracy ("plot") and narrative structure ("plot"). This plot dates back to John Rous's *History of the Kings of England* (1486), which credits the murder of George, Duke of Clarence, to the anxiety of his brother, King Edward, regarding a prophecy that "G" would follow "E" as king: as in the alphabet, so in the monarchy.[19] Raphael Holinshed's *Chronicles* notes that the usurpation of their other brother Richard, Duke of Gloucester, led later Englishmen to reread the prophecy so that the "G" refers to Gloucester rather than George, but Shakespeare was the first to make Richard the author of this "plot."[20] Doing so makes Richard into an ironic, sadistic, narcissistic, and fantastic villain who enjoys advertising the evil he has planned for others in ways they do not understand but the audience does. Richard doesn't flat-out lie. He dissimulates, like an oracle, so his statements are true, but in an unexpected way. He dissimulates to exculpate himself, excusing his crimes by transferring agency onto the interpretive errors of others who do not identify and avert the evil he advertises in advance. Richard usually trumpets his ills by pointing to his body in some backhanded way. Thinking about the human alphabets popular in Renaissance print, we might see Richard's body in the shape of the letter "G." With its arched back, its interrupted perimeter, and its limbs of unequal size, a "G" is an "O" that is "Deform'd, unfinish'd, sent before [its] time / Into this breathing world, scarce half made up." As in the "G" prophecy, throughout *Richard III*, Richard takes a perverse pleasure in pointing to his body to provide his victims with evidence of villainy and then manipulating the meaning of this evidence, executing his schemes while scoffing at his victims' misconceptions.

It has previously caused him intense pain, so why does Richard now enjoy his deformity? In *3 Henry VI*, he sublimated erotic desire to political ambition, but in *Richard III*, his burdensome body is transformed or idealized, so the source of his pain starts producing pleasure. Nothing about his body changes, but it is aggrandized and exalted in his mind. He treats it as a sexual object is treated, gazing upon it, fondling it, gratifying himself by obsessing over it, and running all experience in the world through it. Never mind that Richard is "no[t] made to court an amorous looking glass." He comes to enjoy the sight of his own deformity: "I'll be at charges for a looking glass, / . . . Shine out, fair sun, till I have bought a glass, / That I may see my shadow as I pass" (1.2.255–263). Obsessed with looking at images of himself in shadows and mirrors, the Richard of *Richard III* is a textbook case of Freudian narcissism.

Toward the end of his essay "On Narcissism," Freud explains that a healthy person's mind sets up "an ideal in himself by which he measures his actual ego" (74), preventing the world from becoming one big narcissistic bonanza filled with one self-obsessed Richard III after another: "What we call our *conscience* has the required characteristics" (75). Conscience comes from parents and culture. Since both have taught Richard to interpret his body figurally, however, each is a source of agony. Were Richard to internalize the morals of his family and society, he would hate himself, which Freud says we have instincts to prevent, so Richard must abandon either his natural instinct to love himself or the cultural ideal instructing him to hate himself. The rise of Richard's narcissism, brought about by his inferiority complex, leads to the repression of his conscience.

In a Freudian scheme, repressed consciences often surface in dreams. As his wife, Anne, reports, Richard suffers from "timorous dreams" (4.1.84), and there is a stunning return of Richard's repressed conscience in his nightmare before the Battle of Bosworth. Conscience gnaws at Richard's mind in the form of paranoia, an irrational or even delusional anxiety that someone is out there watching him and judging. Yet paranoia is just an external projection of a conscience that's an internalization of cultural ideals. This confusion of internal and external censors prompts an anxiety in the dreaming Richard, who wakes and asks, "What do I fear? Myself? There's none else by" (5.3.182). Richard is alone—"I am myself alone," he said earlier—but not alone with himself. He has with him the internalized voices judging him to be evil since his birth, which is why Richard has retreated from them and tries to retreat again now: "Then fly," he says, but stops: "What, from myself?" (5.3.185). Freud notes that humans have motor impulses to flee from stimuli that cause discomfort, but flight is impossible when stimuli come from within. You can't outrun yourself, as Richard discovers when his own conscience, rather than his culture, calls him a villain. Unable to escape, he worries that he might kill himself—"What, myself upon myself" (5.3.186)—unable to differentiate the organic aspects of his mind from his total identity, resulting in what modern psychologists call dissociative identity disorder. There are two Richards in this speech: one speaking for instinct, "Alack, I love myself" (5.3.187), and another for conscience, "Alas, I rather hate myself" (5.3.189). This ambivalence indicates the internalization of the exchange Richard has previously experienced as a conflict between himself and others. The *I and you* of this conflict becomes an "I and I," as Richard says in the quarto editions, representing his split subjectivity, or "I am I," as the line reads in the folio, this Richard trying to reassemble his subjectivity in a singular and stable self: "Richard loves Richard, that is, I [and/am] I" (5.3.183). Whichever line we hear, Richard lacks the vocabulary to describe the mental turmoil he is experiencing, so his soliloquy is steeped in contradiction: "I am a villain. Yet I lie; I am not" (5.3.191).

According to Freud, "The final form of the work of repression in the obsessional neurosis is a sterile and never-ending struggle" (115), which seems to be what is happening in Richard's final soliloquy. It may never end, but Freud's point is that it begins with repression, an etiology that extends back further in Richard's case. In the long causal logic of this interpretation, Richard's disability leads to his stigmatization, his stigmatization to his conscience, his conscience to his inferiority, his inferiority complex to (in *3 Henry VI*) his sublimation of sexual fulfillment and (in *Richard III*) his narcissism and claims of exceptionalism, his narcissism to the repression of his conscience, repression to crime, crime to guilt, guilt to paranoia, and paranoia to the return of his repressed conscience in a stunning dream-vision that prompts a full-blown schizophrenic soliloquy. From a Freudian perspective, the tragedy of *Richard III* is that the mental collapse seen in Richard's final soliloquy is the inevitable outcome of that man born into that moment, of the natural instincts of a person with physical disabilities coming into ceaseless and irreconcilable conflict with the cultural ideals of a stigmatizing society.

IV. Stigma as Magic, Again

Was Richard's causal interpretation Shakespeare's interpretation of deformity, as it was Bacon's? Is the causal interpretation a good interpretation of deformity? It certainly appeals to a modern mind committed to the logic of cause and effect, which Tylor, Frazer, and Freud present as the antidote to "magical thinking." Richard's soliloquies brim with the language of logic: "then" four times in his first soliloquy in *3 Henry VI* (3.2.134, 146, 163, 165), "for" twice (3.2.154, 173), and "since" once (3.2.165). His first soliloquy in *Richard III* pivots on a logical triplet, "And therefore since" (1.1.28). The soliloquies sound logical but aren't. The one in *3 Henry VI* voids intense introspection in an incoherent conclusion contradicting the premise that originates the argument. Richard claims that he can have no pleasure in politics and so must seek it in love. He continues with the false though understandable conviction that he can have no pleasure in love because he is disabled. He ends with a return to the already discredited option of political ambition, previously spurned because too many heirs separate him from the crown, but now he believes that the only option he has left in this world is to destroy everyone more fortunate than himself.

It clarifies the lapse in Richard's logic to consider what Tylor and Freud say about the two kinds of magical thinking. Both operate, Freud writes, through "the association of ideas."[21] The first kind is homeopathic magic, which works according to similarity between what one does and what one wants to happen. A primitive man imitates rain in a dance to get rain or tortures an effigy that looks like his enemy. The second kind is contiguous magic, which uses something once in contact with someone, such as a lock of hair, to effect a change on that person. These two logics—similarity and contiguity—reflect the two readings of Richard's body. In the first, his deformity at birth is a sign of his villainy in life, based on a common aversion to each in Lancastrian England—a figural logic of similarity. In the second, deformity is not the sign but the cause of villainy, which develops out of Richard's resentment for his body at birth and its stigmatization—a causal logic of contiguity. The latter reading shifts from a spiritual to a psychological model of stigma, but Freud notes that the logic of cause and effect is not immune to magical thinking: "Some of the primitive belief in omnipotence still survives in men's faith in the power of the human mind, taking account, as it does, of the laws of reality" (110). Richard is still thinking magically when reading villainy as the inevitable outcome of deformity. And we are thinking magically if we accept his account of himself.

Richard's soliloquies about his deformities are also about his confusion, as in the first in *3 Henry VI*, when he is "like one lost in a thorny wood" (3.2.174). When Richard says that he will "hew [his] way out with a bloody axe" (3.2.181), he commits himself to treason, murder, and tyranny as the antidote to pain and suffering. He confuses a hypothesis about deformity—it is "a Cause, which seldome faileth of the Effect"—for a law of nature. Clearly, deformity doesn't always end in villainy. The core of Richard's soliloquies is not only deformity but also deception—deception of himself, deception of the other characters, and deception of the audience as well:

> Why, I can smile and murder whiles I smile,
> And cry "Content!" to that which grieves my heart,
> And wet my cheeks with artificial tears,
> And frame my face to all occasions.
> I'll drown more sailors than the mermaid shall;
> I'll slay more gazers than the basilisk;
> I'll play the orator as well as Nestor,
> Deceive more slyly than Ulysses could,
> And, like a Sinon, take another Troy.
> I can add colors to the chameleon,
> Change shapes with Proteus for advantages,
> And set the murderous machiavel to school. (3.2.182–193)

This soliloquy might be the first modern depiction of disability, but it ends up looking backward to the Tudor Vice, whose language Richard uses to celebrate his skills of deception. The Vice was the son of Satan, the root of all evil, the lord of misrule, the fool of the festival, and a chorus commenting on himself and others. The keynote of the character was deception. Crafty and dexterous, the Vice saw seduction as sport, disguising himself and posing as his victim's friend, dedicating himself to his friend's welfare, and then lying, cheating, cogging, and stealing to bring about his friend's destruction. Audiences knew that the Vice relished dissimulation and intrigue because he explicitly said so as often as he could in soliloquies of considerable length, with an energetic bravado, much like Richard.

The causal reading of Richard's deformity is unsustainable because Shakespeare attributed it to a man whose articulation of it climaxes in a self-congratulatory celebration of his commitment to duplicity, with Richard touring a gallery of literary liars—Nestor, Ulysses, Sinon, Proteus, Machiavelli. In *Richard III*, we cannot happily accept Richard's causal reading of his deformity when only moments later he brags about being "subtle, false, and treacherous" (1.1.37), using "lies well steeled with weighty arguments" (1.1.147). Anyone wanting Richard's deformity to be the cause rather than the sign of his villainy must acknowledge that this is how Richard asks us to read his body in the same breath that he tells us how much he loves to lie. When Richard says to us in the audience—during the intimacy of soliloquy—that he "cannot prove a lover," he is lying. Maybe he's confused. Maybe he's working through some things. Maybe he's got some self-doubt. But the most straightforward reading of that line, in light of Richard's celebrations of duplicity, is that he is lying to us in the audience, who may be accustomed to seeing the Vice figure deceive other characters on stage but aren't accustomed to being lied to themselves. "He accomplishes his greatest deception of all," as Lindsay Row-Heyveld writes, "the seduction of the audience."[22]

Richard does not give an unambiguously accurate explanation of his true character, as the Vice traditionally did. The truth communicated by Richard's speech is that the causal interpretation of deformity is deeply confused. Richard gives his opinion, which is influenced by his involvement in the drama, which means that it's not Shakespeare's opinion, not the author's voice breaking through the dramatic illusion to tell his audience how to interpret the character. Instead, exactly like the Lancastrians' figural interpretation, Richard's causal interpretation is a perspective, one attributed to a character whose deep involvement in a painful series of events inflects his attitude toward deformity. Exploiting the confidence audiences place in the dramatic character who addresses them directly, Shakespeare turned the Vice's deception of other characters on the audience. Richard seduces us just as he seduces Lady Anne; he deceives us as he deceives his brothers. Audiences are manipulated into accepting Richard's reading of his body because it comes in a soliloquy expressing his pain and suffering; sympathy for Richard's plight transforms into a willingness to accept his interpretation of things. In a fascinating evolution in the character of the Vice, we in the audience are the victims of Richard's deceit. We don't simply witness the power and allure of evil as it ensnares characters on stage. By speaking directly to us, Richard makes us think that he is our friend, that he is dedicated to our welfare, but then he lies to us when telling us to accept his causal interpretation of deformity. We succumb to the seduction of evil and sanction it, especially in the theater, where the same thing always happens at the end of Richard's soliloquies: raucous, joyous, appreciative applause.

V. Shakespeare and the Sociological Model of Stigma

In sum, Shakespeare's first tetralogy juxtaposes the Lancastrians' spiritual model of stigma, which sees deformity as a God-given sign of villainy, with Richard's own account of his body, which sees deformity as the cause rather than the sign of his villainy, a psychological model of stigma embraced by later essayists from Bacon to Freud. This movement from sign to cause, from metaphor to metonymy, can be seen as progress from medieval to modern ways of thinking, but Shakespeare questions each model equally: the spiritual by ascribing it to Richard's mortal enemies, whose hatred infects their interpretation, and the psychological by ascribing it to Richard himself, a habitual liar and murderer. So, what, ultimately, is the meaning of physical deformity in Shakespeare's first tetralogy? What does it stand for? What did Shakespeare believe?

In 1815, August Wilhelm von Schlegel became the first to say that we need not choose between spiritual and psychological models.[23] Over the next two centuries, many who have addressed Richard's body (E. W. Tullidge, Henry Norman Hudson, E.M.W. Tillyard, Bernard Spivack, Joseph Pierce, Robert Ornstein, Michael Kahn, Maurice Hunt, E. Pearlman, Linda Charnes, Michael Hattaway, James Siemon, and David Houston Wood, to name a few) have insisted that both interpretations, the figural and the causal, are represented in Shakespeare's plays.[24] True, but neither interpretation is endorsed by Shakespeare; both are examples of magical thinking. Shakespeare's representation of the figural and causal interpretations of deformity in his first tetralogy is neither an *either/or* nor a *both/and*. It's a *neither/nor*. He endorses neither the spiritual nor the psychological model of stigma. There is no authorized interpretation of deformity in Shakespeare's first tetralogy other than the exposure of specious thought—what might be seen as a sociological model of stigma.

Starting in *2 Henry VI*—not with Richard's body itself but with his enemies' comments on it—Shakespeare's plays suggest what is called the "social model" of disability, first articulated by the Union of the Physically Impaired Against Segregation: "It is society which disable[s] physically impaired people. Disability is something imposed on top of our impairments by the way we are unnecessarily isolated and excluded from full participation in society."[25] Shakespeare started with "the discursive construct of the disabled figure," to quote Rosemarie Garland-Thomson, so audiences are "informed more by received attitudes than by people's actual experience of disability."[26] Richard, "determinèd to prove a villain," finds that—to quote Tobin Siebers—"social attitudes and institutions determine, far greater than biological fact, the representation of the body's reality," but also that "the challenge is to function," leading Richard, like Siebers, to search for "ways to represent pain."[27] Shakespeare showed Richard's personal disability experience and, in Katherine Schaap Williams's words, "a frenzy of interpretive fervor about what Richard's body really means."[28] Hobgood extends this line of thought to the surprising "invisibility" of Richard's most visible of bodies: "His habitus comes to contain so many possibilities for meaning that it actually fades from view; the precise, disabled body that prompts such intense attention from spectators, in the end, gets erased by over-signification."[29]

It is not only disability that is symbolic in Shakespeare's first tetralogy but also attempts to make sense of disability, *stigma*, the spiritual model pointing back to the misconceptions of medieval theology, the psychological model gesturing forward to the foibles of modern rationality. In these plays, stigma stands for the breakdown of thought during social interactions involving someone with a visible physical disability. Although that disability may be irrelevant to the animosity between two people, it becomes the venue for expressions of anger and hatred. Margaret does not hate Richard because he is deformed; she articulates her hatred through stigma. When the rhetoric of stigma—repeated often enough—meets a certain spirituality, it transforms into a theory, whitewashing social discrimination by crediting it to nature or God. Faced with the massive stakes of this stigma, someone like Richard may use it to excuse or justify bad behavior that has nothing to do with his body. When the stigmatized individual accepts that disability and villainy are connected, even if he disagrees with his stigmatizers about the nature of this connection, stigma can then become a self-fulfilling prophecy. If so, the thought processes of the stigmatized individual are as compromised as those of the stigmatizers, each side pointing to the pain caused by the other and using it as the basis for an aggressive response. In short, stigma stands for revenge, and Shakespeare's first tetralogy—a tragedy of ambition and revenge—dramatizes the social phenomenon of stigma in which bounds are placed on a man with a physical disability, and those bounds are resisted until this social process comes crashing down. In other words, stigma is tragic.

Shakespeare originated the line of thought that culminated centuries later in Erving Goffman's book *Stigma* (1963), which argues that "a language of relationships, not attributes, is really needed."[30] Like Shakespeare's drama, Goffman's theory of stigma avoids the unsatisfactory interpretive frames of spirituality and psychology by turning to a sociology that is deliberately dramaturgical. For Shakespeare and Goffman alike, the meaning of physical disability is found in the social situation in which bodily deviations from assumed norms are negatively valued because humans, both stigmatizers and stigmatized, cannot help but perceive the mutability of nature from our own deeply limited but highly privileged perspectives. In other words, "stigma" is not a physical feature of the body that is discrediting, as Richard's deformity is taken to be by Shakespeare's Lancastrians, whom Goffman would call "the normals" (5). Nor is it the psychologically determining factor that Richard understands it to be. Stigma is the social situation in which a body acquires negative meaning, which Goffman sees as inherently dramatic: "In many cases, these moments will be the ones when the causes and effects of stigma must be directly confronted by both sides" (13). I have sought to show the causes and effects of stigma in Shakespeare's first tetralogy—what causes Richard to be stigmatized and what the effects of being stigmatized are on him. I have argued that magical thinking is the cause and the effect of stigma and that it is magical thinking regardless of whether we see deformity as a spiritual sign or as a psychological cause of villainy. Richard's birth was not an omen of evil, but, by treating it like one, Shakespeare's Lancastrians evoke, create, perpetuate, and aggravate the depraved man they understand themselves to be describing. Richard's deformity does not destine him for villainy, but he thinks it does, and this belief leads Richard to villainy. The figural and the causal interpretations of Richard's deformity, as dramatized by Shakespeare, are examples of a central sociological tenet dubbed the "Thomas theorem": "If men define situations as real, they are real in their consequences."[31]

Like Shakespeare, Goffman sees the origins of stigma in the mistaken belief that someone *is* something based on a hasty generalization of what someone *does*. Imputing identities to others, as when Margaret calls Richard a "stigmatic," overlooks what Goffman argues in his earlier book *The Presentation of Self in Everyday Life* (1959): we are not, essentially, anything. "The self" is a category projected from the outside by others trying to interpret us, not one that belongs to us because it is our essence. We play various roles in society based on the circumstances of the situations in which we find ourselves and our attempts to be seen as one thing or another. Richard may be a "stigmatic," but he is also a son, a brother, a friend, a foe, a clown, a king, a villain, and a victim. Shakespeare's character is captivating specifically because he does not obediently remain within any one of these roles. Goffman argues that stigma, understood as social interaction between so-called normals and those with discreditable differences, is an uncomfortable event for all involved—stigmatizers, stigmatized, and onlookers—because it involves a breakdown in the categories we create to manage social interactions. To simplify social interactions, we create categories of identities—hero, villain, friend, enemy, and so forth, including "stigmatic." The routines of social interaction lead us to anticipate the behavior of those we meet. Anticipations become expectations, and expectations lead to indignant demands. When our categorical thinking encounters the uniqueness of experience, stigma becomes a problem: "In social situations with an individual known or perceived to have a stigma," Goffman argues, "we are likely, then, to employ categorizations that do not fit, and we and he are likely to experience uneasiness" (19). Richard acts in ways—jovial, irreverent, logical, sympathetic—that the stigmatic, as Margaret defines him, isn't supposed to act. Richard does not easily and permanently fit into accessible categories, such as villain or victim, Vice or narcissist, protagonist or antagonist, friend or enemy, comic or tragic. When these categories are applied, as Goffman would expect, he *and* we are uneasy.

Just as Richard pours his displeasure into his soliloquies, we have been putting our own uneasiness with this character into our notes, poems, essays, articles, books, performances, paintings, adaptations, and conversations for more than four hundred years. Our simultaneous revulsion and attraction are captured in Robert McRuer's slogan "Fuck Richard III," meaning *He can fuck off* and *I want to fuck him*.[32] Goffman gives us a way of thinking about what we have been doing with Richard this whole time: "We are likely to attempt to carry on as though in fact he wholly fitted one of the types of person naturally available to us in the situation, whether this means treating him as someone better than we feel he might be or someone worse than we feel he probably is" (18). There is no better way to view the two dominant traditions in the reception history of Shakespeare's *Richard III*. By eliciting a strong sympathy from the audience, the causal interpretation of deformity makes him into "someone better than we feel he might be"; by demanding an intense aversion from the audience, the figural interpretation treats him as "someone worse than we feel he probably is." In the end, while the debate over Shakespeare's attitude toward disability, based on the example of Richard III, has largely questioned whether Shakespeare thought more like Renaissance physiognomists, such as Thomas Hill and Ambroise Paré, or like modern essayists, such as Francis Bacon and Sigmund Freud, the truth is that Shakespeare's thinking was more in line with that of the twentieth-century sociologist Erving Goffman. Shakespeare embraced the position that the spiritual model of stigma he inherited from earlier English culture and the psychological model he invented for modernity are both based on faulty thinking performed by compromised participants in an explosive social encounter. Shakespeare embraced a sociological model of stigma.

3

The Reality of Physiognomy in *Richard III*

Staging rebellion, regicide, and allegiance amid civil war, Shakespeare's *3 Henry VI* is a play about not only where you stand but also how you stand.¹ The house of York stands against the house of Lancaster, as in one scene by Shakespeare, when Richard stands poised to attack John Clifford, who has killed Richard's father and brother but is prepared to stand his ground: "Ay, crookback, here I stand to answer thee" (2.2.96). It's doubly disparaging to Richard's disability, first in the explicit insult of "crookback" and then in the implicit contrast to the speaker's upright stance. Imagine Clifford stomping his foot on the stage, "here," and straightening himself up into a nobleman's posture, "I stand," to draw the distinction, "to answer," between himself and the enemy he dismisses with a disgusted "thee." Here, stigma works as Erving Goffman argues—as a social relationship where a "normal" person delegitimizes difference, with Shakespeare identifying, exposing, and critiquing the mental and moral lapses of "normals," as Goffman does.

But that's not how stigma works in act 4, scene 1, where disability is stigmatized not by a character but by the play itself. Shakespeare—the author of the scene—connected disability to villainy through the symbolism of standing. As the York brothers dispute the newly crowned King Edward's capricious marriage to Elizabeth, one, Clarence, "stand[s] pensive" (4.1.10), while the other, Richard, stands by Edward as the new king speaks the language of tyranny: "My will shall stand for law" (4.1.50). Tyranny is a deformity of monarchy, which Shakespeare symbolized by bringing Richard together with

Edward as Clarence walks away. "Now, brother Richard, will you stand by us?" Edward asks; "Ay, in despite of all that shall withstand you," Richard responds (4.1.143–144). Imagine, as brothers join at center stage and then turn to exit together, Richard eclipsing Edward, the one's deformity expressing the other's tyranny.

The symbolism of standing in *3 Henry VI* prepares us, as we turn to *Richard III*, to ask a very simple question: Did Shakespeare stigmatize Richard's disability? Is stigma something done by the characters in the play or by the author of the play? Does physiognomy have any basis in reality in *Richard III*?

My answers begin with the temple garden scene in *1 Henry VI*, the first scene in the play credited to Shakespeare, where the Wars of the Roses begin as a debate about what truth looks like. When the Duke of York declares, "The truth appears so naked on my side / That any purblind eye may find it out," the Duke of Somerset retorts, "And on my side it is so well appareled, / So clear, so shining, and so evident / That it will glimmer through a blind man's eye" (2.4.20–24). The imagery asks how truth ought to be expressed: as simply as possible or with an artful elegance? York wants a "naked" truth whose purity needs no decoration: truth unadorned by the inventions of humans. Somerset seeks a "well apparell'd" truth, effective adornment enabling accurate expression: truth clothed in a fashion becoming its excellence.

Emphasizing what is "naked" and "well-apparell'd," this chapter considers the status of physiognomy in *Richard III*, especially during the scenes of deception involving Lady Anne, the Duke of Clarence, Clarence's son, Prince Edward, the Duke of York, Lord Hastings, and the crowd who offers Richard the crown. Richard says exactly how he deceives people. He accuses others of his own "secret mischiefs" (1.3.324), and then, when his interlocutors get angry, he pivots:

> But then I sigh, and with a piece of scripture
> Tell them that God bids us do good for evil.
> And thus I clothe my naked villainy
> With odd old ends stol'n forth of holy writ,
> And seem a saint when most I play the devil. (1.3.333–337)

Shakespeare associated Richard's feigned charity with the clothes covering his deformity. Richard's villainy is "naked," innate, attached to his body, plain to see for anyone looking at what nature has made. It is a naked truth but can be "clothe[d]" in a deceptive appearance, a "seem[ing]" or semblance or, as he says elsewhere, a "dissembling look" that disguises a "plain devil" (1.2.236).

I. Essence and Accident in Physiognomy

In "'The plain devil and dissembling looks': Ambivalent Physiognomy and Shakespeare's *Richard III*," Michael Torrey argues that "physiognomy betrays an inevitable ambivalence" and that "it is precisely such ambivalence that we can see in *Richard III*."[2] Torrey is right: there's a contradiction at the core of Renaissance physiognomy and an inconsistency in how appearances convey meaning in *Richard III*. I think it's not entirely accurate, however, to say that these problems are the same, that the drama "mirror[s]" or "reproduces" (126) the discourse.

The absurdity of Renaissance physiognomy was its attempt to explain away mistakes. Physiognomic manuals did some bizarre logical gymnastics upon noticing that connections between certain bodies and certain souls are demonstrably wrong when applied to actual people. The physiognomers claimed their art only interpreted natural inclinations, but those (always bad) inclinations could be expunged by exercise of reason or grace of God. As Thomas Hill bumbles, "I meane we shall not bee deceyued to know the trueth of the naturall disposicion, and yet we maye fayle of the mans condicions."[3] He claims that physiognomy could reveal someone's nature, but not if that "disposicion" is conveyed into the current "condicions" of someone's personality.

This issue never enters Shakespeare's *Richard III*. No one ever says that Richard's deformity indicates a natural inclination toward villainy that may or may not be realized in his actual behavior or averted by exercise of reason or grace of God. *Richard III* represents a deeper problem in physiognomy, one barely visible in the Renaissance but one that vexed the discourse from its beginnings in the classical world to its ends in the eighteenth century. Endorsing physiognomy in his *Prior Analytics* (ca. 350 B.C.E.), Aristotle cautioned readers not to confuse natural inclinations with accidental conditions: "It is possible to infer character from physical features [φυςιογνομονειν], if it is granted that the body and the soul are changed together by the natural affections. (No doubt by learning music a man has made some change in his soul, but this is not one of those affections which are natural to us.)"[4] Aristotle's students expanded his argument in the *Physiognomics* (ca. 300 B.C.E.), outlining three methods: (1) comparing the look of a human to an animal to claim that the human has the spirit of the animal; (2) seeking to identify the characteristics of various races; and (3) interpreting facial expressions. "The last-mentioned method by itself," they wrote, "is defective in more than one respect. For one thing, the same facial expression may belong to different characters: the brave and the impudent, for example, look alike, though their characters are far asunder."⁵ Like Aristotle, his students concluded that "permanent bodily signs will indicate permanent mental qualities," but "those that come and go" are not available for physiognomic interpretation (806a). Thus, in ancient Greece, physiognomy was restricted to the appearances fixed on a body at birth and did not apply to shifting appearances like facial expressions, certainly not to the clothes one wears, which are accidental (as learning music was).

In the Renaissance, however, facial expressions came under the purview of physiognomy. Erasmus considered it "not a very vayne thing to coniecture by the figure of the face and the behaueour of the rest of the bodie, what disposicion a man is of," explaining that physiognomy is done "by the complexion and pleeight of the bodye, and by the proporcion & settyng, or coumpace of the face or visage."⁶ Writing in 1556, Thomas Hill said that souls "are marked by nature in the proporcion and liniamentes of mans body . . . and specially in the face and handes, whiche as it should seme, god hath made open and vncouerable because al men mighte at all tymes see and perceyue them"; in 1571, Hill pointed physiognomers to "the outwarde notes and lines of the face and body."⁷ Richard Huloet's *Dictionarie* (1572) defines physiognomy as "an arte whereby the nature, or disposition of man is knowen, bothe by body and countenaunce."⁸ Even Shakespeare focused on the face the only time he mentioned physiognomy by name:

In Ajax and Ulysses, oh, what art
Of physiognomy might one behold!
The face of either ciphered either's heart;
Their face their manners most expressly told. (*Lucrece*, 1394–1397)

Most of the words used by Renaissance physiognomers referred to the permanent qualities of the face ("figure," "complexion," "pleeight," "proporcion," "settyng," "coumpace," "liniamentes," "notes," "lines"), but some ("behaueour" and "countenaunce") suggested the legibility of facial expressions. As Hill explained, "The face is often taken, and that simplie, for the naturall looke of any: but the countinaunce signifieth, the qualities of the minde," later elaborating, "In a man the face remayneth, but the countenaunce doth alter: so that the countinaunce is named of the Latine worde *Volando*, which properly in Englishe signifieth a flying or vanishing away."⁹

In his 1746 work, James Parsons said that reading facial expressions would be better termed *metoposcopy* ("the proper Actions of the Muscles of the face, and their particular Obedience to the Influence of the Mind"); writing in

1778, Georg Christoph Lichtenberg called it *pathognomy* ("the semiotics of the affects, or the knowledge of the natural signs of the movements of the mind, according to all its gradations and mixtures") in contrast to *physiognomy* ("the ability to find the nature of the mind and heart from the form and constitution of the external parts of the human body, chiefly of the face, excluding all temporary signs of the movements of the mind").[10] Johann Kaspar Lavater's *Physiognomic Fragments* (1775–1778), the last major attempt to defend physiognomy, claimed a reliable science in contrast to the unreliable art of pathognomy: "Physiognomy is the mirror of the Naturalist and the Sage. Pathognomy is the mirror of Courtiers, and Men of the World. Of it everyone knows something, but few understand Physiognomy. Pathognomy has to contend with dissimulation; but Physiognomy is under no such necessity: it is not to be deceived or misled."[11] This could be the thesis of Shakespeare's *Richard III*.

This reading counters the conclusions of the most comprehensive study of the subject, Sibylle Baumbach's *Shakespeare and the Art of Physiognomy* (2008), which focuses on "Shakespeare's poetics of the face."[12] Citing Hill's extension of physiognomy into pathognomy and illustrating Shakespeare's characters inferring emotional states from facial expressions, Baumbach suggests that Shakespeare accepted a version of physiognomy understood as an "art" rather than a "science" (note that *Lucrece* refers to the "art / Of physiognomy"). "Considering the pivotal role of the human face and its rhetoric in Shakespeare's plays," Baumbach writes, inverting Shakespeare's King Duncan, "there *is* an art to find the mind's construction in the face."[13] Elsewhere, however, Baumbach observes that plays such as *Othello*, *The Merchant of Venice*, and *A Midsummer Night's Dream* illustrate the limitations of the "art" by showing the misreading of faces.

Addressed to the art of pathognomy, Baumbach's argument doesn't explain Shakespeare's attitude toward the science of physiognomy and surprisingly doesn't examine *Richard III* in detail. When we do so, her argument is confirmed and complicated: the art of pathognomy is treated as a compromised activity, but *Richard III* treats the science of physiognomy, when directed toward innate bodily features, as a legitimate enterprise. Physiognomy works in *Richard III* when it is the right kind of physiognomy. The play resists a physiognomy of affected appearances in favor of one of natural attributes. According to the artistic design of *Richard III*, the appearance of Richard at birth, his deformity, is an accurate index of the villainy he executes and the tragedy that awaits him, as physiognomy would have it, however repugnant to us this theory might be. The appearances that Richard controls himself, his face and clothes, are not reliable indicators of his nature. He fashions himself to appear humble, friendly, and munificent when really he is dangerous, treacherous, and deceitful. Shakespeare wrote Richard's "naked villainy" into his body, but Richard is acutely aware of the significance of appearances, and he manipulates those he can control—face and clothes—to secure interpretations that benefit his murderous conspiracies. The characters who distrust Richard because they fix their physiognomic eyes on his deformity (Margaret, Elizabeth, the Duchess of York, Stanley, and Richmond) accurately interpret his natural and naked villainy and are rewarded with life, while those who befriend Richard after shifting their attention to his face and clothes (Anne, Clarence, Hastings, Buckingham, and Edward V) are deceived by his dissembling looks and die for doing the wrong kind of physiognomy. Shakespeare's treatment of Richard's appearance amounts to an anatomy of villainy in which innate physical bodies instantly announce the ethical character of a person, while affected appearances mislead and deceive. "Whether Richard actually is or is not what he seems depends on which aspect of his seeming a character or an audience member considers," as Joel Slotkin puts it. "Seeming, therefore, fluctuates in diagnostic value throughout the play."[14]

This dynamic creates traps for critics, as when the most insightful analyst of *Richard III* in recent years, Katherine Schaap Williams, argues that "physiognomic interpretation is undermined or mistaken" in the play because "his body never stays the same."[15] This reading grows from Williams's argument that Shakespeare created more questions than he answered when characterizing Richard with the words "deformed" and "deformity." What exactly does "deformity" look like? It's such an abstract concept that it could be anything. "Shakespeare's play differs from his historical source in refusing to specify the exact details of Richard's body," Williams writes, yet the body of Shakespeare's Richard compiles many of the legends Shakespeare inherited.[16] Richard's two-year gestation in his mother's womb described by John Rous became the breach delivery described by Thomas More, which in Shakespeare's *3 Henry VI* becomes Richard's statement "I came into the world with my legs forward" (5.6.71). The "crochebake" first described by William Burton became one shoulder that was higher than the other according to Rous, More, and Polydore Vergil, which becomes in Shakespeare's plays the description of Richard as a "crookback" (*2H6*, 5.1.89sd in Quarto; *3H6*, 1.3.75) with a "foul misshapen[ness]" (*3H6*, 2.2.136) and a "misshaped trunk" (*3H6*, 3.2.170) that is "not shaped for sportive tricks" (*R3*, 1.1.14) and "scarce half made up, / And that so lamely and unfashionable" (*R3*, 1.1.21–

22). The withered arm invented by More became the lame hand threatening to rake out Richmond's heart in *The True Tragedie*, and then the "hell-governed arm" of Shakespeare's Richard (*R3*, 1.2.67), whose "arm / Is like a blasted sapling withered up" (*R3*, 3.4.67–68) because nature "shr[u]nk [his] arm up like a withered shrub" (*3H6*, 3.2.156). The protruding back invented in More's Latin text becomes in Shakespeare's Richard a "heap of wrath, foul indigested lump" (*2H6*, 5.1.157) and the "envious mountain on [his] back" (*3H6*, 3.2.157), "an undigested and deformèd lump" (*3H6*, 5.6.51), a "shoulder [that] [i]s ordained so thick" (*3H6*, 5.7.23) that it draws comparisons to a "bunchbacked toad" (*R3*, 1.3.245 and 4.4.81). The toothed birth described by Rous and More, which became the gnawed lip described by Vergil and Richard Rainolde, as well as the boar's tusks and frothy jaws in *A Myrroure for Magistrates* and Thomas Legge's *Richardus Tertius*, becomes in Shakespeare's plays statements about a toothed birth—"Teeth hadst thou in thy head when thou wast born" (*3H6*, 5.6.53), "O, Jesus bless us, he is born with teeth!" (*3H6*, 5.6.75), "He could gnaw a crust at two hours old" (*R3*, 2.4.28), "That dog, that had his teeth before his eyes" (*R3*, 4.4.49)—and the "venom tooth" (*R3*, 1.3.290) that "gnaws his lip" (*R3*, 4.2.27). Perhaps extrapolating from the unequal shoulders and arms of earlier Richards, Shakespeare seems to have himself invented the "legs of an unequal size" (*3H6*, 3.2.159) that "disproportion [Richard] in every part" (*3H6*, 3.2.160), making him "curtailed of this fair proportion" (*R3*, 1.1.18), as well as the accompanying limp such that "dogs bark at [him] as [he] halt[s] by them" (*R3*, 1.1.23) because he "halts and [is] misshapen thus" (*R3*, 1.2.250).

The almost clinical specificity in Shakespeare's enumeration of Richard's impairments allows David Houston Wood and Allison P. Hobgood to read Richard's body—quite apart from the dominant early-modern discourses of physiognomy and monstrosity—as medically explicable, as responsive to the emerging early-modern science of human anatomy.[17] I'll admit that I'm not entirely sure how best to adjudicate between the malleability that Williams sees in Richard's body and the abundance that I have emphasized, but saying that "Richard's 'deformity' is not static" (770), leading to our "inability to categorize Richard's body clearly" (760), adopts the viewpoint that the character himself promotes. Critics, like the characters in *Richard III*, can be deceived by Richard's "dissembling looks." As Williams writes elsewhere, "There is not much Richard can't do, and to do things, he puts his body on view, using the multiple interpretations and expectations it prompts to achieve his ambition."[18]

II. The Anatomy of Villainy in the Wooing of Anne

Lady Anne's safety depends on her adherence to her figural interpretation of Richard's body. At first, it positions her in opposition to him. She mourns the loss of her father-in-law by redistributing the legend of Richard's deformity to his progeny:

> If ever he have child, abortive be it,
> Prodigious, and untimely brought to light,
> Whose ugly and unnatural aspect
> May fright the hopeful mother at the view,
> And that be heir to his unhappiness. (1.2.21–25)

Anne asks for more than misfortune for the man who murdered Henry VI. With the word "prodigious," learned from her mother-in-law, Queen Margaret (*3H6*, 1.3.75), Anne wants providential reparations for the injustice of Henry's death. Anne therefore scolds Richard as one of Satan's lieutenants. Just as Margaret maligned "that devil's butcher, Richard" (*3H6*, 5.5.78), Anne employs the language of demons to say that Richard is a "fiend" (1.2.34), "devil" (1.2.45), "foul devil" (1.2.50), "devilish slave" (1.2.90), and "dreadful minister of hell" (1.2.46) who "hast made the happy earth [his] hell" (1.2.51). She allegorizes his moral character by naming him "homicide" (1.2.125) and animalizes his misshapenness by calling him "hedgehog" (1.2.102), adding a vertical component by claiming Richard will be "damned for that wicked deed" (1.2.103). She "*spits at him*" (1.2.144sd) and sends him away with an invective citing the ocular evidence of her anger: "Out of my sight! Thou dost infect my eyes" (1.2.148). "Anne's appeal is to the 'natural' eye, which in this context is inseparable from the play's relentlessly visual moral iconography," as Linda Charnes observes. "In making a plea for 'plain' vision, Anne implores the lords to read Richard as the obvious."[19] Richard's moral character is clear as day, Anne fumes—*just look at his hump!*

Richard also says *Look at my hump!* when claiming Henry's murder has been hoisted "upon [his] guiltless shoulders" (1.2.98), the same shoulders Anne sees physiognomically as a sign of guilt. Shakespeare then toyed around with Anne's physiognomy, filling this scene with questions about truth and falsity, qualities coordinated with Richard's body and face. Richard's false love "prompts [his] tongue to speak" (1.2.170). When Anne "*looks scornfully at him*" (1.2.170sd), he asks her to interpret his body. He throws open his shirt to show his "true breast" (1.2.175). "Tongue" is false; "breast" is true. "I lay it naked," he says (1.2.177). According to the stage direction, "*He lays his breast open; she offers at with his sword*" (1.2.178sd). When Anne sees Richard's naked body, she wants to attack it. How does she end up Richard's fiancé some twenty lines later? Why does she forsake her figural interpretation of his deformity? Anne later says that she "look'd on Richard's face" (4.1.70) and "grew captive to his honey words" (4.1.79). Richard's "naked" body is a physiognomic sign of his "true" character, his "face" and "tongue" (which produce "words") sites of deception.

Richard earlier located his duplicity in his face during his paean to hypocrisy in *3 Henry VI*: "Why, I can smile and murder whiles I smile, / . . . And frame my face to all occasions" (3.2.182–185). In *Richard III*, he cons Anne into marriage by saying his "tongue could never learn sweet smoothing word" (1.2.168). He tricks the Woodvilles into trusting him by saying that he "cannot flatter and look fair, / Smile in men's faces, smooth, deceive, and cog" (1.3.47–48). Of course he can: he's doing it as he speaks. Richard draws attention to the deformity that means that he "cannot . . . look fair" and then to the disability that means that he cannot "duck with French nods and apish courtesy" (1.3.49). Physiognomically, Richard's bite is figured in his toothed birth, his murders in his withered arm, his envy in his mountainous hump, and his iniquity in his unequal legs. But his ability to obscure his true character is figured in his face. His "tongue" and "smile" are the anatomical origins of the words he uses to deceive his enemies. Villainy is figured in his body at birth, the deceptions that dissemble this villainy in the appearances he can control.

Shifting her eyes from Richard's body to his face, Anne drops her sword and calls him a "dissembler" (1.2.184). To dissemble is not simply to lie. Lies make false claims. In dissembling, lies look like truth. Oracle-like, truth is given, but in a way that likely leads to misinterpretation. The word "dissemble" is a variation on *dissimulate*, a negation of the Latin *similis*, "alike." Anne calls Richard a "dissembler" because he *dis-assembles* the figural meaning of deformity right before her eyes. He takes apart what Lancastrian England has *assembled*, or put together: a likeness between deformity and villainy. Or, to take another turn on this word, Richard *de-symbolizes* his deformity. The warring prefixes, *de* ("apart") and *syn* ("together") indicate Richard's struggle to destroy the figural meaning of deformity that Plantagenet England has put together. Anne puts deformity and danger together when she sees Richard's naked body; Richard rends them by shifting attention to his smiling face. Once Anne admits that she does not know how to read his appearance, he shoves his deformity back in front of her eyes. He shows her "this hand, which for thy love did kill thy love" (1.2.189), the same withered hand he had at birth—according to Tudor lore—the hand that has stabbed her husband and father-in-law.

In the Tudor chronicles, Richard's right hand is both misshapen and murderous. Rous's statement about Richard's shoulders, "the right being higher than the left," grew into the "right hand" that fidgets with his dagger in Vergil's *English History* and the "lame hand" that wants to rake out Henry Tudor's heart in *The True Tragedy*. In Shakespeare's *3 Henry VI*, Richard's "arm" is "bound to revenge" (2.4.2–3), as he shouts at John Clifford, who has recently killed Richard's father. During the Battle of Towton, when Richard comes upon Clifford, already slain, he holds up his withered hand and vows:

> If this right hand would buy two hours' life,
> That I in all despite might rail at him,
> This hand should chop it off and with the issuing blood
> Stifle the villain. (2.6.79–82)

The image of Clifford choking to death on the blood gushing from Richard's severed, deformed arm gives an almost autonomous agency to that appendage. His deformities seem to compulsively answer the murderous call of an otherworldly evil.

In *Richard III*, Anne once knew the figural significance of Richard's "hell-governed arm" (1.2.67), but not after he de-symbolizes his deformity. Her new uncertainty about his body introduces doubt about where his character is truly "figured":

> ANNE I would I knew thy heart.
> RICHARD 'Tis figured in my tongue.
> ANNE I fear me both are false.
> RICHARD Then never man was true.
> ANNE Well, well, put up your sword. (1.2.192–196)

Anne fears that Richard is false, but she should have been certain and would have been had she adhered to the figural interpretation she so passionately affirmed earlier. By shifting the site of the "figure" in his body from his arm and his hump to his face and his tongue, Richard makes his appearance illegible, not only to Anne but also to modern commentators who encounter the complexity of physiognomic interpretation in *Richard III* and conclude that it is incoherent. We must keep Anne's demise in mind. She ends up married to and murdered by a monster because she strays from her figural interpretation of Richard's body, and Shakespeare's point seems to be *don't do that*. As Lindsey Row-Heyveld writes, the play "rewards those characters who respond to Richard and his body with suspicion and punishes those who respond with credulity or charity."[20]

The wooing of Anne ends with Richard's second descant on his own deformity, which works as he said it would in his opening soliloquy. It's an aside referring to what is central from a peripheral position. The center is the assumption that beauty and virtue go together, represented by Prince Edward, Anne's former husband, whose virtues are enumerated before and after his appearance, beauty emanating goodness: "A sweeter and a lovelier gentleman, / Framed in the prodigality of nature, / Young, valiant, wise, and no doubt right royal" (1.2.242–244). While Edward is *prodigal*, "lavish" in his beauty, Richard is *prodigious*, "monstrous" in his deformity. For Anne to look upon Richard after Edward is for her to "abase her eyes on me," Richard says, fixated on the visual aids of moral valuation: "On me, whose all not equals Edward's moiety? / On me, that halts and am misshapen thus?" (1.2.246–250). Richard asks how Anne could love the monster he has been made into by the Lancastrians. To them, his stigma is a sign of danger, as Richard observes when he reviews the evidence that ought to have dissuaded Anne from accepting him: he has killed her husband as well as her father-in-law, whose bleeding corpse lies right before her eyes. "Having God, her conscience, and these bars against [him]," Richard is amazed that he was able to seduce Anne: "And I no friends to back my suit withal / But the plain devil and dissembling looks" (1.2.235–236). Imagine Richard tapping his shoulder as he says that his suit has nothing to "back" it, for his deformity is what makes Richard a "plain devil," according to Lancastrian physiognomy.

But Richard has mastered "dissembling looks." Celebrating his ability to overcome the body given to him by nature with an alternate appearance he has fashioned in his face, Richard sardonically pretends to be handsome: "I do mistake my person all this while! / Upon my life, she finds, although I cannot, / Myself to be a marv'lous proper man" (1.2.252–254). Anne never says that Richard is beautiful, but he ventriloquizes this idea as the ironic implication of her absurd physiognomy: because of his deformity, she has feared and hated him, but now that they are engaged, she must admire his appearance. This ironic affectation of beauty epitomizes the new form of villainy that comes in *Richard III*. In his first soliloquy, Richard said that he is "no[t] made to court an amorous looking glass," but after his seduction of Anne, he finds himself irresistibly attractive: "I'll be at charges for a looking glass, /

And entertain a score or two of tailors / To study fashions to adorn my body" (1.2.255–257). Like his face, Richard's "fashions" are an appearance he can compose and control, in contrast to his deformity. If his body at birth is cast in his shadow, the veneer he covers it with can be seen in a mirror. Richard longs to look upon both images, to descant on the deformity he sees in his shadow and to gaze at his dissembled appearance in his mirror. These two images, shadow and mirror, conclude Richard's second descant on deformity: "Shine out, fair sun, till I have bought a glass, / That I may see my shadow as I pass" (1.2.262–263). Richard wants the sun he has identified as the source of stigma to shine brighter than ever before. He develops a perverse pleasure in seeing the sign of his villainy, according to physiognomy, as he "pass[es]" for a virtuous man by changing his appearance. It delights Richard to descant upon deformity as he dissembles it.

III. Narcissistic Physiognomic Revisionism in Richard's Rise to the Throne

Shakespeare saturated *Richard III* with confirmations of the physiognomic reading of Richard's deformity. The imprisoned Clarence dreaming of sinking into hell is sent thither by a halting Richard: "Methought that Gloucester stumbled, and in falling / Struck me, that thought to stay him, overboard / Into the tumbling billows of the main" (1.4.18–20). If Clarence catching his halting brother represents aid offered to someone with a disability, Clarence's death as a result shows what happens to those who misread deformity in *Richard III*. In this play, deformity leads to death, misshapenness to murder, connections Clarence only apprehends unconsciously in dreams.

Richard simultaneously displays and dissembles his deformity while deceiving Clarence and his son. First, Clarence can't believe it was Richard, not Edward, who ordered his execution: "For he bewept my fortune, / And hugged me in his arms, and swore with sobs / That he would labor my delivery" (1.4.244–246). Visualizing this moment, we see Clarence enveloped in one of the physical signs of Richard's villainy, his deformed "arm," yet deceived by his words ("swore") and tears ("sobs"). As his villainy is enacted, Richard shows his deformity to us in the audience—villainy confirming the physiognomic meaning of deformity—but does so behind Clarence's back, obscuring that sign from Clarence's vision, which focuses on Richard's face.

Richard repeats the deception to convince Clarence's son it was Queen Elizabeth who provoked King Edward to order the execution: "And when my uncle told me so, he wept, / And pitied me, and kindly kissed my cheek"

(2.2.23–24). Richard's deception of Clarence is exactly replayed in the quartos, which have "hugged me in his arm" in place of "pitied me." Imagine Richard stooping to hug his nephew, his hump bristled up above the boy, his "arm" on display behind the boy's back, in front of the audience's eyes. Shakespeare exhibits Richard's deformity as Richard outmaneuvers the physiognomic reading of it, demonstrating the virtuosity of his villainy, providing intrigue for an audience who is now in on the joke. Clarence's boy, however, focuses on Richard's face, his eyes ("wept") and mouth ("kissed").

"Think you my uncle did dissemble?" the boy asks his grandmother, the Duchess of York (2.2.30). She insists that facial affectations allow Richard to dissemble the villainy his body signified at birth: "Oh, that deceit should steal such gentle shapes, / And with a virtuous vizard hide foul guile" (2.2.26–27). There's a corporeal subtext in the idea that virtue and vice are "shape[d]," and in the etymologies of "visor" and "vice." A *visor*, from the French *vis*, "face," is a helmet's frontispiece, brought down to cover one's face, while *vice*, from the Latin *vitium*, "fault," is imperfection in either the moral or physical sense.[21] Richard covers his vice with a visor, his faults with his face, his misshapenness with his masks, his defects with his deceits. To Bassanio in *The Merchant of Venice*, "There is no vice so simple but assumes / Some mark of virtue on his outward parts" (3.1.81–82), but Clarence and his boy misread Richard by focusing their physiognomy on his face, overlooking his body.

Richard blames Clarence's murder on "some tardy cripple" (2.1.89), deflecting attention from himself but, simultaneously, redirecting attention to deformity and its physiognomic significance.[22] With his other nephews, Edward's boys, Richard continues this narcissistic physiognomic revisionism, which reminds audiences of the figural meaning of his body even as it is altered. As David Mitchell and Sharon Snyder observe, "This is not just a matter of *overcoming* liability, but of *employing* apparent liabilities as weaponry in the rhetorical dispute over his intentions and ambitions."[23]

First, Richard accuses the Woodvilles of the villainy he himself is guilty of as he speaks: "Those uncles which you want were dangerous. / Your grace attended to their sugared words" (3.1.12–13). Richard's charge of false rhetoric *is* false rhetoric, but his villainy is deeper than deceit or hypocrisy. He reminds the audience, if not the others on stage, of his deformity as he performs the very villainy it is supposed to signify, which he's claiming it doesn't:

Sweet Prince, the untainted virtue of your years
Hath not yet dived into the world's deceit.
No more can you distinguish of a man

> Than of his outward show, which, God He knows,
> Seldom or never jumpeth with the heart. (3.1.7–11)

Richard says that Edward has read his other uncles physiognomically, that this is a naïve aesthetic, that they have deceived him by fabricating a pleasing front, and that they were really out to get him—what Richard is doing to Edward at that moment. Clearly, Richard is lying about the relationship between the appearance and actions of Edward's other uncles. They appeared friendly because they were friendly. If Edward were to interpret all uncles physiognomically, he would know whom to trust. "Outward show[s]" are all Edward needs. Shakespeare made Richard's rejection of physiognomy part and parcel of the villainy signified by his deformity according to the physiognomy he himself rejects yet events of the play endorse.

Prince Edward's younger brother, the Duke of York, also misreads Uncle Richard's body. At dinner one evening, it was observed that young York was outgrowing his older brother, to which Richard (a diminutive child himself) snarked, "Small herbs have grace, great weeds do grow apace" (2.4.13). Richard reverses the moral significance of his own appearance in contradistinction to the stigma levied at him, claiming that his smallish size signifies virtue, not vice. When York relates this story to Richard's mother, however, she insists that the physiognomic reading of Richard is the right reading:

> The saying did not hold
> In him that did object the same to thee.
> He was the wretched'st thing when he was young,
> So long a-growing and so leisurely
> That, if his rule were true, he should be gracious. (2.4.16–20)

Defending Richard, the archbishop of York proffers an anti-physiognomic reading—"And so no doubt he is, gracious madam"—proposing a Richard who combines deformity with integrity, but the Duchess demurs: "Let mothers doubt" (2.4.21–22). Catching her physiognomy, the young York wishes that he had teased Richard about his toothed birth and, when an embarrassed Queen Elizabeth chides her son for stigmatizing his uncle, Grandam excuses him: "Be not angry with the child" (2.4.36).

Summoned to London, young York remembers the Duchess's physiognomic distrust of deformity. Once Richard refers to the lad as a "little lord" (3.1.122), York becomes "cross in talk," Prince Edward says, apologizing for his younger brother: "Uncle, your Grace knows how to bear with him" (3.1.126–127). Taking a page from Richard's playbook, York attacks Richard with equivocations that attempt to reassemble the stigma Richard has been dissembling:

> You mean to bear me, not to bear with me.
> Uncle, my brother mocks both you and me.
> Because that I am little, like an ape,
> He thinks that you should bear me on your shoulders. (3.1.128–131)

The image evoked is an ape on the back of a jester at an Elizabethan fair.[24] Considering the Tudor Vice who often "*rideth away on the Devils back*," as in Ulpian Fulwell's *Like Wil to Like*, we can see the smallish, apish, churlish York as a Vice on the back of Richard, himself identified with the Vice only fifty lines earlier (3.1.82), here promoted to Devil.[25]

Buckingham notes that York mocks his own puny size to cloak the insult about his uncle's shoulders (3.1.132–135), generating one of the most inscrutable moments of stigma in *Richard III*. At the theater, it can be the biggest laugh of the night. The precocious little York may, as in Dominic Cooke's *Hollow Crown* (2016), act out the image of his disabled uncle carrying him around.[26] If audiences laugh, however, they do so at the image of a young boy mocking a disabled person. That's horrible: I would never laugh at that out on the street. In the modern theatrical tradition, beginning in the Victorian age with Henry Irving's 1877 performance, also represented by Laurence Olivier, York's insult is the one time Richard is shut down by stigma.[27] He has nothing to say. Amid all his narcissistic villainy, Richard feels the pain of stigma. If we sympathize with him in this scene, which is easy to do, we surprise ourselves by disliking the moment we have been awaiting: an unwavering physiognomy of Richard that sees past the falsity of his face to the truth of his body.

The plot against Hastings is the most extensive example of narcissistic physiognomic revisionism. It starts with Catesby lobbying Hastings to join their conspiracy by joking that Richard could make a halting world surefooted:

> [HASTINGS] What news, what news, in this our tott'ring state?
> CATESBY It is a reeling world indeed, my lord,
>   And I believe will never stand upright
>   Till Richard wear the garland of the realm. (3.2.36–39)

Richard's body bends back upon itself, can buttress nothing, looks nothing like the ideal body of the king, but Catesby descants on Richard's deformity. Hastings indignantly rejects Catesby's plan to put Richard on the throne, and, as punishment, Richard makes Hastings the butt of his physiognomic jokes during the subsequent scene of the divided councils.

It starts with Richard's head henchmen, the Duke of Buckingham—whom Richard has called "My other self, my counsel's consistory, / My oracle, my prophet, my dear cousin" (2.2.150–151)—asking, "Who is most inward with the noble Duke?" (3.4.8). The Bishop of Ely says what Buckingham already knows—that Buckingham himself "should soonest know his mind" (3.4.9). Tutored by Richard in physiognomic revisionism, Buckingham's response diverts attention from Richard's body to appearances Richard can control—specifically, his face: "We know each other's faces; for our hearts, / He knows no more of mine than I of yours, / Or I of his, my lord, than you of mine" (3.4.10–12). Because a physiognomy of Richard's body exposes his natural and naked villainy, his agent, Buckingham, who knows Richard better than anyone, claims that his own physiognomy of Richard has failed.

Picking up Buckingham's physiognomy of the face, Hastings misreads Richard as a trustworthy friend by focusing on Richard's face:

> His grace looks cheerfully and smooth this morning.
> There's some conceit or other likes him well
> When that he bids good morrow with such spirit.
> I think there's never a man in Christendom
> Can lesser hide his love or hate than he,
> For by his face straight shall you know his heart. (3.4.48–53)

If so, Stanley asks, "What of his heart perceive you in his face / . . . today?" (3.4.54–55). Unaware of Richard's plan to decapitate him, Hastings responds that Richard is not offended with any of them, "For were he, he had shown it in his looks" (3.4.57). The "looks" Hastings focuses on are the "dissembling looks" of Richard's face. It is, however, the "plain devil" that Hastings sees when Richard enters to accuse his brother's lovers of witchcraft by claiming that they "have prevailed / Upon my body with their hellish charms":

> Then be your eyes the witness of their evil:
> Look how I am bewitched. Behold, mine arm
> Is like a blasted sapling withered up.
> And this is Edward's wife, that monstrous witch,

Consorted with that harlot, strumpet Shore,
That by their witchcraft thus have markèd me. (3.4.61–72)

Shakespeare took this episode from More's *History*, which explains the absurdity of Richard's accusation: "He plucked vp hys doublet sleue to his elbow vpon hist left arme, where he shewed a werish withered arme and small, as it was neuer other. . . . No man was ther present, but wel knew that his harme was euer such since his birth."[28] Since everyone knows Richard's arm has always been deformed, they are astonished when he brings that deformity before them as evidence that Queen Elizabeth and Lady Shore are villains, not him. As usual, Richard's physiognomic revisionism is coupled with narcissism: calling Queen Elizabeth "monstrous" draws attention to his own monstrosity even as he modifies its meaning. A skeptical Hastings begins to propose a punishment "if they have done this deed," and Richard erupts: "'If'? . . . Talk'st thou to me of 'ifs'? . . . Off with his head!" (3.4.73–75). As in the wooing of Anne, Richard narcissistically gives the council the evidence of his villainy, according to a physiognomic interpretation, but then bullies them into his own reading of his body, which is demonstrably wrong, given the evidence *at hand*.

This is the example Williams offers when arguing that "*Richard III* undermines physiognomic readings since other characters misinterpret Richard's own visage, to their political downfall."[29] But, according to the logic of *Richard III*, Hastings's reading of Richard's face is not physiognomy, or at least is the wrong kind of physiognomy. If the play undermines that physiognomy of affected appearances, it also affirms—shockingly, disturbingly—the physiognomy of essential attributes that sees congenital deformity as an emblem of evil.

The following scene showcasing the hypocrisy and theatricality of Richard and Buckingham figures their duplicitous histrionics in their clothes and faces. First, they appear in costume, "*in rotten armor, marvelous ill-favored*" (3.5.1sd). Richard and Buckingham have written, rehearsed, and staged a scene in which an army allied to the traitor Hastings is storming the Tower, and they are its last defense. Echoing his claim to "add colors to the chameleon" (*3H6*, 3.2.191), Richard asks if Buckingham is ready for their greatest performance:

Come, cousin, canst thou quake, and change thy color,
Murder thy breath in middle of a word,
And then again begin, and stop again,
As if thou were distraught and mad with terror? (3.5.1–4)

Richard's question is remarkable for its sensitivity to an actor's respiration, "breath" and "word[s]" the output of the mouth, the mouth set in the face, the face the seat of Richard's deceit. Buckingham's response is a continuation of the paean to hypocrisy in Richard's first soliloquy from *3 Henry VI*, beginning where Richard left off, with the braggadocio's exclamatory "tut":

> Tut, I can counterfeit the deep tragedian:
> Speak, and look back, and pry on every side,
> Tremble and start at wagging of a straw,
> Intending deep suspicion. Ghastly looks
> Are at my service, like enforcèd smiles,
> And both are ready in their offices
> At any time to grace my stratagems. (3.5.5–11)

Like Richard's celebration of homicidal hypocrisy—"Why, I can smile and murder whiles I smile" (*3H6*, 3.2.182)—Buckingham's vivacious boast after the beheading of Hastings locates his hypocrisy in his face, specifically his "enforced smiles."

Richard points to his eyes when the mayor of London arrives to ask about Hastings: "So dear I loved the man that I must weep. / I took him for the plainest-harmless creature" (3.5.24–25). Hastings looked "plain," like "simple, plain Clarence" (1.1.118), which physiognomically meant that he was "harmless"—which is true—but Richard, "the plain devil," claims that Hastings was hiding his treachery behind a false front. Richard is describing himself. Shakespeare even circled back to the Duchess's line about the visor hiding vice, having Richard claim that Hastings did the same: "He daubed his vice with show of virtue" (3.5.29). Richard accuses Hastings of the physiognomic revisionism he himself performs, narcissistically reminding himself, Buckingham, and the audience of his ability to shift shapes despite being branded a villain by nature.

With each deceit, Richard grows more brazen, as when claiming that his brother Edward is a bastard, "Which well appeared in his lineaments, / Being nothing like the noble duke my father." (3.5.91–92). It's Richard who has markedly different "lineaments," this word drawing attention to the curved and uneven lines in Richard's shoulders, spine, and limbs. Buckingham relays the absurd accusation to the people: "Withal, I did infer your lineaments, / Being the right idea of your father, / Both in your form and nobleness of mind" (3.7.12–14). Buckingham revises both sides of the physiognomic equation, replacing deformity and villainy with comeliness and nobility. In addition to its sense as "correct," the word "right" has moral and geometrical meanings, "proper" and "straight," but the deformed villain Richard represents neither rectitude. His mother says that his brothers Edward and George look like their father—"two mirrors of his princely semblance"—while Richard, "one false glass," does not (2.2.51–53).

Thomas More, not Shakespeare, was the first to characterize Richard's conspiracy as bad theater, the audience aware of the illusion, excusing it as the keeping up of courtly decorum.[30] Shakespeare emphasized the tension between the costume Richard dons and the deformity he and his agents repeatedly mention. Richard enters aloft, Bible in hand, churchmen on either side, while Buckingham acts as expositor for the crowd:

> Two props of virtue for a Christian prince
> To stay him from the fall of vanity.
> And see, a book of prayer in his hand,
> True ornaments to know a holy man. (3.7.95–98)

"Props of virtue" is the language of theater, but the discourse of disability is also present, those "props" being crutches keeping Richard from "fall[ing]." Taking appearances as indications of a man's nature, Buckingham's comments are overtly physiognomic, yet he directs attention to the appearances Richard elects to show—the prayer book—not those he had at birth. Buckingham claims essences where there are only accidents or "ornaments," which are characterized as "true."

Pretending to persuade a mock-obstinate Richard to accept the crown, his agents offhandedly allude to his deformity. Buckingham designs a "holy descant" (3.7.48), this odd word, "descant," throwing audiences back to its only other instance in the play, Richard's "descant on [his] own deformity." Catesby says that Richard is "divinely bent to meditation" (3.7.61) when he means "bent to divine meditation," a transposition acknowledging the figural interpretation where Richard has been "divinely bent" by God. Richard draws attention to his appearance, feigning concern that he is "disgracious in the city's eye" (3.7.111). Buckingham calls Edward's boys bastards by calling them "the corruption of a blemished stock" (3.7.122), a description equally suited to the physiognomic reading of a Richard whose body commemorates the familial strife of the Wars of the Roses. Most blatantly, recalling Catesby's "reeling world," Buckingham treats Richard as the orthopedic remedy for a misshapen nation:

> This noble isle doth want her proper limbs,
> Her face defaced with scars of infamy,
> Her royal stock graft with ignoble plants,
> And almost shouldered in the swallowing gulf
> Of dark forgetfulness and deep oblivion. (3.7.125–129)

Why do Richard, Buckingham, and Catesby repeatedly refer to deformity in their attempts to court him for the crown? Two possibilities: first, that Shakespeare intended these allusions to be consciously made by characters aware of what they were doing; or second, that he didn't, that they're Shakespeare suggesting—through imagery—that Richard's deformity was transferred to the entire nation when he became king of England. Maybe deformity is omnipresent in *Richard III*, not only in Richard's psychological turmoil but also in Shakespeare's imagery, because, as Goffman theorizes, stigma consumes attention, turning ordinary events into fraught situations that run everything through stigma.[31] Stigma can suck up an author's attention, manifesting in unexpected, unrelated places.

From the other perspective, imagine Richard instructing Buckingham and Catesby to brush upon his deformity during the scene of his election, doing so because he enjoys reminding his victims of his stigma. Imagine this narcissism as a progressive disease that began when he displayed his body to us, Anne, his family, and his friends and now crests as Richard descants on his deformity in front of the gathered citizens of London. When Buckingham offers him the crown, Richard's rejection is narcissistic and physiognomic, saying that he cannot accept it, "so mighty and so many my defects" (3.7.159). When Catesby implores Richard to accept Buckingham's offer, Richard says that he is not shaped for royalty: "Alas, why would you heap this care on me? / I am unfit for state and majesty" (3.7.203–204). Richard only accepts the crown, he tells Buckingham, "since you will buckle fortune on my back" (3.7.226). In each line, Richard points the crowd to the deformity that signifies his criminal character according to the aesthetic ideology of Plantagenet England, making them responsible for their own downfall because they do not follow the physiognomy they have invented and earlier attached to him.

His deformity signifies his villainy, but his villainy is not just deceit, hypocrisy, crime, treason, treachery, and tyranny. His villainy volleys the physiognomy others have hurled at him back at them, using their obsession with appearances to draw their attention to the appearances he can control and manipulate—his face and clothes—to produce an image of virtue in contrast to the image of vice found in his physical body at birth. Thus, the height of Richard's villainy is his acquisition of support and power through the very same means by which he has been stigmatized and discredited—by exploiting the prominence of the visual in ethical judgment—making his victims responsible for their own deaths, transposing his guilt to them, by providing them with the evidence of his villainy—his deformity—and then dissembling its meaning.

IV. Shakespeare's Tudors and the Structure of Stigma

If Queen Margaret can stand for the Tudor historians who, hostile to Richard III, first stigmatized his deformity in the sixteenth century, her daughter-in-law, Lady Anne, stands for the later Tudors who perpetuated the figural reading of his body, handing it down from generation to generation. Anne's desire for God to send Richard to hell—"Either heaven with lightning strike the murd'rer dead, / Or earth gape open wide and eat him quick" (1.2.64–65)—seems learned from Margaret, who concludes her career stigmatizing Richard with a plea for heaven to finalize the narrative implied when she first called Richard a "stigmatic" way back in *3 Henry VI*:

> Earth gapes, hell burns, fiends roar, saints pray,
> To have him suddenly conveyed from hence.
> Cancel his bond of life, dear God I pray,
> That I may live and say, "The dog is dead." (4.4.75–78)

Shakespeare marked Anne's learning of Richard's coronation, realizing her mistake in marrying him, with a symbolic stigmatization of sorts. She wishes the "golden metal that must round [her] brow / Were red-hot steel to sear [her] to the brains" (4.1.59–60), burning a mark onto her forehead to signify guilt. This stigma in the ancient sense—a mark made by civic authorities on the body of a criminal—is a refraction of the stigmatization of Richard in the Tudor chronicles, which read the political crimes of his adulthood back into his body at birth, changing stigma from a punitive practice performed by humans into a supernatural system of signification.

In act 4 of *Richard III*, the social circulation of stigma extends to Anne's aunt, Cecily Nevil, the Duchess of York, Richard's mother, and to Anne's sister-in-law, Cecily's daughter-in-law, Elizabeth Woodville, former queen of England. Elizabeth asks Margaret—one former queen of England whose family has been murdered and disinherited to another—to "help [her] curse / That bottled spider, that foul bunch-backed toad" (4.4.80–81), a callback to Margaret's earlier images of Richard as a "bottled spider" (1.3.241) and a "poisonous bunch-backed toad" (1.3.245). Teaching Elizabeth magical thinking, Margaret tells her to imagine a world polarized into good and evil and to exaggerate each—"Think that thy babes were fairer than they were, / And he that slew them fouler than he is" (4.4.120–121)—which Elizabeth does when Richard arrives to charm her as he did Anne.

Just as Margaret earlier demonized Richard as a "stigmatic" (*3H6*, 2.2.135), a "devil" (*R3*, 1.3.117), a "cacodemon" (1.3.143), and a "son of hell" (1.3.229) because "sin, death, and hell have set their marks on him" (1.3.292), Elizabeth envisions Richard as of the devil's legion:

> Hid'st thou that forehead with a golden crown
> Where't should be branded, if that right were right,
> The slaughter of the prince that owed that crown
> And the dire death of my poor sons and brothers? (4.4.140–143)

Like Anne, Elizabeth processes Richard's villainy through stigma, not the one he had at birth, but the one he should have because of his criminality, a "brand[ing]" to identify a criminal. This branding evokes the mark of the beast, the false prophet or "beast from the earth" from Revelation 13.11–17, often equated with the Antichrist. Exercising the authority of Satan, animating his image, and killing those who will not worship it, the Antichrist was the king of false kings, sometimes appearing as a grisly monster wearing a crown; those marked by the beast on their right hand or forehead would receive God's wrath when the rider on the horse arrived to defeat their army (keep in mind, looking ahead, that Richard famously doesn't have a horse at the Battle of Bosworth). Used to characterize the historical Richard by his first historian, John Rous, the Antichrist is an apt image for Shakespeare's Richard because, like the Antichrist, Richard covers his deformed body with the ornaments of royalty.

When Elizabeth asks, "Shall I be tempted of the devil thus" (4.4.418), she becomes the only character other than Margaret, Anne, or Richard himself to call him a "devil." These four and the Duchess also identify Richard's destiny as "hell," the only characters to do so. In these moments, Elizabeth is not reading Richard physiognomically, as Margaret and Anne did earlier. Instead, like the Duchess, Elizabeth's animosity toward Richard is expressed in stigma, calling him "spider," "toad," and "devil," or saying that she will not give her daughter to Richard "unless [he] couldst put on some other shape" (4.4.286). At the end of their exchange, Richard's narcissistic physiognomic revisionism seems to have worked on Elizabeth, who says that she will go to her daughter on Richard's behalf. The subsequent scene reveals that Elizabeth has engaged her daughter to the Earl of Richmond, Henry Tudor. The wooing of Anne is not repeated but revised by the wooing of Elizabeth: where Anne forsook her figural interpretation and fell victim to Richard's ruse, Elizabeth remains firm. Where the former died, the latter survives.

Margaret, Elizabeth, and the Duchess each stigmatize Richard and avoid his homicidal dash through the royal family. Anne's disappearance shows that Richard has no problem killing women. The deaths of Anne, Clarence, Hastings, Buckingham, and Edward V are corollaries to the survival of Margaret, Elizabeth, and the Duchess: the characters who befriend Richard because they see signs of virtue in his face die because of their bad physiognomy, and those stigmatizing Richard's deformity, distrusting his every action, are rewarded with life. The stigmatizer who most vexes Richard, the young Duke of York who dies in the tower, is an exception to this rule. At the same time, allowing his older but no wiser brother Edward to silence him (3.1.126–127), York dies because he—like Anne—did not (or could not) stick to the course of action his stigmatizing spirit suggested he should follow.

The survival of the stigmatizers in a drama drenched in death provides a structural confirmation of the efficacy of physiognomy in *Richard III*. It explains why the fathers of the Tudor dynasty—Lord Stanley and the earl of Richmond—both survive the wrath of Richard. Rather, since history dictated their survival, it explains why Shakespeare made Stanley and Richmond stigmatizers. First, like Clarence's dream, Stanley's dream that "the boar had razèd off his helm" (3.2.10) connects murder with misshapenness, be it (for Clarence) the limp of a lame man or (for Stanley) the hunchback of a wild boar. Like Clarence's dream, Stanley's is not taken seriously; it is ignored as a trifle of the perturbed mind, dismissed as a superstitious nightmare with no basis in reality and no significance:

> I wonder he's so simple
> To trust the mock'ry of unquiet slumbers.
> To fly the boar before the boar pursues
> Were to incense the boar to follow us
> And make pursuit where he did mean no chase. (3.2.25–29)

Hastings concludes that "the boar will use us kindly" (3.2.32) only a few scenes before Richard chops off his head, as Stanley's dream predicted. In *Richard III*, Shakespeare repeatedly presented a surface that is natural, skeptical, and rational, which modern audiences are apt to embrace because it matches up with the world as we experience it. But this surface has no structure in *Richard III*. The structure of events in this play suggests a world that is magical, figural, supernatural. According to the internal logic of the play, Hastings's dismissive interpretation of Stanley's dream is a *bad* interpretation, which Hastings later acknowledges, adding another supernatural sign of his own:

> Stanley did dream the boar did raze his helm,
> And I did scorn it and disdain to fly.
> Three times today my footcloth horse did stumble,
> And started when he looked upon the Tower,
> As loath to bear me to the slaughterhouse. (3.4.82)

By partnering Stanley's stigmatization of Richard as a boar with his superstitious dream and then reconfiguring such premonitions as Stanley's dream and Hastings's stumbling horse as valid evidence, Shakespeare's play asks audiences to view stigma as a legitimate supernatural phenomenon.

After his defection, Stanley again stigmatizes Richard as a "deadly boar" (4.5.2) in the very speech that establishes the Tudor myth by announcing the union of the red rose and the white in the marriage of Richmond and Elizabeth's daughter. Richmond has been paying attention to his stepfather's language about "this foul swine":

> The wretched, bloody, and usurping boar
> That spoiled your summer fields and fruitful vines,
> Swills your warm blood like wash, and makes his trough
> In your embowelèd bosoms. (5.2.7–10)

Stanley and Richmond's stigmatizing of Richard as a boar is not the figural reading of Margaret and Anne. Like the Duchess and Elizabeth, Stanley and Richmond speak a stigma that is more rhetorical than analytical, and one suited to their political function in the play: they plan to replant with pink the English garden of red and white roses the boar has uprooted.

If Richmond takes up Stanley's stigmatization of Richard's royal seal, the future Henry VII also inherits the stigma Margaret established with her first and last words on Richard. At the start of the play, she scolded Richard to heel, "stay, dog" (1.3.215), later using this canine conceit to describe his character physiognomically ("when he fawns, he bites" [1.3.289]) and his soul figurally ("a hellhound that doth haunt us all to death" [4.4.48]), until at last she begged God to let her live to say, "The dog is dead" (4.4.78). This conceit is recalled when the figure cast by Richard's deformed birth is fulfilled for the final time, meaning that its tragic significance is finally reversed, with Richmond repeating Margaret's words nearly *verbatim*: "The day is ours; the bloody dog is dead" (5.5.2). In writing *Richard III*, Shakespeare made the stigmatized Richard of the Tudor myth into the "carnal cur" of Margaret's curses and then remade Margaret's curses into the triumphant pronouncement of Henry Tudor.

Richmond doesn't simply repeat Margaret's language; he inherits the logic in her spiritual model of stigma. While she says that Richard is a "minister of hell" (1.2.46) and "all [its] ministers attend on him" (1.3.293), Richmond's soldiers are "ministers of chastisement" (5.3.113), and he is the Lord's "captain" (5.3.108). He stirs his army with the theology of a just and active God, the dark side of which has been voiced by Margaret. He states the political theology of the Tudor myth, claiming the authority of divinity and the ancient constitution or "good old cause" of England: "God and our good cause fight upon our side" (5.3.238). Richmond calls Richard "God's enemy," making himself a figure for Christ, asserting divine justice: "If you fight against God's enemy, / God will, in justice, ward you" (5.3.251–252). Richmond voices the brighter, more uplifting Christian providentialist political theology that is the corollary to Margaret's vengeful spirituality of stigma.

When Richmond begins his final speech of reconciliation with the noble treatment of his foes in battle—"Inter their bodies as become their births" (5.5.15)—it's hard not to think of the historical Richard III's corpse stripped, flung over a horse, paraded around, and stabbed up the ass. As Philip Schwyzer has discussed, "The theme of Richard's posthumous humiliation looms surprisingly large in the Tudor popular tradition, larger indeed than that of his reputed deformity."[32] But the violence against Richard's body after death and the myth of his deformed body at birth form a single unit, writing Richard into other myths of good conquering evil. As Schwyzer points out, the connection between Richard's deformity and humiliation was explicitly made two decades after Shakespeare's play by John Speed: "For a miserable spectacle the space of two dayes [he] lay naked and unburied, his remembrance being as odious to all, as his person deformed, and lothsome to be looked upon."[33]

Why did Shakespeare make the parents of the Tudor dynasty—Stanley, Richmond, Elizabeth—stigmatizers? The obvious answer is that, historically speaking, the Tudors invented the stigmatized and demonized Richard III, who was more monster than man. Shakespeare reattributed the figural interpretations of Richard's body done by the Tudor historians to the founders of the dynasty that commissioned those histories. By turning the claims of the Tudor myth into Margaret's language and logic of vengeance and then turning Margaret's curses back into the Tudor myth proclaimed by Richmond at the end of the play, Shakespeare suggested that the Christian eschatology of the Tudor myth can be seen as the *nemesis* of Senecan tragedy, whose representative is Margaret. "I am hungry for revenge," she bellows (4.4.61). Stigma is revenge. It always is. But Shakespeare could have made that point without writing a plot that makes the figural interpretation of deformity a good interpretation. When you live in the world that Shakespeare created for his first tetralogy, basing your attitude toward Richard on a figural interpretation of his deformity allows you to survive his bloody dash through the English nobility.

Shakespeare made stigma real in his first tetralogy, or at least the lens used by the characters who survive the tragedy to establish a new, secure social order at the end of the play. Shakespeare provided a structural confirmation of the propriety of stigma, one disturbing to modern audiences and critics who think that stigma is bogus and harmful. Given this structural confirmation of stigma in *Richard III*, the question for modern audiences is elevated from *Do you accept or reject stigma?* to *Do you accept or reject the image of reality that underwrites stigma?* As Shakespeare illustrated, stigma is created and perpetuated by a spirituality that posits God as a divine judge rewarding the virtuous, punishing the wicked, and stigmatizing the extremely wicked with physical signs of their evil natures. Because Shakespeare validated physiognomy according to the reality of *Richard III*, the acceptance or rejection of physiognomy is also the acceptance or rejection of that reality, and vice versa.

The challenge is that stigma implicates a religious sensibility—call it Christianity—that remains present in modern culture, often seen as a force of good. To despise the practice of stigma in Shakespeare's *Richard III* is to call some of the basic tenets of Christianity into question. In Shakespeare's first tetralogy, stigma is so interwoven with spirituality that a rejection of the rhetoric and practice of stigma amounts to a rejection of the theology and metaphysics of spirit. Perhaps that is why no one really took issue with the figural interpretation of Richard's deformity until the middle of the eighteenth century—except maybe Shakespeare himself.

4

The Unnatural Age of Margaret

*Antiquating the Spiritual Model
of Stigma in* Richard III

Is Shakespeare with us or against us? That question confronts anyone who studies *Richard III* and who sees stigma as a repugnant social tradition and stain on history. In writing the foundational representation of disability in English literature, did Shakespeare endorse—intentionally or unwittingly—the tradition of stigma from earlier culture and literature? Or reject stigma with a forward-thinking sensibility? Was Shakespeare a stigmatizer or a critic of stigma? And how did his treatment of stigma connect to other concerns, such as politics and religion?

Answers start to take shape in the second scene of *Richard III*, when Lady Anne points to the murdered King Henry's mutilated corpse and voices the superstition that a dead body's wounds bleed afresh in the presence of its murderer. This is the first (but not last) time the text of *Richard III* presents a dramaturgical ambiguity that must be addressed to stage the play. Decisions determine the dramatic reality of a performance, which frames an audience's interpretation of Richard's body in that performance. If Henry's wounds do not bleed, suggesting that Anne is undergoing a fit of superstitious hallucination—brought on by the traumatic loss of her husband, father-in-law, and king—then the dramatic reality is naturalistic, and an interpretation of Richard's disability should be too. In this case, the causal interpretation—viewing disability as the cause rather than the sign of Richard's villainy—is the *right* interpretation.

If Henry's wounds bleed, however, the play acquires a supernatural dramatic reality that supports Anne's subsequent treatment of Richard's body as a figure of evil fulfilled in murder:

> Blush, blush, thou lump of foul deformity,
> For 'tis thy presence that exhales this blood
> From cold and empty veins where no blood dwells.
> Thy deeds, inhuman and unnatural,
> Provokes this deluge most unnatural.
> O God, which this blood mad'st, revenge his death!
> O earth, which this blood drink'st, revenge his death!
> Either heaven with lightning strike the murd'rer dead,
> Or earth gape open wide and eat him quick (1.2.57–65)

Anne's curse follows the structure of figural realism described by Erich Auerbach. She starts with a "deformity" that she then connects to a seemingly unrelated "deed." To Anne, the inhuman murder of Henry VI fulfilled the figure cast by Richard's unnatural birth. Both remain concrete historical events—Richard was born deformed in 1452 and murdered Henry in 1471—but these events now signify each other, and together they signify something in the future that will be the definitive, compensatory event. When God's hand reaches into history to strike Richard down, or Earth swallows him into Hell, the providential power organizing the universe in a rational, just, and felicitous arc of history will be revealed as the final and fullest meaning of Richard's deformity.

Shakespeare gave stigma metaphysical implications in *Richard III*: the way you interpret disability signifies and is sustained by your understanding of reality. To embrace the figural interpretation is to live in the supernatural world of myth and spirit; to adopt a causal interpretation takes you into the natural world of body and behavior. In *Richard III*, and in life, stigma has extraordinarily high stakes, since voicing your interpretation of disability often means declaring what kind of world you think you live in.

I. The Metaphysics of Stigma in Shakespeare's First Tetralogy

Richard and Margaret are competing choruses in *Richard III*, each vying for the audience's endorsement, especially on the most important issue in the play, the meaning of Richard's body, the causal reading coming from

Richard, the figural from Margaret. One challenge of *Richard III* is that Margaret's figural interpretations of Richard's body are as accurate as they are offensive: as accurate an account of his character and outcome as they are offensive to anyone who thinks that stigma is a revolting practice. As deluded and harmful as it is to modern audiences, the figural reading is an accurate reading of disability in Shakespeare's first tetralogy, given how Shakespeare represented reality in those plays. Because Shakespeare validated physiognomy according to the reality of *Richard III*, the acceptance or rejection of physiognomy is also the acceptance or rejection of that reality, and vice versa.

Margaret is the spokesperson for the first tetralogy's supernatural dramatic reality. Speaking with Senecan declamation, she experiences the world differently than the rhetorically unimpressive ways we think and speak outside the theater. Her version of reality then disperses throughout *Richard III* when her league of ladies starts conversing as artificially as she does. Shakespeare could write naturalistic speech, but the stilted and rehearsed lines of Margaret's cohort draw attention to the scriptedness of *Richard III*. This is a world that has been written—not by Shakespeare, the implication is, but by some higher power.

On its own, a high rhetorical style does not indicate a supernatural dramatic reality, especially in Elizabethan drama. But Shakespeare's first tetralogy elevates from formulaic lines to formulaic plotlines. Portents and prophecies accurately anticipate events, as in "that fatal prophecy" from Henry V that structures the two tetralogies: "That Henry born at Monmouth should win all, / And Henry born at Windsor lose all" (*1H6*, 3.1.199–200). In *Richard III*, Margaret's curses create a foreshadow-and-fulfillment pattern. They always take effect, with one exception, and are often recalled upon fulfillment. Out on the street, curses are words of ill will that alleviate our woe in the therapeutic act of expression, but in *Richard III*, prophecies, portents, and curses ascend into the ether, where sits the author of events, whether God or Shakespeare, who heeds their call.

Sometimes Shakespeare's first tetralogy brings portents on stage right before our eyes. In scenes probably written by Christopher Marlowe, Joan's fiends physically appear in *1 Henry VI* (5.3.8–29), as does the spirit Asnath in *2 Henry VI* (1.4.22–39). In a scene from *3 Henry VI*, probably by Shakespeare, the York brothers see *"three suns appear in the air"* (5.8sd in Octavio). Shakespeare adapted this marvelous moment from Edward Hall's chronicle, but there's a difference.[1] Where Hall reported (with some skepticism) what Edward believed that he saw, Shakespeare made the suns' appearance an actual, perceptible, historical event. The spectacle of the three suns is related to the other significant spectacle on stage at that moment—Richard's body. The figural interpretation of prodigies like Richard is allied with the figural interpretation of prodigies like the three suns, based on what Richard says when he sees them: "In this the heaven figures some event" (2.1.32). Like Richard's deformed birth, the suns "figure" some future that will fulfill the figure. Shakespeare presented the suns as real in his text, not reported skeptically as in Hall's, thereby surprisingly and uncomfortably endorsing the theology of figures.

A stage representing the portent of the three suns as an actual event makes the figural interpretation of disability a viable interpretation, even if it's odd and offensive to modern ways of thinking. Shakespeare wrote a play that, in its structure, condones figural interpretation. That means that our task, as audiences, shifts from accepting or rejecting the figural interpretation of disability to accepting or rejecting the version of reality that makes figural interpretation possible.

This supernatural dramatic reality culminates in the fearful symmetry of the final act of *Richard III*, with its two tents, two orations, even the two names in the battle of Richard versus Richmond, the former a villain opening the play with a speech about "grim-visaged war" (1.1.9), the latter a hero closing it with one about "smooth-faced peace" (5.5.33). The tent scene cuts the stage in half and polarizes morality into clear-cut camps of good and evil. Where Shakespeare's source, *The True Tragedy of Richard the Third*, had Richard report his nightmare, Shakespeare brings the ghosts of Richard's victims physically onstage. The antitheses in their messages—"despair and die" for Richard (5.3.126), "live and flourish" for Richmond (5.3.130)—use a rhetorical formalism to suggest a supernatural dramatic reality. Richard then plans to march "if not to heaven then hand in hand to hell" (5.3.311). The "*exeunt*" after Richard's comically bad oration to his soldiers is an Elizabethan version of the demons parading into the hellmouth at the end of the English mystery plays.

Questions of chronology and collaboration complicate the issue—scholars think that *2* and *3 Henry VI* were written first and that *1 Henry VI* was a prequel written in 1592, which Shakespeare and company revised around 1595—but, in terms of the narrative told, the tetralogy starts with creatural conflicts here on Earth in *1 Henry VI* and then grows more otherworldly as it unfolds. The first scene in *1 Henry VI*, probably by Thomas Nashe, does not show the "ghost" of Henry V (1.1.52), nor "comets, importing change of times and states" (1.1.2), nor "the bad revolting stars / That have consented unto Henry's death" (1.1.4–5), nor "the subtle-witted French / Conjurers and sorcerers" that "by magic verses have contriv'd his end" (1.1.25–27). This scene parodies the foolish men who superstitiously believe in such silliness. "Tush, man, abodements must not now affright us," Edward IV says in *3 Henry VI* (4.8.13) to his brother Richard, whose body has been treated as an "abodement." God does not oversee the action at the start of the tetralogy, but every time an evil character dies, it becomes easier to believe that the "heavens are just and time suppresseth wrongs," in the words of Queen Margaret (*3H6*, 3.3.77), the voice of this providential theology. By alternating between superstitious statements meant to mock a too simplistic spirituality and more serious theological statements about divine providence borne out by the play, Shakespeare complicated the dramatic reality of the first tetralogy. But it's not simply that, to quote Nicholas Brooke, *Richard III* presents "a simultaneous perception of two utterly different and opposed scales of value, the historical and the tragic."[2] I think that Shakespeare chose a side.

II. Margaret's Old Age

While Shakespeare's first tetralogy establishes a supernatural dramatic reality, its association with old Queen Margaret suggests that Shakespeare was satirizing the spirituality that envisions such a world. He only wrote a supernatural dramatic reality that supports the figural reading of Richard's body into *Richard III* to characterize it as old and ugly. Shakespeare made an aged and withered Margaret the representative of the retrograde spirituality of the Tudor myth so that audiences would see that spirituality—literally see it—as old and ugly.

Margaret plays a part made famous by her countrywoman, Joan de Pucelle of *1 Henry VI*.[3] In scenes written mostly by Nashe and Marlowe, possibly during or after Shakespeare's composition of *Richard III*, Joan was first beautified, literally, in her adolescence when the virgin Mary transformed her from a "black and swart" troll into a "beauty" (1.2.84–86). She is stunning at the start of *1 Henry VI*: the French dauphin "burn[s]" with "desire" when he sees her (1.2.108). To English eyes, however, Joan is an "ugly witch," "hag, enchantress," and "miscreant," in the Duke of York's words (5.3.34, 42, and 44). When York captures Joan, she pleads, "Give me leave to curse awhile" (5.3.43), and at that moment, for the first time, Margaret of Anjou appears—perhaps a connection created when *1 Henry VI* was revised after Shakespeare wrote *Richard III*.

As female French warriors scourging their English enemies and prophesying the plots of Shakespeare's plays, Joan and Margaret share a kinship extending from nationality to personality. "Assigned am I to be the English scourge," Joan says in *1 Henry VI* (1.2.129); in *2 Henry VI*, Margaret becomes "England's bloody scourge" (5.1.118). Joan is "that railing Hecate" (*1H6*, 3.1.63)—in league with the demon that oversees the "supernatural soliciting" in *Macbeth* (1.3.132)—and Margaret a "railer" (*3H6*, 5.5.38). Their invective includes "the spirit of deep prophesy," which Joan enjoys: "What's past and what's to come she can descry" (1.2.55–57). With "the help of hell" (2.1.18), Joan accesses the occult to serve a structural function in the plotting of *1 Henry VI*, as when she delays the death of Lord Talbot because "[his] hour is not yet come" (1.6.13). According to the dauphin, Joan's "promises are like Adonis' garden, / That one day bloomed and fruitful were the next" (1.7.6–7). This efficacy extends to the Margaret of *Richard III*, when she assumes the role of the first tetralogy's French prophetess.

Shakespeare also repeated Joan's physical degeneration in the much longer life of Margaret. Just as Joan became an "ugly witch" and "hag enchantress," Margaret becomes a "foul wrinkled witch" and "hateful withered hag" in *Richard III* (1.3.163 and 211). As Thomas Heywood wrote, using the language of stigma, witches "are for the most part stigmaticall and ouglie, in so much, that it is growne into a common Adage, *Deformis vt Saga*, As deformed as a Witch."[4] Perhaps Margaret's hideousness explains why Richard recoils in horror when she steps out of the shadows in *Richard III* (she responds, "Villain, do not turn away" [1.3.162]) and why Richard reacts by drawing attention to the visual ("What mak'st thou in my sight?" [1.3.163]).

The old, ugly, even deformed Margaret of *Richard III* is nearly unrecognizable as the beauty who smiled and curtsied her way into *1* and *2 Henry VI*, catching the eye of her future husband, King Henry, and future lover, the Duke of Suffolk. When Suffolk first "*gazes on her*" in *1 Henry VI* (5.4.1sd), "beauteous Margaret" (5.6.2) is the "fairest beauty" (5.4.2), a "gorgeous beauty" (5.4.20) and "beauty's princely majesty" (5.4.26) who is "gracèd with external gifts" (5.6.3). Suffolk introduces Margaret in *2 Henry VI* as "the fairest queen that ever king received," and Henry swoons to see a "beauteous face" whose "sight did ravish" him (1.1.16–32). In *3 Henry VI*, however, Margaret becomes the "she-wolf of France," "an Amazonian trull" marked by unfeminine military prowess, as the Duke of York complains: "Women are soft, mild, pitiful and flexible; / Thou stern, obdurate, flinty, rough, remorseless," (1.4.111, 114, and 141–142). Suddenly her "share" of "beauty" is "small" (1.4.128–129), and "Helen of Greece was fairer far" (2.2.146). She was beautiful in the first two parts of *Henry VI*, but in the third, "[her] face is vizard-like, unchanging, / Made impudent with use of evil deeds" (1.4.116–117). As she becomes "more inhuman, more inexorable, / Oh, ten times more than tigers of Hyrcania" (1.4.154–155), Margaret's body becomes more inhuman, figured as a "tiger's heart wrapped in a woman's hide" (1.4.137). Morally and physically, Margaret hardens into the "Iron of Naples" (2.2.139).

If the beauty queen of *1* and *2 Henry VI* is ugly by *3 Henry VI*, she's downright hideous by *Richard III*, where she is unnaturally old. In the stage directions, it is specifically "*old Queen Margaret*" (1.3.110sd and 4.4.1sd) who brings her "wretched self" (1.3.202), "ancient sorrow" (4.4.35), and "seniory" (4.4.36) back to *Richard III* to prophesy the tragic end of Plantagenet England. She enters behind the action, commenting upon it, but she is also behind the times, in two senses. First, Margaret is, to quote Maurice Charney, "the voice of history and moral conscience reminding us of the crimes of Richard."[5] Second, Margaret is the voice of the ancient theology insisting that God will reward virtue and punish vice. Her ghostly body is the "index of a direful pageant" (4.4.85), Shakespeare granting her the vocabulary of tragedy to describe the events of the play, from "a dire induction" to "the consequence" that "will prove as bitter, black, and tragical" (4.4.5–7).

According to Shakespeare's sources, Margaret was gone from England by the time of her appearance in act 1 of *Richard III* and dead by the time she shows up in act 4. Hall related how Edward IV captured Margaret after the Battle of Tewkesbury in 1471, and her father ransomed her back to France in 1473 (the actual date was November 13, 1475):

> Toward thende she was vexed with troble, neuer quyet nor in peace, & in her very extreme age she passed her dayes in Fraunce, more lyke a death then a lyfe, languisshyng and mornyng in continuall sorowe, not so much for her selfe and her husbande, whose ages were almost consumed and worne, but for the losse of prince Edward her sonne.[6]

Even after he "waft[s] her hence to France" at the end of *3 Henry VI* (5.7.41), Shakespeare was so struck by Hall's account of Margaret's old age that he anachronistically brought her back in *Richard III*, where she haunts the drama, in Hall's words, "more lyke a death then a lyfe."

With Margaret coming from beyond the grave, the iconography of the character Dethe in Middle English and Tudor drama helps us envision her appearance and its significance. In the N-Town cycle of the Corpus Christi plays, Mors describes himself—"I be nakyd and pore of array / And wurmys knawe me al abowte"—and the woodcut introducing the morality play *Everyman* (1485) shows a skeletal Dethe dressed in rags, holding the lid of a coffin.[7] Marlowe addressed "the vglie monster death . . . pale and wan"; *The Lamentable Tragedie of Locrine* (1595) describes "Blacke vgly death with visage pale and wanne"; and Robert Yarington cribbed from Shakespeare's *Richard III* to envision "Thou vgly monster, grim imperious death, / Thou raw-bonde lumpe of foule deformitie."[8] Shakespeare himself called Death a "Hard-favored tyrant, ugly, meager, lean . . . Grim-grinning ghost, earth's worm" (*Venus and Adonis*, 931–933), a "rotten carcass . . . old" with "rags" (*King John*, 2.1.456–457), "the lean abhorrèd monster" (*Romeo and Juliet*, 5.3.104), with an "empty eye" (*MOV* 2.7.63) inside the "ugliest mask" (*2H4*, 1.1.66); a "dark spirit" (*Coriolanus*, 2.1.149); and "an ugly monster" (*Cymbeline*, 5.3.70). Imagine Margaret empty-eyed, ugly, and grim, with pale skin ghostly and gnawed; thin, boney, and waning away; dressed in rotten black rags; even deformed or monstrous. Thus, she steps into *Richard III*, screeching, "Which of you trembles not that looks on me?" (1.3.159).

In the Renaissance, Death was incarnated in human, female form in the iconography of witches, which regularly relied upon imagery of disability.[9] According to Reginald Scot's *The Discouerie of Witchcraft* (1584), witches were "commonly old, lame, bleare-eied, pale, fowl, and full of wrinkles."[10] Of the witch Duessa, Edmund Spenser wrote that "more vgly shape yet neuer liuing creature saw."[11] The woodcut for *A Most Wicked Worke of a Wretched Witch* (1592) shows a woman with a crouched neck and a cane.[12] The woodcut for *The Wonderful Discouerie of the Witchcrafts of Margaret and Phillip Flower* (1619) shows a woman with crutches and misaligned shoulders.[13] *The Wonderfull Discouerie of Elizabeth Sawyer* (1621) shows her hunched over and leaning on a cane, while the play based on this story, *The Witch of Edmonton* (1621), describes Sawyer as "poor, deform'd and ignorant, / And like a Bow buckl'd and bent together"; the play was not published until 1658, with a woodcut that shows Sawyer with a large hunchback and a cane.[14] Meanwhile, the woodcut for *A Certaine Relation of the Hog-Faced Gentlewoman Called Mistris Tannin Skinker* (1640) makes the witch explicitly monstrous, giving her a pig's head.[15]

Recognizing that Queen Margaret is old, ugly, deformed, even monstrous brings her body into relation with the other ugly, disabled, monstrous character in the play, Richard. His stigmatized body is always noticed, hers rarely, but Richard's birth defects and Margaret's old age only make sense together, dialectically, each constituting the meaning of the other. As the oldest and angriest Lancastrian, Margaret is the most frequent and furious champion of the figural interpretation of Richard's disability. Like most Tudor writers, Shakespeare used Richard's disability to envision his villainy, but he also used

Margaret's aged body to envision her figural reading of Richard as an old and ugly aesthetic. Shakespeare did not directly oppose the figural interpretation of disability. His first tetralogy seems to endorse it as good interpretation, given what counts as reality in those plays. Instead, Shakespeare critiqued the entire complex of historical, political, theological, metaphysical, and dramatic systems that make the figural interpretation of disability possible and valid. He mocked the world one must imagine to figurally interpret disability. If Shakespeare critiqued the causal interpretation of disability by attributing it to Richard himself, a confused man and compulsive liar, he satirized the figural interpretation by attributing it to Margaret. Her old age is stage stigma just as much as Richard's deformity is. Shakespeare used one stigma to critique the production and perpetuation of another: he satirized the aesthetics that promote the beauty of virtue and the deformity of vice, even as—paradoxically—he used this aesthetic to make this point.

III. The Ugliness of the Weird Sisters

We are on shaky, highly speculative ground here, but there is corroborating evidence. *Richard III* was not the last time Shakespeare stigmatized the tragic chorus of a play by making her unnaturally old and ugly: he did the same with the Weird Sisters in *Macbeth*. Before Shakespeare, the Weird Sisters were beautiful wonders in marvelous apparel, beings from another world: nymphs, fairies, or goddesses of destiny.[16] But Shakespeare reupholstered the Weird Sisters in the iconography of witches, their bodies made wrinkled and withered, their surroundings gloomy and grotesque.

In Raphael Holinshed's *Chronicles*, as in Shakespeare's play, the sisters call Macbeth "Thane of Glamis," "Thane of Cawdor," and "King of Scotland," but then, in Holinshed, they vanish from the story of Macbeth's bloody rise to the throne.[17] In contrast, Shakespeare brought the sisters back, adding an element of calamity to the felicity in their prophecies by attributing to the Weird Sisters the prophecies of Macbeth's death—that he will not be killed by any man born of a woman, nor until Birnam wood comes to Dunsinane—prophecies Holinshed's *Chronicles* ascribe to some random witch, not the Weird Sisters.[18] Thus, where the British chronicles before Shakespeare depict the Weird Sisters as magical, even beautiful beings speaking a fixed and felicitous future, *Macbeth* changed the sisters into something hideous while adding tragic irony to their fortune-telling.

Why did Shakespeare turn the Weird Sisters' beauty to ugliness and add tragedy to their prophecies of prosperity? In the context of King James's recent coronation in 1603, it may be that Shakespeare made the Weird Sisters ugly to illustrate how unattractive the world becomes under the Calvinist doctrine of predestination, which James endorsed, a theology that must disconnect truth and beauty. If predestination is true, it is an ugly truth, which Shakespeare showed by announcing the incontrovertible tragedy of *Macbeth* through the prophecies of hideous hags. Although Shakespeare spent much of his career critiquing the folly of stigma, he himself was not above employing the representational resources of stigma—specifically, the imagery of old age—in the cases of Margaret and the Weird Sisters. Shakespeare's most important depiction of old age, *King Lear*, shows that his aged bodies need not always vocalize a supernatural dramatic reality. But when he made the aged body grotesque—as with Margaret and the Weird Sisters, but not Lear—Shakespeare used the old and withered (and female) body to announce an archaic theology governing a grim course of tragic action.

5

Richard III's Disability after Shakespeare

Discovering the Causal Paradigm

Given the dominance of the "figural" interpretation of Richard III in the sixteenth century (seeing disability as a sign of evil embodied), the "causal" interpretation Shakespeare advanced (repositioning disability as a cause rather than sign of villainy) was a remarkable anomaly. Shakespeare further suggested that these competing interpretations of disability signify competing theological, philosophical, psychological, ethical, and historical systems of behavior and belief. But what impact did Shakespeare's new understanding of Richard have?

This chapter tells the story of Richard's disability in the centuries after Shakespeare. Cultural histories of Richard III tend to come in two varieties: one relates the blackening of Richard's reputation between his death and Shakespeare's plays,[1] and the other surveys the modern performance history of Shakespeare's character.[2] These emphases on the sixteenth century and then the eighteenth century and after elide the remarkable thing that happened to the interpretation of Richard's disability in the seventeenth century: nothing.[3] Nothing changed. That's what's remarkable. But then, in the third quarter of the eighteenth century, Shakespeare's causal interpretation of Richard's disability was not only noticed for the first time in print but, in the short span of about ten years, became the dominant way of thinking about Shakespeare's character.

I. "Your Eyes Advance after Your Thoughts": Perception and Interpretation

To discuss stability and change in the treatment of Richard's deformity after Shakespeare, this chapter returns to Thomas Kuhn's ideas from *The Structure of Scientific Revolutions* (1962). Kuhn positions his notion of a "paradigm shift" against two scientific commonplaces. First is the distinction, traditional since René Descartes, between perception (done by the eyes) and interpretation (by the mind). Second is the notion, put forth by a line of philosophers of science running from Francis Bacon through Auguste Comte to Karl Popper, of scientific progress as an incremental creep toward truth. Kuhn rejects this notion because he denies the Cartesian claim that we all see the same reality, yet some of us interpret it differently. Instead, Kuhn argues, we have a "disciplinary matrix" made up of generalizations, theories, beliefs, values, arguments, and examples that create assumptions and expectations about how the world works (a position advanced in literary studies in Stanley Fish's theory of "interpretive communities").[4] These preconceptions about reality influence the methods and instruments we employ to study our world. If the way we collect information about the world is already conditioned by what we believe and expect to be true, then the act of perception—what we see—is conditioned (some say compromised) by our beliefs, values, assumptions, expectations, methods, and instruments. We only see what we are prepared or expect to see.

The relationship between thought and sight was central to the Shakespeare who wrote that "the mind and sight" can be "commix'd" (*A Lover's Complaint*, 28). He said it best in *Henry V*, invoking the imagination of his audience: "Your eyes advance, / After your thoughts" (5.0.45–46). First you think it, and then you see it, an inversion of the Cartesian priority of perception.

On this contentious point, Kuhn cites psychological experiments showing that "perceiving is a process which results from the stimulation of a prepared or *eingestellt* [positioned] organism."[5] These studies reveal that a person's perceptual field is organized to maximize stimuli relevant to current needs, desires, and expectations and to minimize those inimical. To N. R. Hanson, whom Kuhn cites, "There is a sense, then, in which seeing is a 'theory-laden' undertaking."[6] Kuhn writes that "something like a paradigm is prerequisite to perception itself" (113). A "paradigm" is not simply an interpretation repeatedly arrived at and independently verified until it achieves consensus. It is the image of reality—not interpretation, but perception—almost inevitably created once a certain disciplinary matrix is in place.

Almost inevitably. Anomalous or unexpected facts, data, evidence, and experiences exist but, to Kuhn, are usually suppressed, allowing for the perpetuation of a paradigm. This is what Kuhn calls "normal science," but anomalies are not argued against or willfully ignored. They are not seen at all, or not seen as relevant. Only when an unshakable awareness of anomaly exists do Kuhnian revolutions begin. The acute and repeated difficulty of connecting expectation and experience results in a deeper investigation of the paradigm than ever before. There is a loosening of the disciplinary matrix, a more skeptical reflection upon it. "Scientists have not generally needed or wanted to be philosophers," Kuhn notes (88), but in moments of disciplinary "crisis," they often turn to abstract speculation to shore up assumptions and beliefs.

Thus, a paradigm shift is not a new and improved interpretation. It involves "a reconstruction of the field from new fundamentals, a reconstruction that changes some of the field's most elementary theoretical generalizations as well as many of its paradigm methods and applications" (84–85). New assumptions and expectations bring new methods and instruments of study; a new disciplinary matrix brings new facts, data, evidence, and experience. A new image—perception, not interpretation—of reality emerges. As Kuhn insists, "Scientists do not see something *as* something else; instead they simply see it" (85). If that new perception is viscerally more satisfying to the scientific community (Kuhn uses such terms as "better," "simpler," "neater," "more suitable" [155]), then the older paradigm is replaced in short order. What was previously an anomalous experience comes to be expected, a "paradigm shift."

Turning to the resolution of revolutions, Kuhn notes that there will be holdouts, "lifelong resistance, particularly from those whose productive careers have committed them to an older tradition of normal science" (151). Conversion to a new paradigm does not involve individual scientists changing their minds as much as an older generation of scientists dying out, with a newer generation emerging whose professional training begins after the paradigm shift.[7] Textbooks are rewritten. New methodologies are taught. New instruments are invented. New perceptions of reality. A new disciplinary matrix. A new worldview. A new world. "Though the world does not change with a change of paradigm," Kuhn writes, controversially, "the scientist afterward works in a different world" (121). There's not a change in objective reality, of course, but in the subjective experience of the scientist such that "the data are not unequivocally stable" (121). When challenged on this point, Kuhn responded that "two groups, the members of which have systematically different sensations on receipt of the same stimuli, do *in some sense* live in different worlds" (193). Referencing gestalt psychology and Wittgenstein's popular example, he concludes, "What were ducks in the scientist's world before the revolution are rabbits afterward" (111).

From a Kuhnian perspective, it is wrong to speak of figural and causal "interpretations" of Richard's disability. Kuhn would speak of figural and causal *understandings* that come from situated perception, not deliberate interpretation. In the shift from the early-modern to the modern reception of Richard's disability, the perception itself changed. Shakespeareans before and after the third quarter of the eighteenth century were living in different worlds. Modern audiences didn't see things differently; they saw different things when they saw Richard's disability. The reception history of *Richard III* proves Shakespeare right: your attitude toward stigma signifies your understanding of reality.

II. Richard's Deformity in the Early-Modern Age: The Causal Anomaly and the Figural Paradigm

"Throughout the whole Tragedie," John Milton wrote about Shakespeare's *Richard III*, "The Poet us'd not much licence in departing from the truth of History."[8] Although Shakespeare distanced himself from the Tudor chronicles by suggesting Richard's disability is not the sign but the cause of his villainy, Milton—a careful reader—thought that Shakespeare did not depart much at all. No one even noticed Shakespeare's causal interpretation of Richard's disability (at least not in print) until the middle of the eighteenth century. Shakespeare did not change the conversation. Thus, the early-modern treatment of Richard's disability amounts to a remarkable case of "normal science," *normal* because the continued popularity of the figural interpretation worked as Kuhn says that scientific research usually works—repeating, confirming, and extending but not questioning an established paradigm of thought and suppressing or ignoring anomalies—but also *normal* because it exhibits the understanding of disability promoted by those whom Erving Goffman calls "the normals."[9] The early-modern treatment of Richard III was, to quote Kuhn, "an attempt to force nature into the preformed and relatively inflexible box that the paradigm supplies" (24). Normal science only observes phenomena and articulates theories already supplied by a paradigm. It "does not aim at novelties of fact or theory and, when successful, finds none" (52). Facts and theories not already part of a paradigm are often not seen at all. The following survey of statements about Richard III's body in the century after Shakespeare is heavy on demonstration to throw some real weight behind the claim that Shakespeare's early-modern and modern audiences quite literally didn't see the same thing when they saw Richard's disability.

Texts contemporary with Shakespeare's show that the figural paradigm of the sixteenth century continued to dominate into the seventeenth. Thomas Heywood's *King Edward the Fourth, Part II* (1594), written two years after Shakespeare's *Richard III*, has a Shakespearean Richard say, "I am a true stampt villaine as euer liude."[10] Disability is the "stamp" of villainy, a figure connected to the divinely directed course of Tudor history, the Wars of the Roses: "The crooke bakt Boare the way hath found, / To roote our Roses from our ground" (L4). Before Shakespeare, plays referred to "Richard the Third" in their title, but Ben Jonson's play was titled *Richard Crookback* (1602). It has been lost to history, but the title suggests Shakespeare's earliest audiences saw him contributing to, not counteracting, the Tudor treatment of Richard. Thus, *The Returne from Pernassus* (1601) dramatizes the actor who played Shakespeare's Richard III, Richard Burbage, auditioning young actors and telling one, "I like your face, and the proportion of your body for *Richard* the 3."[11] Richard's body continued to define him, while Shakespeare's fictional Richard all but replaced the historical Richard, as in Richard Corbet's *Iter Boreale* (ca. 1619), when one character "mistooke a Player for a King, / For when he would have said, King Richard dy'd, / And call'd a Horse, a Horse, he Burbage cry'd."[12]

Anomalies existed—there is no deformity in the engraving of Richard (or the accompanying description) in Thomas Talbot's *The True Portraiture of the Countenances and Attires of the Kings of England* (1597)—but Michael Drayton's historical poems carried the figural interpretation from the Elizabethan to the Jacobean age.[13] Richard's episode in *England's Heroicall Epistles* (1597) quotes Shakespeare to call Richard "that foule, ilfauored, crookback'd stigmatick," an editor's note glossing the line with Thomas More's version of Richard's birth.[14] Drayton's *Poly-Oblion* (1613) calls Richard "a monster loth'd, / The man, to hell and death himselfe that had betroth'd," recalling Shakespeare's Richard marked by sin, death, and hell.[15] After Shakespeare, Richard became more, not less, monstrous, as in John Davies of Hereford's 1603 description of Richard as a "*Monster*, not a *Man*," a figure Davies attached to "the flud / Of *Divine Vengeance*."[16]

A Myrroure for Magistrates popularized the figural understanding of Richard III in the sixteenth century, and Richard Niccols's compendium to the *Myrroure*, titled *A Winter Night's Vision* (1610), perpetuated it.[17] Two of the eleven new poems deal with Richard, his villainy, and his disability.

One claims that Richard "from his mothers painful throwes, / Mark't for a plague into the world was brought" (738), the earthly, creatureal event given supernatural significance. In a narrative interlude between this poem and the next, Niccols describes how the murder of the princes fulfilled the tragic figure cast by Richard's congenital malformation: "They dead, their uncles tragedie succeeds: His monstrous birth, his shape, his bloodie deeds" (749). The next poem out-Shakespeares Shakespeare, offering the most extensive figural interpretation of Richard to date. He is "a man-like monster . . . by heau'n and nature in [his] birth accurst" for "Nature by signes vnto the world hath show'd" just as "Heau'n at that time told b'inauspitious stares / Nations far off of Englands ciuil warres," so Niccols's Richard declares:

> Each spectatours eie
> Would by my lookes into my manners prie:
> The bodies ill-shapte limbes are oft defin'd
> For signes of euill manners in the mind. . . .
> I did appeare a most misshapen wight:
> And hard it was to judge, if that my soule
> Or limbes ill fashion'd feature were more foule. (750–751)

The image of Richard in armor printed with this poem figurally connects the deformity of a withered right hand, one finger jutting up unnaturally, with the violence of his left hand, holding a dagger.[18] In a loftier style, Christopher Brooke's *The Ghost of Richard the Third* (1614) catalogues many of the same prodigious signs—horizontal correspondences with a vertical relationship—as when "th'*Almighty Thunde'er*" shakes "Massie Earth" upon Richard's "Monstrous Byrth."[19] In the two decades that followed Shakespeare's *Richard III*, the king's deformity grew in its size and significance, while the figural interpretation grew in explicitness and frequency.

The figural reading of Richard III was codified enough to be a metaphor for Robert Cecil, advisor to Queen Elizabeth and King James, derided as "a little hunchback," "little elf," "pygmy," and "a little, crooked person."[20] Alluding to Shakespeare's "crookback" (*3H6*, 1.3.75), a "bottled spider" (*R3*, 1.3.241) and "dissembler" (1.2.184) who can "smile in men's faces, smooth, deceive, and cog" (1.3.48), one manuscript libel verse calls Cecil a "Dissembling smoothfaced dwarf . . . I know your crookback's spider shapen"[21] After Cecil's death in 1612, another eulogizes him with reference to Richard:

> Heere lieth Robin Crooktback, unjustly reckond
> A Richard the third, he was Judas [the Second] . . .
> Richard, or Robert, which is the worse?
> A crookt back great in state is England's curse.[22]

A third poem reads: "Two R:R:rs two crookebacks of late ruled Englands helme / The one spilte the Royall bloode, the other Spoylde the Realme."[23] There are two layers of figural interpretation in these verses. First, Richard's and Cecil's bodies figure their actions and destinies: disability figures villainy and tragedy. Second, Richard and Cecil (along with Judas) are reiterated character types in a figural patterning of history.

The figural reading of Richard III came to Caroline England when John Beaumont (elder brother to dramatist Francis) wrote the narrative poem *Bosworth Field* (1629). Beaumont uses Shakespearean imagery to show "the Winters storme of Ciuill warre" become "our eternall Spring" after the nation is freed from the "Tyrants iawes" of the "crooked Monster."[24] Another poem from 1638 describes Richard's toothed birth as a "dreaded signe" and "presage of cruelty."[25] We can only imagine how monstrous the main character was in Samuel Rowley's *A Tragedy of Richard the Thirde or the English Prophett with the Reformation*, licensed by Sir Henry Herbert for performance by Palgrave's Men at the Fortune in 1623, but lost to history.[26] Richard III was played by a child actor at the Red Bull Theatre at some point in the early seventeenth century, with Heywood publishing a prologue in 1637 where the boy actor suggests a parallel between his diminutive body and Richard's deformed:

> If any wonder by what magick charme,
> Richard the third is shrunke up like his arme:
> And where in fulnesse you expected him,
> You see me onely crawling, like a lime. . . .
> Hee's tearm'd a man, that showes a dwarfish thing.[27]

Printed in quarto six times and in the first folio, Shakespeare's *Richard III* remained popular enough to earn a performance at court on the queen's birthday in 1634, but soon Shakespeare's play was shelved for nearly two decades, like all drama, during the English Revolution.

During the interregnum, Thomas Wincoll's *Plantagenets Tragicall Story* (1649) warns "men turn'd to Monsters, I shall bring to view" before launching into the figure-fulfillment-vertical-relationship pattern.[28] He mentions

Richard's toothed birth, claiming that Nature was "no Bungler, but a Prophetesse" when it misshaped Richard: "Sin's like a Monster, which is seldome borne / But by some swelling, or excesse of forme" (57). Wincoll connects the figure to a divinely governed course of history that would manifest at the Battle of Bosworth, when "veng'ance wil powre down from Richmonds steel" (44). Wincoll then closes the first book of his poem by remarking how historians will drag Richard through the mud, just as his body was dragged unceremoniously to its burial.

Wincoll was right; Richard continued to bear the slander of seventeenth-century writers on his shoulder. In his sermon at the Palace of Whitehall on the day of Charles II's restoration in 1660, Henry King mentioned precedents in the Bible, Socrates, and Aristotle when noting "our Third Richard's deformed Body and ill aspect made him look'd on as that Prodigy whom all fear'd, none lov'd."[29] The Restoration reopened the theater doors, and John Caryll's play *The English Princess* (1667) reaffirmed the vicious and tyrannical image of Richard, whom one character refers to figurally as "a Monster both in crimes and Shape."[30] John Crowne's *The Misery of Civil War* (1680), adapting the last two parts of Shakespeare's *Henry VI* trilogy, makes Richard's deformity synonymous with "that fowl Monster Civil-War."[31] Crowne's Queen Margaret calls Richard an "ugly Crook-back," both "hideous" and "horrid," before declaring that his "soul cannot be worse than where it is" (12). Many of the insults Crowe throws at Richard come straight from Shakespeare, as when Crowe's Edward IV warns the audience about his brother:

> He is a Hell at whose foul front appears,
> Ill manners, and ill nature, and ill shape,
> Like a three-headed Dog, that barks at all things
> That dare come near him, specially at beauty. (22)

In 1689–1690, Richard was played at Drury Lane by Samuel Sandford, an actor described as someone who "was not the Stage-Villain by Choice, but from Necessity; for having a low and crooked Person, such bodily Defects were too strong to be admitted into great, or amiable Characters."[32]

The figural tradition survived, in part, because the most common way to represent Richard's deformity was in imaginative texts—verse or drama. These kinds of literature have conventions disposing them to figurative language, encouraging writers to position Richard's disability in elevated plots and themes reaching beyond the realm of earthly human experience—this in contrast to, say, historical or critical prose privileging clarity of communication over creativity of expression. As Kuhn observes, someone working from within a paradigm "knows what he wants to achieve, and he designs his instruments and directs his thoughts accordingly" (96). In scientific research, a paradigm is often implicit in the instrument used to gather data. A figural understanding of Richard's deformity led writers to express their ideas poetically, and, in turn, the stylistically heightened medium of poetry led writers to perpetuate the figural understanding. Shakespeare's causal understanding was ignored in the seventeenth century because it was better suited to prose argument than poetic narrative.

Yet the figural interpretation came into seventeenth-century history writing. The poetic apparatus perpetuated the figural paradigm, but the paradigm transcended the apparatus. In 1605, William Camden quoted John Rous's early account of Richard's deformity, adding that Richard's "monstrous birth foreshewed his monstrous proceedings, for he was born with all his teeth, and haire to his shoulders."[33] John Speed's *The History of Great Britaine* (1613) gave a figural reading of Richard, "his inward mind more deformed then were his outward lineaments."[34] John Trussell's *History of England* (1636) quoted Shakespeare to accuse Richard of "cloking his wolvish condition, under the vaile of innocent well-meaning, this Monster of men, backt by the divell and his dissembling lookes."[35] Richard Baker's *Chronicle of the Kings of England* (1643) used the rhetorical resources of poetry to make the argument of physiognomy:

> There never was in any man a greater uniformity of Body and Minde then was in [Richard III]; both of them equally deformed. Of Body he was but low, crooke-backt, hook-shouldred, splay-footed, and goggle-eyed, his face little and round, his complexion swarsie, his left arm from his birth dry and withered: born a monster in nature, with all his teeth, with haire on his head, and nailes on his fingers and toes. And just such were the qualities of his minde.[36]

In 1650, the parliamentarian pamphleteer Henry Parker also used the rhetoric of monstrosity to discuss "Richard the Third, a bloody and cruel man, rather a monster then a Prince."[37] In 1652, the anti-Jacobean courtier Anthony Weldon called Richard "a Monster of lust & cruelty."[38] And in 1683, the cleric William Assheton addressed the "Monster of Mankind the Duke of *Glocester*."[39] These epithets came more out of convenience than sustained argument, for, by this time, the figural interpretation was so dominant that it did not need to be argued. It was an assumption from which interpretation flowed rather than a conclusion toward which interpretation went.

Anti-figural accounts of Richard's disability were not unheard of in the seventeenth century but were—like Shakespeare's plays—anomalies suppressed by the dominant paradigm. Bacon's *The Historie of the Reigne of King Henry the Seuenth* (begun in 1609, finished in 1621, published in 1629) was anomalous simply by not mentioning Richard's deformities. This present absence is significant in light of Bacon's "Essay on Deformity" (1613), which states the causal understanding of deformity as a general theory. Yet neither the work of Bacon nor any other early-modern writer apart from Shakespeare suggested a causal link between Richard's disability and villainy.

Consider William Cornwallis's *Essays of Certaine Paradoxes* (1616), which contains a piece titled "The Prayse of King Richard the Third" in a series of satirical essays celebrating, for example, French pox, nothingness, and debt. Cornwallis recuperates Richard with an anti-figural interpretation, connecting deformity with not villainy but valor (a quite different causal interpretation from Shakespeare's):

> He was crook-backt, lame, il-shapen, il-fauoured. I might impute that fault to Nature, but that I rather think it her bounty: for she being wholly intentiue of his minde, neglected his forme, so that shee influenced a straight minde in a crooked bodie, wherein shee showed her carefull prouidence. For often times, the care to keep those parts well formed, with-draws mens mindes from better actions. . . . With those imperfect limes, hee performed actions most perfectly valiant.[40]

Citing Cornwallis, George Buck's 1646 attempt to disprove the Tudor myth with his *Life and Reign of Richard III* drew attention to the partisan leanings of John Rous, Thomas More, Edward Hall, Raphael Holinshed, and Shakespeare. Buck also cited historians whose work made no mention of any deformity (such as Archibald Whitelaw, Philippe de Commines, John Stow, and the author of the *Croyland Chronicle*) to argue that Richard III was neither deformed nor villainous.[41] This is the view on display in a portrait, dated to around 1660, originally housed in Keevil Manor, now in the National Trust: a Richard with no discernable deformities.[42] In *England's Worthies* (1660), William Winstanley also charged Richard's historians with bias in lamenting the "malicious traducers, who like Shakespear in his Play of him, render [Richard III] dreadfully black in his actions, a monster of nature, rather then a man of admirable parts."[43] Note that when Buck and Winstanley argue that Richard was not deformed—was instead demonized and stigmatized by the Tudors—they say that he was neither deformed nor villainous. These anomalous readings remain somewhat paradigmatic, therefore, insofar as Richard's body and behavior retain an affinity, each now adjusted from a deplorable to an admirable status.

The anomalous Richards of Shakespeare, Cornwallis, Buck, and Winstanley lead to two conclusions. First, if we think about the representation of Richard III's disability as scientific research, then we can say that, while anomalies exist, the figural interpretation that treats Richard's disability as a God-given sign of danger and damnation suppressed anomalous accounts. Consider the notion that a deformed body might lead the man bearing it to compensate with mental and moral excellence, which appears in a reworking of Shakespeare's *Richard III* in John Dryden and Nathaniel Lee's *Oedipus: A Tragedy* (1679). Bickering like Anne and Richard, this play's Eurydice and Creon debate the meaning of his misshapen body, she hurling figural interpretations, he demurring.[44] The debate might indicate the growing debatability of the figural reading of deformity, though Eurydice gets the last word, affirming the figural paradigm. Once Eurydice exits, moreover, Creon admits that her figural reading of his body is the *right* reading—"Tis true, I am / What she has told me, an offence to sight: / My body opens inward to my soul" (7)—which dramatizes the suppression of anomalous readings of Richard's deformity during the seventeenth century. But *why* were anomalous interpretations suppressed by the figural paradigm?

The answer relates to the second conclusion we can draw at this point: even anomalies like the anti-figural arguments from Cornwallis, Buck, and Winstanley understood Shakespeare to be a proponent of the figural paradigm, and, more importantly, the causal paradigm that Shakespeare proposed *wasn't even noticed*. Cornwallis says that Richard was deformed yet virtuous. Buck and Winstanley say that he wasn't deformed at all. But no one says, as Shakespeare did, that Richard's deformity was cause rather than sign of his villainy. The closest anyone came was when one early-modern reader—whose marginalia in a copy of the first folio have survived and been dated to around 1630—wrote the following note at the start of *Richard III*: "Richard acknowledgeing the crooked deformities of his bodie and malice of his mind resolues to Interrupt the Ioyes of the peace of his brether and by putting distrust and dissension amongs them to make each of them ouerthrow other to make him [an] vnlawfull way to the crowne."[45] Hints of a causal reading come through in this reader's emphasis on Richard "acknowledgeing" and "resolu[ing]": the reader is glossing Richard's "I am determinèd to prove a villain," as *I have resolved that I shall be villainous* rather than *God has destined me for villainy*. At the same time, this reader's parallel construction, "the crooked deformities of his bodie and malice of his mind," suggests congruence between body and mind. The reader ignores Richard's other (more explicit) causal interpretation of his deformity in his first soliloquy in *3 Henry VI*, actually suppressing Shakespeare's causal interpretation with a marginal note asserting a figural interpretation, simply writing "his monstrouous deformities" next to Richard's soliloquy (149). These figural interpretations are part of what James Siemon, who has analyzed this reader's marginalia, calls "a clear responsiveness to the Tudor political-dynastic interpretation of history."[46] The anomalous causal understanding of Richard's deformity was suppressed, in part, because it called into question the theoretical foundations of the figural paradigm, such as the Tudor myth and the spiritual model of stigma.

Unless additional evidence is discovered or presented, we can conclude that Shakespeare's causal interpretation of Richard's deformity was totally overlooked in the sixteenth, seventeenth, and early eighteenth centuries. It was not only uninfluential—it was unknown, or at least unacknowledged. Why wasn't Shakespeare's causal interpretation of Richard's deformity noticed, not even as a counterargument to refute, for more than 150 years? A Kuhnian perspective suggests that Shakespeare's anomalous causal interpretation *was not seen* because it was not needed, desired, or expected, given the situation of Shakespeare's early-modern audiences.

The figural paradigm dominated well into the eighteenth century. Richard's soliloquies received no annotations from Shakespeare's earliest eighteenth-century editors, Nicholas Rowe in 1709 and Alexander Pope in 1725. There's no need to pile up quotations, but the figural paradigm was articulated by Paul de Rapin in 1725, John Oldmixon in 1726, Edmund Curll in 1736, Guillaume Thomas Raynal in 1751, Charlotte Lennox in 1754, Ferdinando Warner in 1756, William Dodd in 1757, and Tobias Smollett in 1758.[47] The only discernible differences between the figural paradigms of the seventeenth and eighteenth centuries are (1) the paradigm's continued expansion out from imaginative literature into prose histories and (2) an increased awareness of the anomalous anti-figural readings of Buck and his ilk. Historical studies show a mounting recognition that the Tudors had blackened Richard's life and demonized his deformity—a sentiment voiced by Rapin in 1725, Thomas Carte in 1750, William Hay in 1754, and Thomas Mortimer in 1764.[48] When Horace Walpole wrote his ground-breaking *Historic Doubts on the Life and Reign of King Richard the Third* in 1768, his text inaugurated a crisis in historical studies of Richard III because it did not back down from, to quote Kuhn, "the recognition that nature has somehow violated the paradigm-induced expectations that govern normal science."[49] Walpole printed for the first time a story handed down orally: "The old countess of Desmond, who had danced with Richard, declared he was the handsomest man in the room except his brother Edward, and was very well made" (102). Carrying the anti-figural banner, Walpole asks, "Cannot a foul soul inhabit a fair body?" (103).

Literary studies show an increased awareness of the Shakespearean anomaly in the second quarter of the eighteenth century, as in Lewis Theobald's 1733 note on the moment in *3 Henry VI* when Richard stabs Henry as Henry is stigmatizing Richard's deformity, leaving an unfinished line of verse. Offended by the violation of neoclassical rules of meter, Theobald writes, "I can easily see, that this Blank was cause'd by the Nicety of the Players, to suppress an indecent idea."[50] Contra Theobald, it's fairly clear that it is Richard (the dramatic character) rather than Shakespeare's acting company (the historical people) who "suppress[ed]" Henry's figural interpretation of Richard's body. But Theobald views stigma as "an indecent idea." Contrast William Warburton's 1747 note on Margaret's claim that Richard is the "slave of nature and the son of hell. . . . Sin, death, and hell have set their marks on him" (1.3.229, 292):

> The expression is strong and noble, and alludes to the antient custom of masters' branding their profligate slaves: by which it is insinuated that his mis-shapen person was the mark that nature had set upon him to stigmatize his ill conditions. . . . But as the speaker rises in her resentment, she expresses this contemptuous thought much more openly, and condemns him to a still worse state of slavery. *Sin, Death and Hell have set their marks upon him.* Only, in the first line, her mention of his moral condition insinuates her reflections on his deformity: and, in the last, her mention of his deformity insinuates her reflections on his moral condition. And thus he has taught her to scold in all the elegance of figure.[51]

Warburton, whose language acknowledges the relationship between "stigma" and "figure" more clearly than any other writer I have seen, considers these ideas "strong and noble." Nevertheless, when he reads Richard scoffing at "dissembling nature" (1.1.19), Warburton explains that nature is "dissembling" because it joins in Richard two things that do not resemble each other, "a brave soul and a deformed body" (214n2). This incongruity between soul and body challenges the figural paradigm. Between Theobald and Warburton, the newly invented apparatus of the annotated Shakespearean text led to a deeper investigation of the object of study and an increased awareness that something in Shakespeare's representation of Richard's deformity did not quite fit with expectations drawn from the dominant figural paradigm.

Two passages from two intellectual giants of the seventeenth century illustrate the grip the figural interpretation of Richard's deformity continued to hold in the early 1760s. First, writing in 1761, Voltaire used a figural simile to say Richard had "an aspect as hideous as his soul was villainous."[52] Second, writing in 1762, David Hume concluded his chapter on Richard III in *History of England* by reviewing one of the anomalous interpretations of Richard, suppressing it, and using Richard's deformity to summarize his villainy: "This prince was of a small stature, humpbacked, and had a harsh disagreeable countenance; so that his body was in every particular no less deformed than his mind."[53]

From a Kuhnian perspective, the figural understanding of Richard's disability held sway so long into the eighteenth century because a paradigm is only declared invalid if an alternate idea is available to take its place. Until the recognition of Shakespeare's causal interpretation in the third quarter of the eighteenth century, there was no viable alternative to the figural paradigm, so it persisted despite its identified inadequacies. Acknowledging the causal interpretation of Richard's deformity in Shakespeare's text required, in Kuhn's words, "a more than additive adjustment of theory" (53). Until readers started seeing nature in a new way, the causal interpretation was not noticed. That's because the figural interpretation was not an interpretation at all. It was not the conclusion of an interpretive process. It was the basis of that process. With the rise of the causal interpretation in the middle of the eighteenth century, Richard's deformity was not reinterpreted as something else. It was seen as something else.

III. The Shakespearean Revolution

The understanding of Richard's disability underwent a Kuhnian "paradigm shift" in the years between 1765 and 1775. A change of contextual presentation more than textual interpretation, it's really a story of the transition from the frontispiece for *3 Henry VI* in Nicholas Rowe's landmark edition of *The Works of Mr. William Shakespeare* (1709; see Figure 5.1) to William Hogarth's painting of *David Garrick as Richard III* (1745; see Figure 5.3).

Rowe's frontispiece for *3 Henry VI*, an engraving of a theatrical performance, presents a world of black and white, visually and ethically. Richard's

FIGURE 5.1 Frontispiece to The Third Part of King Henry VI, in *The Works of Mr. William Shakespeare*, ed. Nicholas Rowe, vol. 4 (London: Jacob Tonson, 1709).

bubbly, cartoonish humpback, seen in profile, is made to signify the crime he is enacting, the murder of King Henry. That figural connection only makes sense, however, when the world works as it does in Rowe's frontispiece for *Richard III*, depicting the tent scene at the end of the play (see Figure 5.2). Another engraving emphasizing theatrical architecture, with curtains framing the scene, the ghosts of Richard's victims return to curse him, rising through the trapdoor of the stage. In the theater and in the frontispiece, that vertical movement suggests planes of existence above and below the material, creatural world of human experience. Only with a mythical world of spirit "up there" and "down there" can Richard's deformity at birth signify his villainy in life.

Showing seven ghosts visible on stage, Rowe's frontispiece for *Richard III* refers to Shakespeare's original text, not Colley Cibber's 1699 adaptation, which cut Richard's visitors to four.[54] Cibber also replaced Shakespeare's ambiguity with clarity. Shakespeare's tent scene can be interpreted as a ghostly visitation from supernatural forces directing the conquest of good over evil,

FIGURE 5.2 Frontispiece to *The Life and Death of Richard III*, in *The Works of Mr. William Shakespeare*, ed. Nicholas Rowe, vol. 4 (London: Jacob Tonson, 1709).

Richmond over Richard, like a medieval morality play, or as a dream vision projected from Richard's guilty conscious, like a modern psychoanalytic interpretation of nightmares. Using the imagery of both ghosts and dreams, Shakespeare asked audiences to decide what sort of world they think they live in. This ambiguity is tied to the choice Shakespeare requires audiences to make about which is a better interpretation of Richard's disability—the figural or the causal. In a supernatural world with ghosts, the figural interpretation is better. In a naturalized world with only dreams, the causal interpretation is more compelling. Cibber made his choice, clarifying—eliminating—Shakespeare's ambiguity by adding lines that limit interpretation ("'Twas but my fancy" [52], "'Twas but a dream" [53]) and eliminating Richmond's tent and the ghosts that appear to him. Whereas Shakespeare's two tents break the scene's spatial verisimilitude, suggesting a mythological world of good and evil, Cibber's scene is naturalistic, with Richmond's dream merely reported, not staged.

Where Shakespeare posed questions—about reality, about disability—Cibber answered them. Instead of starting with Richard's descant on his deformity, Cibber begins with the murder of Henry VI: instead of a pseudo-allegorical character reminiscent of the Vice announcing his significance directly to an audience, it's a naturalistic interaction among characters remaining within a dramatic illusion regulated by the modern proscenium. That change in theatrical atmosphere encourages a change in the interpretation of Richard's body. Cibber's Richard eventually speaks the soliloquy that opens Shakespeare's play, but not the climactic line, "I am determinèd to prove a villain" (1.1.30). The epitome of Shakespeare's ambiguity, this line invites and sustains two claims about Richard's villainy, forcing audiences to turn their interpretive eyes on the logic of their own moral judgments. In Cibber's text, Richard's causal understanding rules the day, largely because Cibber removed Margaret and her figural understanding from the play, an excision retained in most performances up to the twentieth century. Cibber did not explicitly endorse or even acknowledge the causal interpretation of Richard's deformity, but he changed the dramatic reality of *Richard III* by making the play as naturalistic as possible, changing how disability relates to villainy. The supernatural stage reality Shakespeare suggested allowed audiences to sustain a figural reading of Richard's disability as a God-given sign of his villainy, but Cibber's naturalized stage encouraged a naturalistic, causal interpretation.

From 1741 to 1776, David Garrick starred in Cibber's *Richard III*, acting with a naturalistic style that Cibber, by his own admission, could not achieve. Commemorated in Hogarth's painting, *David Garrick as Richard III* (1745), his most famous moment was the tent scene (see Figure 5.3). The combined vision of Cibber, Garrick, and Hogarth looks nothing like the tent scene in Rowe's frontispiece. Rowe's ghosts have vanished from Hogarth's canvas, which shows Richard awaking from a dream. There's no vertical movement—the scene remains here on Earth. The painted scenery of the theater remains, but Garrick was swept away from the stage entirely in Francis Hayman's *David Garrick as Richard III* (1760).[55] This Richard roams a fully naturalized landscape, dead horse and all, during the Battle of Bosworth. In *David Garrick as Richard III* (1771), Hayman's pupil, Nathaniel Dance-Holland, captured every wrinkle of the aging actor's face as he runs through a Bosworth Field alive with battle.[56]

With the cutting and fading of the ghosts, the supernatural dramatic reality allowing the figural interpretation of Richard's disability faded too. In its place emerged a natural dramatic reality calling for the causal interpretation of Richard's body. Cibber's edits reveal that the eighteenth-century change in

Figure 5.3 William Hogarth, *David Garrick as Richard III* (1745), oil on canvas, 75 × 98 ¾ in., at the Walker Art Gallery (Liverpool, England). Courtesy of National Museums Liverpool, Walker Art Gallery.

---

readings of Richard's body was not an *interpretive* change—it was a *perceptual* change. Eighteenth-century audiences literally saw something different than early-modern audiences—not Shakespeare's *Richard III* but Cibber's, Garrick's, and Hogarth's. Those audiences were, in Kuhn's terms, living in different worlds. The figural and causal understandings of Richard's disability were different perceptions conditioned by the different assumptions and expectations created by the different dramatic realities of these two different plays.

This naturalism inaugurated a period in which conceptual categories were adjusted until the initially anomalous causal interpretation of Richard's disability became standard. Responding to Garrick, Samuel Derrick's *A General View of the Stage* (1759) characterized Richard as "deformed, wicked, perfidious, splenetic, and ambitious."[57] It looks like a figural interpretation at first, but Derrick makes his causal thinking clear: "His drawing a parallel between himself and the rest of human kind, to all whom he finds himself unequal, determines him in villainy" (237).

But it was Samuel Johnson, Garrick's teacher, friend, and roommate from Lichfield, and two notes in Johnson's edition of Shakespeare's *Plays* (1765) that explored the anomalous interpretation of Richard's disability with enough depth and force to inaugurate a paradigm shift. This shift involved a rejection of early-modern metaphysics. Just before delivering his causal interpretation, Johnson mocked the "unlicked bear whelp," the early-modern belief that bear cubs were born as formless masses and then licked into shape by their mothers.[58] Such superstitions were out of step with Johnson's age and with the naturalism of a Shakespeare whom Johnson knew as "the poet of nature."[59] Johnson frames his first causal reading of Richard's disability, in a note on Richard's first soliloquy in *3 Henry VI*, as an example of naturalism:

> Richard speaks here the language of nature. Whoever is stigmatised with deformity has a constant source of envy in his mind, and would counterbalance by some other superiority these advantages which he feels himself to want. Bacon remarks that the deformed are commonly daring, and it is almost proverbally observed that they are ill-natured. The truth is, that the deformed, like other men, are displeased with inferiority, and endeavor to gain ground by good or bad means, as they are virtuous or corrupt. (173n4)

Citing Bacon, Johnson draws the connection between Shakespeare's example of the causal understanding of deformity in Richard III and Bacon's theory of this phenomenon. But with his language of "inferiority" and "compensation," Johnson sounds more like later twentieth-century psychoanalytic critics identifying Shakespeare's Richard as an example of an "inferiority complex." Freud popularized this reading in 1916 with his theory of "the exceptions"— whose anger over some innate disadvantage becomes the basis for immoral behavior—a theory that grew out of a reading of *Richard III*.[60] Johnson and Freud even share the suggestion that Richard's seemingly abnormal behavior is actually typical. Where Johnson wrote that "the deformed, like other men, are displeased with inferiority," Freud thought that "we all think we have reason to reproach Nature and our destiny for congenital and infantile disadvantages" (315). For Johnson and Freud, Shakespeare's play appeals to our indignation toward nature through Richard's causal interpretation of his disability. Freud, thinking and writing in a twentieth-century vocabulary, was really just practicing a paradigm discovered by Johnson in 1765. Kuhn calls it "mop-up work" (24). Johnson was a literary critic, Freud a psychologist, but they were working with the same disciplinary matrix. Just as literary criticism worked its way into Freud's psychology, psychological considerations came into Johnson's criticism.

Johnson's causal reading of Richard's disability was no accident or idiosyncrasy. It was part of a recognizable pattern in Johnson's thought, articulated again when Johnson turned to the opening soliloquy of *Richard III*: "Shakespeare very diligently inculcates, that the wickedness of Richard proceeded from his deformity, from the envy that rose at the comparison of his own person to others, and which incited him to disturb the pleasures that he could not partake."[61] *Proceeded, rose, incited*: this is the language of consequentiality, chain reactions, causes and effects rather than figures and fulfillments. The repetition of this reading in Johnson's two notes can stand for the moment in Richard's cultural history when the causal interpretation of his disability shifted from the anomalous to the expected. This paradigm extended from Johnson's notes on Richard to Falstaff, who is both a stigmatized character (Prince Hal mocks Falstaff's obesity) and a stigmatizer himself (Falstaff mocks his friend Bardolph's rosacea):

> This is a natural picture. Every man who feels in himself the pain of deformity, however, like this merry knight, he may affect to make sport with it among those whom it is his interest to please, is ready to revenge any hint of contempt upon one whom he can use with freedom.[62]

Again, Johnson describes the causal interpretation of disability as naturalism, an understanding fueled by the naturalistic acting of his friend Garrick.

Kuhn notes that paradigm shifts often occur in the hands of a small group of closely connected practitioners, and Johnson's reading of Richard emanated out through his students, not only Garrick but also Elizabeth Montagu, George Steevens, and Elizabeth Griffith. Note that, other than Lennox in 1754, Montagu and Griffith are the first female writers to appear in this cultural history: talk about a paradigm shift. Eleven years Johnson's younger, Montagu was a woman of means and the founder of the Bluestocking Society, a literary discussion group including Johnson, Garrick, Griffith, and Walpole that met at Montagu's house in London. It's not hard to imagine their discussions turning to Richard III and Garrick and Johnson presenting their causal interpretation of Richard to the group. That interpretation made its way into Montagu's *Essay on the Writings and Genius of Shakespear* (1769):

> The learned Sir Thomas More in his history of the Crook'd-Back Richard, tells, with the garrulity of an old nurse, the current stories of the king's deformity, and the monstrous appearances of his infancy, which he seems with superstitious credulity to believe to have been the omens and prognostics of his future villainy. Shakespear, with a more philosophical turn of mind, considers them not as presaging but as instigating his cruel ambition.[63]

The causal reading was "natural" to Johnson, "philosophical" to Montagu. Either way, it could explain why the old figural reading was wrong. In mocking the political mythology and "superstitious credulity" of the Tudor historians, Montagu shows how the paradigm shift was bound up with new understandings of history and reality.

Kuhn recognizes that some holdouts from a supplanted school of thought will meet a new paradigm with "lifelong resistance" (151). Writing in 1770, Francis Gentleman thought that "it was certainly well judged to make [Richard's] external appearance on the stage, emblematic of his mind," and in a text written that same year but not published until 1785, Thomas Whately said that "the deformity of his body was supposed to indicate a similar depravity of mind; and Shakespeare makes great use both of that, and of the current stories of the times concerning the circumstances of his birth, to intimate that his actions proceeded not from the occasion, but from a savageness of nature."[64] Gentleman's separation of the historical Richard III from Shakespeare's character and Whately's argument against the causal interpretation convey a deep awareness of anomaly, a feeling that these figural interpretations are now arguing uphill.

If Johnson shared the causal reading of Richard with Montagu through the Bluestocking Society, it would have come to Steevens when he and Johnson collaborated on an edition of Shakespeare's plays. Writing for the *General Evening Post* in 1772, just before their joint edition appeared, Steevens delivered a causal interpretation, though his tone was different from his mentor's:

> [Shakespeare] makes so needless a devil of the crook'd-back monster (since we must subscribe to the general opinion of Richard's deformity) that he actually raises our ridicule, where he obviously wishes to excite the abhorrence of his auditors. Who, for instance, can resist the impulses of risability when Richard, as a reason for his crimes, acquaints us that he wants to make his mind a fit companion for his body?[65]

Johnson may have sympathized with Richard's causal reading of his own body, and Steevens may have found it repulsive, but both recognized its presence in Shakespeare's text, which didn't happen before the third quarter of the eighteenth century. In his editorial notes, Steevens continued to distinguish between *us* and *them*. Of Margaret's suggestion that Richard is an "Elvish-marked, abortive, rooting hog" (1.3.227), Stevens notes condescendingly, "The common people in Scotland (as I learn from Kelly's *Proverbs*) have still an aversion to those who have any natural defect or redundancy, as thinking them *mark'd* out for mischief."[66] Of Hastings's stumbling horse (3.4.84), Steevens informs his modern readers that "to stumble was anciently esteem'd a bad omen" (88n2). For the burning blue light in Richard's "I am I" soliloquy (5.3.180), Steevens notes that "it was anciently supposed that fire was a preservative against evil spirits" (155n9). "Anciently" in these notes means *in Shakespeare's time*, with Steevens quoting John Lyly (1553–1606) and Thomas Nashe (1567–1601) to illustrate his comments. They were living in different worlds.

Griffith's *The Morality of Shakespeare's Drama Illustrated* (1775) clinches the paradigm shift, saying things about Richard's disability not said only a decade earlier as if they could never have been otherwise. Griffith's book was inspired by Montagu's *Essay on the Writings and Genius of Shakespear* and alludes to Walpole's *Historic Doubts* when noting that "the deformity of Richard . . . has lately, from a concurrence of contemporary testimonies, been rendered problematical at least, by a learned and ingenious author."[67] Turning from the historical Richard III to Shakespeare's character, Griffith repeats and refines the Johnson circle's causal interpretation:

> Our poet, zealous for the honour of the human character, most artfully contrives to make Richard's weakness appear to arise from a resentment against the partiality of Nature, in having stigmatized him with so deformed a person, joined to an envious jealousy towards the rest of mankind, for being endowed with fairer forms, and more attractive graces. (311)

The grammatical structure of Griffith's sentence, with its relative clauses, captures how late-eighteenth-century critics started viewing Richard's body as the start of a chain reaction. Because of his congenital malformations, Richard is ostracized from society, which brings about issues of inferiority, which leads him to react hostilely to a world that will not accept him.

With their discovery and articulation of the causal reading, Johnson and his circle produced an interpretation of Richard's disability able to attract the next generation of readers, and the figural understanding was promptly relegated to the status of historical curiosity. William Richardson in 1785, August Wilhelm von Schlegel in 1808, Samuel Taylor Coleridge in 1810, and Søren Kierkegaard in 1843 are only the most famous of the writers who elaborated upon the causal interpretation of Richard III in the years after Johnson.[68] The figural interpretation did not disappear completely—voiced, for example, by William Hazlitt in 1817[69]—but it shifted from paradigmatic to anomalous and was suppressed by the dominant causal paradigm.

Some charts can show the dominance of the figural paradigm in the early-modern age and the sharp break that occurred in the third quarter of the eighteenth century. In Figure 5.4, during the early-modern era—defined as the time between Rous and Hume (1484–1764)—more than two-thirds of all discussions of Richard III that I've seen advance a figural interpretation of his disability: fifty-three figural interpretations compared to eleven sources that do not mention any deformity, eight explicitly anti-figural interpretations, and only two causal interpretations (Shakespeare's *3 Henry VI* and *Richard III*). The dominance of the figural paradigm is even more pronounced if we cut out the pre-paradigm period (which includes most of the sources that don't mention deformity) and the second quarter of the seventeenth century (when the anti-figural argument starts picking up steam). In the years between 1510 and 1725, figural interpretations compose more than 80 percent of statements about Richard III (forty out of forty-eight).

On the righthand side of Figure 5.4, the chart for the modern era shows how swiftly and decisively the figural paradigm fell from favor in the third quarter of the eighteenth century. Figure 5.5 further shows that, in modern literary criticism, the causal interpretation of Richard's deformity replaced the figural interpretation as the dominant paradigm. In the nineteenth and twentieth centuries, a long list of historians writing in the wake of Buck and Walpole—William Hutton, Sharon Turner, Caroline Halstead, John Heneage Jesse, James Gairdner, Thomas Legge, Clements Markham, Paul Murray Kendall, and Charles Ross—articulate an anti-figural paradigm arguing that Richard wasn't deformed, wasn't evil, or wasn't either.[70] Pseudo-legal texts, such as Josephine Tey's popular mystery novel *The Daughter of Time* (1951), in which an English detective goes into his nation's history to investigate the charges against Richard, and a mock trial presided over by U.S. Supreme Court Chief Justice William H. Rehnquist in 1997 find Richard *not guilty* of murdering the princes in the Tower and often not physically impaired, citing the legal maxim *falsus in unus, falsus in omnibus*: "If a witness is found to have testified falsely about one matter, it may be inferred that his testimony

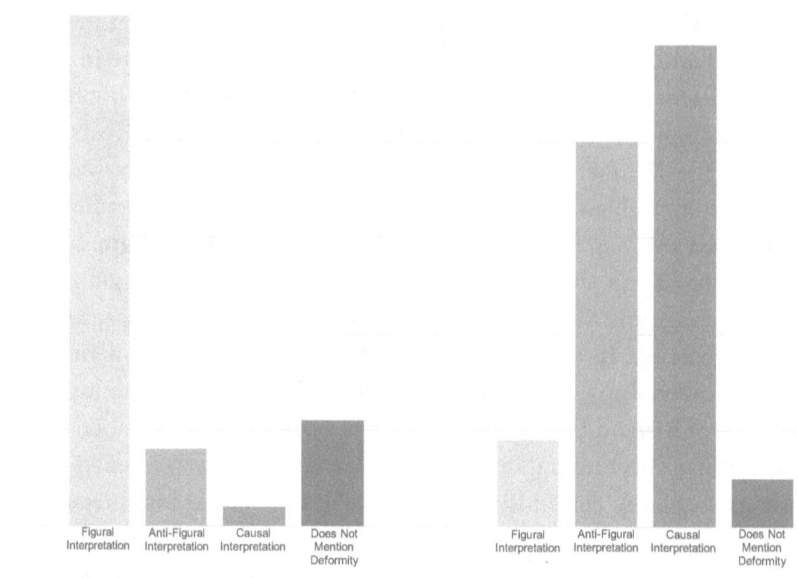

FIGURE 5.4 Representations of Richard III's Deformity, 1484–2011.

as to other matters is false as well."[71] Taken together, anti-figural and causal statements in the modern age (1765–2011) outnumber figural interpretations of Richard's deformity by a margin of ninety to nine in the materials I have looked at.

Figure 5.5 presents the modern period in two charts to emphasize that, after the third quarter of the eighteenth century, what was a singular discourse split in two—study of the historical person and study of Shakespeare's character. Seventeenth-century historians saw Shakespeare as a fellow historian telling the story of Richard III (and succeeding or failing, based on the later historian's attitude toward the figural interpretation of Richard's disability). In the eighteenth century, historians started seeing Shakespeare as an artist who had embellished history for political purposes. These modern historians pursued and refined the anti-figural argument without getting into the causal argument that presupposes a deformity in Richard III that many of them denied. Literary critics involved in the nascent Shakespeare industry started seeing his history plays as objects worthy of study as literature, not as history. Shakespeare shifted from an interpreter of history to something historical that needed interpretation. The feeling from historians that something in the figural paradigm had gone seriously wrong came to a head at precisely

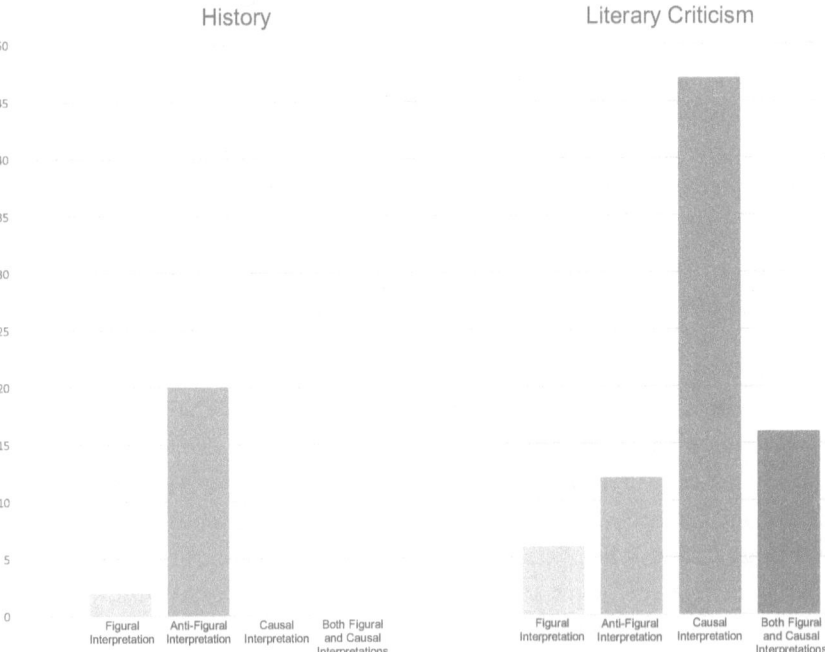

FIGURE 5.5 Representations of Richard III's Deformity, 1765–2011.

the moment when literary critics first started noticing Shakespeare's causal interpretation of Richard's deformity.

In sum, the third quarter of the eighteenth century was a time when conceptual categories were adjusted until the initially anomalous causal interpretation of Richard's disability became the anticipated interpretation. The embrace of this causal interpretation in the mid-eighteenth century can be described as a "paradigm shift," not only because it was rapid rather than cumulative, occurring in the span of about ten years, but also because it was administered by a small, young, and closely connected community of researchers (including several women, a novel development) whose apparatuses of interpretation brought them to see Richard's body in a whole new way. It was not a paradigm shift in the sense that there was a change in interpretation. Instead, there emerged new objects of interpretation: the *Richard III* of Cibber's adaptation and Johnson's edition. In both cases, Shakespeare's text came packaged in a new frame—Cibber's naturalistic theater or Johnson's editorial commentary—that encouraged the causal interpretation of Richard's disability. It was a change in perception. An Elizabethan audience seeing or reading *Richard III* saw something different than the eighteenth-century person seeing Cibber's adaptation or reading Johnson's edition. These were not two different interpretations of the same text. They were two different reactions to two different perceptions of Richard's disability that were different because the circumstances of reading and seeing created different texts to be interpreted. It was not the interpretation that changed but the object of interpretation itself.

IV. Different Worlds: Dramatic Reality in Modernity's *Richard III*

The late-eighteenth-century paradigm shift in readings of Richard's disability occurred alongside a change in how the tent scene was understood, drawn, and staged. While Shakespeare allowed the visitation to be either ghosts or a dream, and Cibber encouraged the dream reading, the Johnson circle explicitly argued that it is a dream. Johnson reprinted Warburton's note that Richard's conscience "takes advantage of his sleep, and frights him in his dreams."[72] Montagu wrote a long chapter "On the Praeternatural Beings," looking especially at the Ghost in *Hamlet*, apologizing for Shakespeare's superstitions by arguing that they are "allegorical beings" suited to "an age that affected abstruse learning."[73] Steevens gave a literary history of the Tudor chronicles that relates Richard's disturbed dreams developing into Shakespeare's "phantoms, speaking in their particular characters, on the stage."[74] And Griffith frankly stated that "the Ghosts here are not to be taken literally; they are to be understood only as an allegorical representation of those images or ideas which naturally occur to the minds of men during their sleep."[75] Shakespeare set the scene at night, when Richard and Richmond are dreaming, she noted, "which intirely removes the seeming absurdity of such an exhibition" (320–321). Griffith elsewhere declared that Elizabethans misunderstood the mind: "admonitions of conscience [were] taken for supernatural emotions" (77). Johnson's circle really was living in a different world than Shakespeare's early-modern audiences.

Shakespeare's audiences lived in the world depicted by Henry Fuseli, whose work always demonstrates a flair for the supernatural and, around 1769, shows the ghosts rising vertically through the trapdoor of the stage to haunt a sleeping Richard, candle burning in the center of the image to indicate the supernatural.[76] This paradigm representing the tent scene as the "ghost scene" includes another Fuseli drawing, lost to history, but preserved in James Neagle's engraving, which shows some almost comically bedsheeted ghosts stacked vertically, one on top of the other, a candle burning on the left of the image.[77] There is also a late-eighteenth-century sketch by a little-known artist known as the Master of the Mallet that shows an alert Richard visited by a King Henry VI who seems to be stepping down from heaven on stairs of clouds, past a burning candle.[78] And there is William Blake's early-nineteenth-century watercolor painting of the translucent ghosts stretched out vertically around a fully awake Richard swinging his sword through their immaterial presence, a candle burning off to the left.[79]

But the paradigm soon shifted, perhaps symbolized by Fuseli's 1777 sketch of *Richard III Visited by Ghosts*. The starkly black-and-white right side of the image shows a swirl of vertical movement, indicating the presence of the supernatural, while the lightly sketched left side shows Richard's visitors in a horizontal train, one holding a mirror with lines drawn to Richard's head, suggesting projections of his guilty conscience.[80]

By the late eighteenth century, Shakespeareans were altogether embarrassed by what Edward Capell called in 1779 "that awful scene of the '*Ghosts*' rising."[81] Like Hogarth, the Danish Nicolai Abildgaard's 1787 painting shows Richard waking from a nightmare, visitors nowhere in sight because they were only in his dreams.[82] Abildgaard returned to the scene in the 1780s, now depicting the ghosts, but only because Richard is sleeping, and they are an image in his mind, indicated by the horizontal patterning of the visitors; there are no burning candles.[83] Nor are there candles or ghosts in William Hamilton's homage to Hogarth in *John Phillip Kemble as Richard III* (ca. 1787).[84] The visitors in Thomas Stothard's late-eighteenth-century drawing of the tent scene are placed around the head of a sleeping Richard's bed to indicate a dream.[85] Similarly, William Sharp's 1794 engraving shows ephemeral visitors coming into focus, peeking into Richard's tent from outside, moving toward the viewer on a horizontal plain rather than up from below on a vertical plain.[86] As a 1798 article in the *Monthly Mirror* insisted, "It should be remembered that we have here only *the representation of a vision*; it is not intended that we should consider these objects as spirits which *actually* appeared to the naked and material eye of *Richard*, but as the terrific formations of sleep acting upon his imagination."[87] This article notes that the 1794 *Macbeth* at Drury Lane featuring John Philip Kemble totally eliminated, for the first time ever, the ghost of Banquo, making Macbeth look upon vacant air.[88] The ghosts of Richard III's victims were also vanishing from the stage. Audiences even saw them disappear before their eyes in Edmund Kean's 1814 production of *Richard III*.

Initially, Kean's tent scene presented ghosts rising through the trapdoor in the stage, as in Rowe's frontispiece, but William Hazlett's review complained that this supernatural gesture was ludicrous in the modern age: "We wish the introduction of the ghosts through the trap-doors of the stage were altogether omitted. The speeches, which they address to Richard, might be delivered just as well from behind the scenes. These sorts of exhibitions are only proper for a superstitious age; and in an age not superstitious, excite ridicule instead of terror."[89] Hazlitt sought to disembody the visitors completely, but Kean settled for bringing them in from the sides of the stage, "behind a gauze or tissue, at the back of the tyrant's couch."[90] A similar performance was engineered at Covent Garden: "The young princes appear at the back, but the shades of *King Henry* and *Lady Anne* come in at the sides, with a sort of serial mist." Visually blurring the visitors with gauze made them the fuzzy images of a dream. Bringing them in behind the sleeping Richard, framed by his bedposts, made them projections of his troubled mind. Similarly, Charles Heath's 1816 engraving of Henry Howard's drawing frames the visitors in Richard's canopy behind him; we only see them because we are seeing into Richard's dreams.[91] Later in the nineteenth century, Alexandre Bida's painting also positions the visitors behind Richard, here fully awake, making them hallucinations rather than dreams, a mentally distraught Richard clutching his head, trying to get the voices out.[92] If Kean's initial tent scene with the ghosts evoked the vertical movement of supernatural drama in the premodern ages, as represented by Rowe's 1709 frontispiece, the revised staging of a dream or hallucination indicated the purely horizontal world of naturalized modern drama depicted in Hogarth's 1745 painting of Garrick. Thus, Kean's biographer remembered his tent scene as "filled with a radiance altogether new to the stage"—a dream, not a ghostly visitation: "As he recovered from the dream he burst forth upon the audience with a meridian splendour which would have shed additional glory on Garrick's representation even as handed down to posterity by Hogarth."[93]

V. The Disciplinary Matrix of Early Disability Studies

The shift in performances and illustrations of the tent scene in *Richard III* was, like the discovery of the causal interpretation of Richard's disability, fallout from the eighteenth-century transition from the declamatory acting style of Thomas Betterton and James Quin to the naturalism of David Garrick and Charles Macklin. As theater historians such as Jean Benedetti note, Garrick's career marks "the birth of modern theatre," which might be dated to 1741, the year Garrick and Macklin debuted in London.[94] While disciplinary histories are always complex, sometimes idiosyncratic, experts in several disciplines relevant to the interpretation of Richard's disability have identified their moments of modernization in the mid-eighteenth century.[95]

Broadly speaking, in European thought, there was a shift from the metaphysics of the scholastics and rationalists to the empiricism of David Hume and the idealism of Immanuel Kant. Replacing speculation on the beyond with theories of truth and virtue based on observable phenomena, these thinkers called spirituality into question, disrupting the theological basis of figural interpretation. Erich Auerbach, the literary historian whose account of figural interpretation I have relied upon, sees Kant as the birth of the modern representation of reality in Western literature: "It was precisely the German intellectual development during the second half of the eighteenth century which laid the aesthetic foundation of modern realism."[96] Auerbach contrasts the horizontality of modern realism with the verticality of premodern figural interpretation: "In the modern view, the provisional event is treated as a step in an unbroken horizontal process; in the figural system the interpretation is always sought from above; events are considered not in their unbroken relation to one another, but torn apart, individually, each in relation to something other that is promised and not yet present."[97] Like Richard's visitors in modern takes on the tent scene, modern literature remains on a horizontal plane. And modern audiences thinking about Richard's disability are, to quote Auerbach, "able to explain to a certain extent every single historical fact by its immediate causes and to foresee to a certain extent its immediate consequences, moving so to speak on a horizontal plane."[98]

Consequently, figural interpretation lost its purchase on disability in the modern age. Earlier theories of physiognomy and monstrosity gave way to teratology (the scientific study of birth defects), orthopedics (the branch of medicine dealing with the treatment and prevention of skeletal and muscular abnormalities), and disability studies (a field in the humanities addressing the social aspects of impairment). Each discipline had a watershed moment in the middle of the eighteenth century—in keeping with disability historians such as Michel Foucault, Henri-Jacques Stiker, Lennard J. Davis, Rosemarie Garland-Thomson, David M. Turner, and Essaka Joshua, who identify the late eighteenth century as an intellectual turning point and the early nineteenth century as a social turning point in England.[99]

In physiognomy, skeptical and satirical essays had been written by the likes of Michel de Montaigne and Joseph Addison.[100] But they did not curb the massive popularity of texts such as Giambattista della Porta's *On Human Physiognomy* (1586), which was published in more than twenty editions in several languages across Europe by 1655, and Johann Kaspar Lavater's four-volume *Essays on Physiognomy* (1775–1778), with sixteen German, fifteen French, and twenty English editions appearing within forty years of its original publication.¹⁰¹ The most prominent dissenting voices had ties to the English critics responsible for the paradigm shift in the treatment of Richard III's disability. In 1746, Hogarth's friend James Parsons published *Human Physiognomy Explained*, a lecture series delivered to the Royal Society that sought to flip physiognomy on its head, arguing that the only thing available for interpretation is facial expressions (as recorded in muscle memory) and not innate bodily features.¹⁰² Written in 1763, John Clubbe's *Physiognomy*—dedicated to Hogarth, who provides the frontispiece—spoofs the field by suggesting that moral character could be weighed by placing heads on a scale.¹⁰³ But it was Johnson and Garrick's friend Georg Christoph Lichtenberg whose critique of Lavater in *On Physiognomy, Against the Physiognomist* (1778) marked a turning point to the decisive philosophical refutations of physiognomy by Kant in 1798 and Hegel in 1807.¹⁰⁴ Lichtenberg argued against the coordination of physical and moral attributes by presenting Lavater with an image of the homely Samuel Johnson.¹⁰⁵

As physiognomy lost philosophical credibility, two medical fields—teratology and orthopedics—gained scientific support. Teratology grew from advances in embryology. In 1651, the English scientist William Harvey proposed the theory of epigenesis to counter the prevailing theory of preformation. Where preformation held that male sperm contained a tiny homunculus such that the human body possessed its shape, fully formed but in miniature, from the moment of conception, Harvey's epigenesis argued that parts of the body develop and augment successively. Thus, congenital malformations are caused by arrested development during a fetus's embryonic stage. According to historian of teratology Josef Warkany, "Although the principle of embryologic arrest was expressed by Harvey, it was not applied by many during the next 150 years, after which this explanation for congenital malformations became most popular."¹⁰⁶ The most notable embryological debate about congenital impairment occurred in the third quarter of the eighteenth century, when the German physiologist Caspar Friedrich Wolff, arguing that "monsters are not the immediate work of God, but of nature," dealt a death blow to the theory of preformation presented by the Swiss anatomist Albrecht von Haller.¹⁰⁷ It was only a matter of time until the French father-and-son team of Étienne and Isidore Geoffroy Saint-Hilaire founded the discipline of teratology (Isidore coining this term in 1832 to avoid the baggage of the discredited discourse of "monstrosity").¹⁰⁸

Orthopedics was founded in 1741 by the French physician Nicolas Andry and then systematized in William John Little's landmark lectures *On the Deformities of the Human Frame* (1843–1844).¹⁰⁹ Little, himself physically disabled, was the first physician to hazard a medical diagnosis of Shakespeare's Richard III, a parlor game that became popular in the second half of the twentieth century.[110] In this line of thought, the consensus is, as Donald Miller and Ethel Davis write in a 1969 essay titled "Shakespeare and Orthopedics," that "if modern corrective measures had then been available to the infant who was to become Richard III, history might have told another story in England."[111]

As this statement indicates, orthopedics contributed to the medical model of disability, which views all manner of bodily impairment as a medical problem to be fixed or cured, an attitude roundly rejected by the modern disability studies that became popular in the 1990s. Arguably, disability studies was founded in the third quarter of the eighteenth century by Hay, an English member of Parliament and author of *Deformity: An Essay* (1754), a response to Bacon's "Of Deformity" (1613), which generalizes the causal interpretation of disability Shakespeare suggests in Richard. Even after Shakespeare and Bacon, however, the figural understanding of disability dominated discourse through the early eighteenth century, as I have documented in the reception of Richard III and as also evident in the treatment of Alexander Pope.

Pott's disease, a form of tuberculosis affecting the spine, stunted Pope's growth, a physical characteristic detractors metaphorized in their assessment of his mind and manners. In one figural interpretation from Mary Wortley Montagu, Pope had "the Emblem of [his] crooked Mind, / Mark'd on [his] Back, like *Cain*, by God's own Hand."[112] John Dennis, another critic, said that "his Form is the best Index of his Mind," elaborating elsewhere that Pope's body "'tis the mark of God and Nature upon him, to give us warning that we should hold no Society with him, as a Creature not of our Original, nor of our Species."[113] To one final detractor, Pope had a "Mind so suited to its vile Abode":

> It seems the Counterpart by Heav'n design'd
> A Symbol and a Warning to Mankind:
> As at some Door we find hung out a Sign,
> Type of the Monster to be found within.[114]

These accounts of Pope's body are not simply metaphors claiming correspondence between physical and mental attributes. Each statement enchants this metaphor by ascribing it to divinity ("God" or "Heav'n"), illustrating Auerbach's "vertical" component of figural interpretation. Perhaps Pope had these figural interpretations in mind when writing his most famous lines:

"Know then thyself, presume not God to scan, / The Proper study of mankind is Man."[115]

As metaphysics flattened in the eighteenth century, the figural interpretation of disability lost its grip. One essay titled "Deformity Not Always a Sign of an Ill Man" (1746) argues that, while the example of Richard III *does* exhibit a figural dynamic, that dynamic does *not* extend to all people with physical disabilities:

> The common received axiom, that obliges men to mark, or beware of those that God hath marked with any signal deformity, does not constantly hold true with respect to all men; for tho' some of them are perverse and wicked in their inclinations; yet we find others so affable, courteous and honest, that nature seems to make amends for the disadvantageous figure of their outsides, by endowing them with excellent qualifications within.[116]

William Hay saw himself as such an exception. His *Deformity: An Essay* argues against both the verticality of the figural interpretation and the horizontality of the causal interpretation. For Hay, both views are symbolic understandings of deformity that need to be trashed, or strongly qualified. The difficulties a physically disabled person encounters in their social interaction often foster emotions of resentment and hostility, Hay argues, but they can also fashion perseverance, independence, and humility. Thus, he entertains an inversion of Juvenal's maxim *mens sana in corpore sano*, "a good mind in a good body," to suggest "*ut fit mens recta in corpore curvo*, for an upright mind in a crooked body."[117]

As an early example of disability studies—coming from "arguably the first writer in the history of English literature to conceptualize and articulate physical disability as a personal identity," Helen Deutsch says[118]—Hay's 1754 essay is remarkable for two reasons. First, it was written by a disabled person, anticipating the emphasis on personal experience in later disability studies, such as Randolph Bourne's "The Handicapped—By One of Them" (1911) and James Charlton's *Nothing about Us without Us* (1998).[119] Second, Hay directed readers from deformity to disability—"Bodily Deformity is visible to every Eye; but the Effects of it are known to very few"—anticipating the distinction between *impairment* and *disability* in later disability studies. Hay argues against Bacon's thesis that deformity is "a cause which seldom faileth of the effect," but they both look at the "effects" of deformity. While Bacon sees villainy as the probable effect, Hay as one possible effect, both are dealing with the logic of cause and effect.

The third quarter of the eighteenth century was *the* moment for disability in the English-speaking world. One index to the influence of Hay's thought is Johnson's comments on Pope's disability in 1779, shortly after the paradigm shift in understandings of Richard III. Johnson begins with an amateur orthopedic diagnosis presenting Pope's disability as not the cause but the effect of disease: "He was of a constitution originally feeble and weak, and as bodies of a tender frame are easily distorted his deformity was probably in part the effect of his application."[120] Johnson then narrates how deformity became a cause: "By natural deformity or accidental distortion his vital functions were so much disordered that his life was a 'long disease'" (382). Pope had headaches, was sensitive to cold, wore a brace in his bodice, and required an attendant to dress. These effects of impairment caused certain personality flaws, Johnson claims: "The indulgence and accommodation which his sickness required had taught him all the unpleasing and unsocial qualities of a valetudinary man. He expected that every thing should give way to his ease or humour, as a child whose parents will not hear her cry has an unresisted dominion in the nursery" (383). In contrast to early-eighteenth-century statements about Pope's body, Johnson never intimates that it is anything other than a creatural issue remaining here on the horizontal plane of material cause and effect.

Another index to the rise of disability studies in the modern age is the treatment of deformity and disability in the works of Lord Byron, informed—like Hay—by his own perspective as a disabled writer. "The Morning Post, in particular, has found out that I am a sort of Richard III," he wrote, "Deformed in mind and body."[121] Byron's unfinished play, *The Deformed Transformed* (1824), alludes to Shakespeare's *Richard III* several times—opening with the protagonist's mother cursing him as a "hunchback," "incubus," "nightmare," "abortion," "monstrous sport of nature," "hedgehog"—only to pivot to a causal interpretation of deformity tinged with Romantic heroism:

> Deformity is daring.
> It is its essence to o'ertake mankind
> By heart and soul, and make itself the equal—
> Aye, the superior of the rest. There is
> A spur in its halt movements, to become
> All that the others cannot, in such things
> As still are free to both, to compensate
> For stepdame Nature's avarice at first.[122]

A third index is the disgust, fascination, and respect variously shown for Joseph Merrick, the Elephant Man.[123] A fourth is the new literary characters whose disfigurements brought about various virtues and vices—Victor Hugo's Quasimodo, his Gwynplaine, and Gaston Leroux's Phantom of the Opera, for instance.[124] These examples suggest that, during this time, serious cultural reflection on disability lived largely in literature until twentieth-century academics, such as Alfred Adler, Beatrice Wright, Erving Goffman, and Leslie Fiedler, took up disability as a psychosocial concern.[125] Then, disability studies became a field in its own right toward the end of the twentieth century, led by scholars such as Henri-Jacques Stiker, Lennard Davis, Rosemarie Garland-Thomson, Simi Linton, David Mitchell, Sharon Snyder, Ato Quayson, and Tobin Siebers.[126] From Hay and Johnson to Byron and Merrick to Hugo and Leroux to the social psychologists and disability scholars, these thinkers have many disagreements about the nature and implications of physical disability, but all work with the logic of cause and effect traceable back through Hay to Bacon and, ultimately, Shakespeare's Richard III.

As such, twentieth- and twenty-first-century readings of Richard's body have done what Kuhn calls "mop-up work" on the causal paradigm. These readings—the psychoanalytic reading popular in the twentieth century, the disability studies reading popular in the twenty-first century, and the medical reading culminating in the 2012 discovery and diagnosis of Richard's scoliosis—extend our understanding of Richard's body while still operating within the causal paradigm established in the third quarter of the eighteenth century. The language of cause and effect is now the only game in town, and it allows us to tell the totality of the story of Richard's body, reaching as far back as the historical Richard's birth.

According to the osteologists who analyzed Richard's recovered skeleton, he was born healthy but developed an idiopathic adolescent-onset scoliosis in his teenage years. He was not hunchbacked but was physically impaired, probably noticeably. His right shoulder was higher than his left, though it could have been hidden by a skilled tailor. His scoliosis probably caused Richard chronic pain, and perhaps disability. But stigma was certainly present, if not during Richard's life, then soon after his death. His Tudor enemies and their descendants demonized him, treating his impairment as a congenital abnormality rather than one developed later in life. This backdating of deformity to Richard's birth allowed the Tudors to rope the discourses of monstrosity and physiognomy into their representations, with the mythologized figural interpretation of Richard III emerging as a standard paradigm in sixteenth-century literature and culture. As disability scholars have pointed out, however, the sixteenth century also included advances in the scientific treatment of birth defects, leading to an instability in the discourses of deformity and disability. This instability contributed to a density, a complexity, and a certain rehumanization of Richard in Shakespeare's plays, as epitomized by the suggestion of a causal interpretation of his disability.

Here, the logic and language of cause and effect can shift from explaining the history resulting in Shakespeare's creation of a literary text to explaining the events in that text. From a modern scientific perspective, the character created by Shakespeare (one deformed at birth, never mind the historical Richard III), during gestation in his mother's womb, underwent an abnormal cellular epigenesis—either (using the technical terms of teratology) a *malformation* (caused by a disorder of tissue development) or a *deformation* (caused by mechanical stress to normal tissue), thus with an etiology either genetic or environmental—resulting in a severe congenital abnormality. From a psychoanalytic perspective, the child's physical impairment was met with disappointment and rejection from his mother, which fostered feelings of shame and inferiority in the child. If in childhood Richard was denied familial love, in adulthood he was denied sexual love, due either to a physical disability related to his congenital condition (e.g., impotency) or to the laws of attraction. Envious of others valued for their fair features, Richard compensated for his perceived organic inferiority by sublimating the pursuit of sexual gratification to the pursuit of pleasure from other sources. He established his worth as a warrior and politician, which might have been successful were it not for his arrested, childlike moral development, manifesting in antisocial behavior. He became sensitive, obstinate, narcissistic, resentful, contemptuous, bitter, angry, and vindictive, a pathological state leading to frustration, immorality, and crime. He stifled his guilt by justifying or rationalizing his wrongdoing as his right, given the wrong done to him by nature, this repression facilitating his descent from wickedness into psychopathy. He became a paranoid, perverse, misogynistic, incestuous child murderer who, upon the return of his repressed conscience, experienced a full-scale schizophrenic breakdown shortly before his death in battle.

In telling that story in that way—as a series of causes and effects—I am simply the latest practitioner of the causal paradigm discovered in the third quarter of the eighteenth century. In addition to the development of theatrical naturalism in English theater, the rise of realism in European literature, the death of physiognomy and monstrosity, the birth of teratology and orthopedics, and the first suggestions of disability studies, the paradigm shift in the understanding of Richard III referred to other previously discussed developments that occurred in the third quarter of the eighteenth century. In history, there was the shift from accepting to rejecting the Tudor myth that occurred with Walpole's *Historic Doubts* (1768). In ethics, there was the separation of natural and moral evil that solidified after the Lisbon earthquake of 1755. The paradigm shift in the understanding of Richard's deformity occurred in conjunction with—and because of—a change in the "disciplinary matrix" in play. There was, to quote Kuhn, "a displacement of the conceptual network" (102) through which Shakespeare's readers viewed the world and his text.

As argued at the start of this book, due to Shakespeare's irony, his plays do not provide any stable grounds of interpretation, so early-modern audiences turned to the most readily available grounds—their own beliefs about disability, villainy, reality, and history. Between the early-modern and the modern ages, those beliefs changed. At the start of the eighteenth century, it was artistically, historically, ethically, philosophically, and theologically conventional to interpret Richard's disability as a sign of his moral, mental, or spiritual deformity. Anomalous anti-figural interpretations of Richard's deformity were suppressed by the figural paradigm because they threatened the foundations of the disciplinary matrix in play. The causal interpretation of Richard's deformity was not noticed because it was not needed, desired, or expected, given the situation of Shakespeare's early-modern audiences. During the age of "normal science," readers neither tested nor sought to confirm the guiding lights of their disciplinary matrix. They believed what Shakespeare's Queen Margaret believes about disability, villainy, history, and reality, so they embraced her figural interpretation of Richard's body. Those beliefs all changed, however, midway through the eighteenth century, when it became artistically, historically, ethically, philosophically, and theologically *un*conventional to see Richard's body as a sign of his soul, mind, or manners. The causal interpretation not only was recognized for the first time in print but quickly became the dominant way to read Richard's body. Trying to determine whether one of these paradigm shifts happened first and thus held priority over the others is a fool's errand. Each recursively involved—influencing and being influenced by—the others, each referenced during the discovery of the causal interpretation of Richard's deformity. So, why did the cultural assumptions and beliefs about a number of issues related to the interpretation of Richard III's disability all change in the eighteenth century? In a word, *modernization*.

VI. Modernization as Gestalt Switch

This conclusion may sound obvious or innocuous, but it allows us to theorize what modernization was by taking the cultural history of Richard's disability as a representative example. Modernization is often described as the rise of the age of reason and science (to replace religion), democracy (to replace monarchy), capitalism (to replace feudalism), and urbanization (to replace country living).[127] Each of those phenomena, however, was a function of the rise of a new mode of understanding why things happen. If we were to extrapolate outward from the example of Richard's disability, we would say that modernization was not a gradual, incremental change but a moment in the third quarter of the eighteenth century when the dominant habits and beliefs related to etiology and hermeneutics—the study of causes and the theory of interpretation—shifted from figural to causal ways of thinking. Anomalies always exist, but before the modern age, things were commonly understood to be determined according to their relationship to an immaterial world thought to be imperceptible but figured—pointed to—by the things seen before our eyes. In the modern age, material things are usually understood to be determined according to their relationship to other material things in a huge, interconnected chain of causes and effects. Things previously understood to be signs that figured became, in modernity, things caused and effected. It was what Kuhn calls a "paradigm-induced gestalt switch" (120), the *figural gestalt* of thought in the premodern age replaced by the *causal gestalt* of thought in the modern age.

This moment in the cultural history of Richard III was destructive as well as constructive. Kuhn could be describing the reception history of Shakespeare's *Richard III* in the third quarter of the eighteenth century when he writes that a new paradigm is "seldom or never just an increment to what is already known," for "its assimilation requires the reconstruction of prior theory and the re-evaluation of prior fact" (7). The paradigm shift in interpretations of Richard's disability that occurred in the mid-eighteenth century was more than just a paradigm shift. It occurred in concert with several other shifts in historical, philosophical, ethical, and artistic contexts; it was a massive cultural realignment suggesting that Shakespeare was right when he indicated that one's interpretation of disability is closely bound up with one's understanding of reality.

If so, then the causal paradigm and its disciplinary matrix were not just incompatible but, in fact, incommensurable with the figural paradigm and its assumptions, values, beliefs, instruments, and techniques. The paradigms exhibited completely different orders of interpretation. The fundamental truths grounding the interpretive process were different. How an idea was deemed compelling was different. Both paradigms had built-in defense mechanisms always able to explain why the other interpretation was wrong, and wrong in a way that confirmed the dominant paradigm. The figural paradigm rejected Richard's causal interpretation of his disability as one of the lies and villainies that the figural paradigm predicted. The causal paradigm explained the figural interpretation of Richard's deformity as the social injustice that brought about the villainy it purported to describe. Each interpretation could refute the other because they did not share a common reality that might be invoked to adjudicate the truth of a position. The two paradigms were not competing interpretations of the same thing; they were different images of reality produced through different disciplinary matrices representing different worldviews.

The *both/and* argument, recognizing both the figural and causal understandings of deformity simultaneously at play in Shakespeare's first tetralogy, may appear at times anomalously in the modern age—August Wilhelm von Schlegel in 1808 or E.M.W. Tillyard in 1944—but it caught on noticeably in the 1990s and, in the twenty-first century, with the rise of disability studies, has become the dominant paradigm.[128] Committed to recognizing different interpretations coming from different perspectives rather than advancing its own, that argument displays a *historical gestalt* of etiology and hermeneutics. To be sure, these are paradigms, not absolutes. After the discovery of Richard's skeleton, observing the "gleeful voyeuristic reconsideration of whether Shakespeare was 'right' in his assessment of Richard as a villain," Marcela Kostihova noted how often—to this day—"our culture insists on coherence between personal appearance and moral interiority."[129] If we allow for anomalies but recognize dominant paradigms, the figural, the causal, and the historical gestalts are the shapes of thought, respectively, in the premodern, modern, and postmodern eras.

6

Richard III's Disability in Modern Performance

The Changing Bodies of Character and Actor

The last chapter moved from analyzing an eighteenth-century paradigm shift in understandings of Richard III's disability to theorizing what modernization was. The guiding principle is that Shakespeare is so prominent in modern culture that examining receptions of his works over time can launch cultural studies of modernity. Looking at some subcultures, this chapter illustrates the viability of this method, theorized in the conclusion as the "anthropology of audience," by telling the story of Richard III's disability on stage in the modern English-speaking world and beyond.

Performance histories of *Richard III* often do one of two things: (1) summarize various aspects of stage productions over time[1] or (2) focus on film in the twentieth century.[2] Concentrating specifically on Richard's disability guides analysis in two ways. First, it narrows scope, comparing many texts and identifying patterns over long periods of time. Second, it directs attention away from film, where little new happens with Richard's disability, to theater, first in the nineteenth century, and then in recent productions from the twenty-first.

These two eras have obvious differences but one thing in common: both involve modern theater practitioners trying to make sense of Shakespeare trying to make sense of Richard trying to make sense of his body. The refraction of interpretation in these efforts results in big-picture questions about whose frame of reference should govern the character: the modern audience's, Shakespeare's, Plantagenet England's? Analysis reveals not simply what different theater practitioners did with Richard's disability in different places at different times but what it was like to encounter Shakespeare amid those shifting circumstances. Shakespeare's reception becomes an opportunity to identify competing cultural paradigms and narrate cultural change over time. So, the sections below work from close readings of Richard's disability on stage to generalizations about larger phenomena—(1) the nineteenth-century Shakespearean history play, (2) the diversification of Shakespearean theater that started in the nineteenth century and continues today, (3) the politicization of Shakespeare from his era to ours, and (4) twenty-first-century disability theater. That makes this chapter both a conclusion to the cultural history of Richard's disability that has been the concern of this book up to this point and a transition to the approach to Shakespeare theorized in the conclusion, the "anthropology of audience."

I. The Disappearing and Reappearing Hump: Richard on Stage in the Nineteenth Century

The first woman to play Richard III was a Mrs. Le Fevre at a benefit on her behalf in London on March 4, 1782. Little is known about her, but a surviving drawing shows no discernable disability (see Figure 6.1). Indeed, when we line up late-eighteenth- and nineteenth-century actors playing Shakespeare's Richard III in chronological order, we see the size of his hump decrease down to nothing over the first half of the century before growing back up over the second half. It's not immediately obvious why this would happen. Mainstream English attitudes about physical disability moved in the nineteenth century from hostility toward acceptance. That linear trend does not align with the ebb and flow of Richard's hump. It's relevant that nineteenth-century historians became increasingly convinced that the historical Richard III was not disabled, but that trend continued up to the 2012 discovery of Richard's skeleton. Why did the English theater re-deform Richard at the end of the nineteenth century when historians of the time hadn't?

An anthropology of nineteenth-century Shakespearean theater reveals that the disappearance and reappearance of Richard's hump signify shifting attitudes about theatrical authenticity: the size decreased in the first half of the century because English theaters wanted to be faithful to history, and it increased in the second half because they wanted to be faithful to Shakespeare. For the Shakespearean history play, the early nineteenth century was an age of historical fidelity, while the late nineteenth century was one of textual fidelity.

The disability inherited from the eighteenth century, primarily David

FIGURE 6.1 *Portrait of the actress Mrs Le Fevre, in character as Richard III* (London: Torre, 1782), etching and stipple, 225 × 173 mm, at the British Library (London, England). © The Trustees of the British Museum.

Garrick's performance and paintings of it, had uneven shoulders and a noticeable mound protruding up, sometimes backward. After Garrick retired, John Philip Kemble took up Richard at Drury Lane in 1783. Depicted in Gilbert Stuart's 1786 portrait, Kemble played Richard with a large hump, taking up one-third of Stuart's canvas, covered in the folds of a black cloak, angling out behind Richard and to the side, toward the viewer, who can easily connect the mournful look on Richard's face to his disability.³ Kemble's portrayal was also the model for two James Northcote illustrations. In the first, Richard is slope-shouldered on both sides, his chest caving in on itself, as he looks anxiously at the young princes he plans to murder.⁴ The second replays the same scene, now pulling Richard's right shoulder up even with his nose, positioning it at a seemingly impossible angle.⁵

In contrast, Joseph George Holman's 1787 Richard III was athletic with even shoulders.⁶ Annabel Scratch's *Caricature of John Quick as Richard III in "Richard III"* (1790) shows a spry Richard, "an actor of quick conceptions," with no discernible impairment.⁷ It's difficult to tell whether Richard in Henry Singleton and William Nutter's 1792 engraving has any deformity at all or just a cape draped over equally aligned shoulders.⁸ And an anonymous painting shows John Bannister's 1794 Richard a little off-kilter in his posture, but with square, even shoulders.⁹ At the turn of the nineteenth century, therefore, there were two models for playing Richard: the older, more established deformed character and the newer, less prominent version with no impairment.

The next two Richards, George Frederick Cooke and Edmund Kean, nicely illustrate this instability in the size of the hump. Cooke's Richard began at Covent Garden in 1800; the earliest image, Robert Dighton's *Mr. Cooke* (1800), shows a mountainous hump protruding out backward, head and neck off-center on his body.¹⁰ Writing in 1802, Charles Lamb complained that Cooke played too much of "the *monster Richard*," not enough of "the *man Richard*, whom Shakespeare drew."¹¹ A later, more famous image of Cooke, the American Thomas Sully's 1811 *George Frederick Cooke as Richard III* (see Figure 6.2), shows even shoulders: a hump may be hiding behind Richard, but it's not emphasized in the portrait. Other, less magisterial depictions of Cooke's Richard—several engravings and an anonymous undated portrait—similarly show straight shoulders and no hump.¹² Cooke's hump decreased with the passage of time, at least in visual representations of it, which also happened with Kean's Richard, premiering at Drury Lane in 1814.

In an article near the beginning of Kean's run, Leigh Hunt noted an "enormous and bolster-like pad" on the actor's leg to suggest deformity.¹³ The most famous painting, John James Halls's *Edmund Kean as Richard in "Richard III" by William Shakespeare* (1814), gives a mountainlike shape to Richard's shoulders, his coat hanging off a back protruding impossibly far out from his body.¹⁴ But Samuel Drummond's *Edmund Kean as Richard III* (1814; see Figure 6.3) shows even shoulders in an athletic position, with additional reviews noting that Kean only indicated deformity by suggesting disabilities (carrying a walking stick, for example) and supplying the psy-

FIGURE 6.2 Thomas Sully, *George Frederick Cooke as Richard III* (1811), oil on canvas, 60.5 × 95 in., at the Philadelphia Academy of Fine Arts (Pennsylvania).

FIGURE 6.3 Samuel Drummond, *Edmund Kean as Richard III* (1814), oil on canvas, 80 × 48 in., in the Raymond Mander and Joe Mitchenson Theatre Collection at the University of Bristol (England).

chological effects.¹⁵ George Clint's painting of Kean as Richard shows only a slight shoulder mound that might be missed if one isn't looking for it and, like the etchings of Cooke, little or no deformity.¹⁶

With Cooke and Keen, a deformity that started out as obvious and unavoidable diminished over time, which occurred more generally in the nineteenth century. There is no visible deformity in an illustration of Thomas Cobham's Richard III, which first appeared at Covent Garden in 1816.¹⁷ In 1817, Kean's "rival Richard" at Covent Garden, Junius Brutus Booth, had equal shoulders.¹⁸ William Charles Macready's 1819 Richard at Covent Garden did have a raised left shoulder, from which Richard's arm hung awkwardly at a right angle.¹⁹ Significantly, Macready was the first to try restoring Shakespeare's original text—Colley Cibber's version had dominated the stage since the start of the eighteenth century—but Macready's project failed, being staged only twice and then retired. And Macready would be the last noticeably deformed Richard on the London stage for some time.²⁰

While an early-nineteenth-century engraving of Richard in a printed book—shoulders askew, kneeling before Lady Anne—shows the textual tradition maintaining a deformed Richard, there is no discernible impairment in illustrations of Richard from the theatrical tradition.²¹ Illustrations of Edwin Forrest from 1827 to 1837, Charles Freer around 1830, a Mr. Wightman around 1833, James Prescott Warde in 1833, Samuel Phelps from 1837 to 1849, Charles Kean from 1838 to 1854, and James Holloway in 1856 present able-bodied Richards in athletic poses reminiscent of the Edmund Kean lithographs (see Figure 6.4).²² Similarly, illustrations such as *J. B. Roberts as Richard III* (ca. 1854), *Mr. C. Kean as Gloster* (ca. 1857), *Mr. J. W. Wallack as Gloucester* (ca. 1858), and *Edwin Forrest as "Richard III"* (ca. 1860) show Richard standing still, square shoulders, equal legs, invoking the poses of Cooke and Kean, but now with no deformity.²³

Most importantly, Charles Kean—famous for his theatrical historicism that sought to deliver authentic scenery and costumes for Shakespeare's plays—based his production on a book illustrated by two antiquaries, Charles F. Tomkins and James Robinson Planché, who scoured the documentary evidence to correct the historically inaccurate costuming of the play, allowing for the possibility of a disability, but making very little of its significance.²⁴ As Kean's production suggests, in the mid-nineteenth century, performances of *Richard III* brought the body of the king into line with the conclusions of the historicism of that age: Richard III, slandered by the Tudor dynasty, actually was not deformed. "For the hump back and crooked form, I think we have no adequate authority," wrote Sharon Turner in *The History of England during the Middle*

FIGURE 6.4 George Edward Madeley, *Mr. Charles Kean as Richard the IIIrd* (London: G. E. Madeley, 19th c.), colored lithograph, 10 ½ × 7 ½ in., at the Folger Shakespeare Library (Washington, DC). Image from Folger Digital Image Collection.

Ages (1823).[25] Caroline Amelia Halsted's *Richard III. as Duke of Gloucester and King of England* (1844) agreed: "His . . . deformity may vanish under the bright influence of that searching examination into historical truth, that firm resolution of separating fact from fiction, which peculiarly characterize the present enlightened period."[26] The greatest emblem of this un-deformed mid-nineteenth-century Richard is an engraving now at the Folger Shakespeare Library (see Figure 6.5), its statuesque quality more a response to the historical Richard III than the theatrical or textual traditions of Shakespeare's character.[27]

But that historically oriented performance created problems, as Edwin Forrest learned. According to his friend and biographer, James Rees, Forrest based his costume for Richard on a lithograph that appeared in the Paston Letters, a five-volume collection of manuscripts from the Wars of the Roses, "this being historical, and taken in connection with the flattering description of the old Countess of Desmond, who had danced with [Richard] when he was Duke of Gloster, and is stated to have declared that he was the handsomest man in the room except his brother, King Edward."[28] Thus, Forrest "conveyed the idea of [Richard's] deformity more by words than the presentation of an actual picture" (254). His Richard wasn't deformed (see Figure

FIGURE 6.5 *Richard III* (mid-19th c.), engraving, 10 ¾ × 7 in., at the Folger Shakespeare Library (Washington, DC). Image from Folger Digital Image Collection.

6.6), but Rees objected: "We called Mr. Forrest's attention to the portrait of Richard, as drawn by Shakespeare, and it was from this he should fashion his person; indeed, the very language required it" (254). The stigma levied at Richard's body in Shakespeare's text makes no sense if Richard isn't disabled. Rees's narrative of his conversation with Forrest is worth quoting at length:

> "Your Richard," we observed, "will never be popular if you insist upon representing him in the light the Countess of Desmond places him."
> "But her description, and that of Sir Thomas Moore, are historical."
> "True; but it is not Shakespeare. . . ."
> "True; yet, if tradition had not thrown around the character these objectionable features, would not my version be more acceptable to the audience?"

FIGURE 6.6 *Mr. Edwin Forrest as Richard III* (1855), engraving, 7 × 9 ¾ in., The Rare Book & Manuscript Library, University of Illinois at Urbana-Champaign.

"No, for tradition has given to the stage a Richard; you must trace it back to Shakespeare, even to the first representative under the eye of the immortal author himself. You cannot depart from this. Had Kean, Booth, and Cooper changed this traditionary picture, we question if Richard III. would be as popular as it is now. It is the character that renders it great; take that away, and what is left?"

"This, I admit, is a strong argument, but still I cannot so distort Richard."

"Then, let me advise you to present him in the two pictures, one historical, the other Shakespeare."

"How so?"

"You make him history from the first to the last. Why not make him Shakespeare up to the wooing of Lady Anne? He is here in all his deformity, for she says:

'Blush, blush, thou lump of foul deformity.'

"These words will not apply to your Richard, but to that of Shakespeare's. Still, the lady listens to his vows, and is won by a tongue that can wheedle the devil."

"Well, what then?"

"Why, after this, follow history. Carry out the words of Richard; change your dress, and appear 'a very proper man, as fashioned by a score of tailors.'" (255)

Rees's two Richards—one deformed, one not—captures the tension actors felt in the middle of the nineteenth century: they were pulled in different directions by Richard III as understood by historians and *Richard III* as written by Shakespeare.

Later nineteenth-century productions re-grew Richard's hump to be accurate not to history but to Shakespeare. Productions shifted from historical accuracy to textual accuracy, even if the text, they thought, was false to history. Richard's right shoulder started creeping back up in an illustration of *Mr. G. V. Brooke as the Duke of Gloster* (he played the role from 1842 to 1865), or his left shoulder started dipping back down in *Mr. Couldock as Richard III* (he played Richard around 1851).[29] The theatrical tradition was coming back in line with the textual tradition, represented by illustrations of noticeably deformed Richards by John Gilbert and J. A. Wright, because productions were being faithful to the text.[30] In *Edwin Booth as Richard III* (1872; see Figure 6.7), Richard has a left shoulder jutting up unnaturally, as memorialized in his costume, in possession of the Folger Shakespeare Library, cut to have the left shoulder higher than the right.[31] Noting that "Booth restored Shakespeare's *Richard the Third* to the stage in 1876–77," one critic wrote, "There was no distortion, whether of limp, or hump, or costume."[32] This critic doesn't mean there was "no distortion" in Richard's body: there was a massive deformity. There was "no distortion" to Shakespeare's image of a deformed Richard, even if Shakespeare's Richard was a distortion of history. Text supplanted history as guiding authority.

In *Mr. Barry Sullivan as Richard III* (1876), Richard has a crabbed neck with a noticeable hump out behind him.[33] In *John McCullough as Richard III* (ca. 1877), his left shoulder jumps up the canvas while the right dips down.[34] Mounted at the Lyceum in London in 1877, Henry Irving's Richard was more nuanced, emphasizing Richard's deformities more "by means merely of

FIGURE 6.7 Henry Linton after John Hennessy, *Edwin Booth as Richard III* (1872), at the Folger Shakespeare Library (Washington, DC). Image from Folger Digital Image Collection.

rounded shoulders and a halting walk."[35] The right heel on Irving's boots was stacked higher than the left to capture the character's limp.[36] Edwin Long's *Henry Irving as Richard, Duke of Gloucester* (1877; see Figure 6.8) depicts a noticeably raised left shoulder, which was exaggerated in caricatures of the actor.[37] Irving in London in 1877 and Booth in New York in 1878 both did away with Cibber's adaptation, fully restoring Shakespeare's text for the first time in nearly two hundred years.[38] The return to Shakespeare meant a return to a disabled Richard. Theatrical and textual traditions came back in line. On the theatrical side, Richard Mansfield portrayed Richard in 1889 with a towering right shoulder, "a hump like a camel," said one critic (see Figure 6.9).[39] On the textual side, Edwin Austin Abbey's painting of *Richard, Duke of Gloucester, and the Lady Anne* (1896) portrayed a grotesque, spiderlike Richard bunched up in his shoulders.[40]

Theatrical and textual traditions having reunited by the end of the nineteenth century, most of the great English and American Richard IIIs of the early and mid-twentieth century were basically riffs on Booth's, Irving's, and Mansfield's camel-hump shoulder: Frank Benson (1886–1915), Robert Mantell (1904), Martin Harvey (1910), Frederick Warde (1912), Robert Atkins (1915), John Barrymore (1920–1929), Baliol Holloway (1921–1930), George Hayes (1928), Walter Hampden (1934), Emlyn Williams (1937), John Laurie (1939), Basil Rathbone (1939), Donald Wolfit (1942–1944), Laurence Olivier (1944–1955), Richard Whorf (1949), José Ferrer (1953), Alec Guinness (1953), Marius Goring (1953), George C. Scott (1957), Robert Helpmann (1957), Paul Daneman (1960), Christopher Plummer (1961), Vincent Price (1962), Ian Holm (1963–1964), Alan Bates (1967), Norman Rodway (1970), Al Pacino (1973, 1979), John Wood (1979), and Ron Cook (1983).[41] But there were three noteworthy moments for Richard's disability in twentieth-century performance. First, Jürgen Fehling's 1937 production in Berlin costumed Richard's deformity to mock Joseph Goebbels. On the backdrop of henchmen dressed as Nazi stormtroopers, "Fehling, a passionate anti-Nazi . . . took a devilish pleasure in turning the last scion of the house of York into a likeness of the club-footed Minister of Propaganda."[42] Second, Olivier's film juxtaposed Richard's deformity with Olivier's sex appeal (Olivier loved to look at his own legs, prominently displayed here in tights).[43] Although his main prosthetic was not a hump but a long pointy nose, Olivier's Richard was disabled, halting intermittently. Third, Holm used a prosthetic boot to accommodate a clubfoot, while Goring and Rodway added iron braces to Richard's legs and torso, modern medical prosthetics cast back upon Shakespeare's medieval play.[44] But for much of the twentieth century, Richard's costume remained

FIGURE 6.8 Edwin Long, *Henry Irving as Richard, Duke of Gloucester* (1877), oil on canvas, 57 × 40 in., at the Museum and Gallery at Bob Jones University (Greenville, SC).

FIGURE 6.9 *Mr. Richard Mansfield as King Richard III* (London: Stereoscopic, 1889), photograph, 5 3/8 × 4 in., at the Folger Shakespeare Library (Washington, DC). Image from Folger Digital Image Collection.

largely the same: pseudo-medieval garb, stuffed-up shoulder, twisted hand, clubfoot, limp.

If there was a twentieth-century stasis in Richard's costume, the nineteenth-century productions I've examined show not just that Richard's deformity changed over time but that it changed in conjunction with shifting desires and obligations of theatrical performance. In the first half of the nineteenth century, performances of the Shakespearean history play sought to be accountable to history; in the second half, to Shakespeare. Theatrical historicism continued well into the twentieth century—most notably in William Poel's productions for the Elizabethan Stage Society—but the example of Richard III shows that theatrical historicism was unsustainable. Thus, in an 1896 review, George Bernard Shaw scoffed simultaneously at Richard's "incongruous conventional appendages, such as the Punch hump" and "the solemnity of those spectators who feel bound to take the affair as a profound and subtle historical study."[45]

Behind the shift away from theatrical historicism was a recognition that Shakespeare's plays are not history, nor need they be. The point was no longer to stage the story of Richard III, using Shakespeare's text because he had told the story best, with alterations as needed (a la Cibber). The point was now to stage Shakespeare's text—to tell his story, regardless of its historical accuracy, as a stand-alone narrative. The Richard III of history and the one of literature, previously seen as part of the same discourse, were cordoned off into separate realms. It wasn't that academic historians at the end of the nineteenth century believed that Richard wasn't deformed but that theater practitioners believed that he was. Rather, the Richards of history and of Shakespeare were wholly different things—not different versions of the same thing but objectively unique, belonging to separate spheres of thought and incommensurable with each other. There were two different Richards—the one of literature and the one of history—who look radically different, one deformed, one not.

In the second half of the nineteenth century, English theater practitioners realized that their productions of Shakespeare's history plays were staging neither reality nor even a representation of reality, but rather a representation of a representation. The nineteenth-century representation of Shakespeare's sixteenth-century representation of fifteenth-century English history could not connect back up with the original events because Shakespeare had distorted the line of sight. A rigid historicism in Shakespearean theater is absurd because Shakespeare's history plays are already ahistorical. It's not just that Shakespeare's own acting companies used sixteenth-century costumes to present medieval history; it's that Shakespeare dramatized medieval history as it was understood in the Elizabethan age. As Richard Schoch writes, "Shakespeare's own historicized status thus unwittingly betrayed the errancy of Charles Kean's theatrical medievalism: that the Middle Ages could not be authentically restored because it was always already mediated through an Elizabethan perspective."[46] To properly historicize a Shakespearean history play, one would present it not as it occurred in medieval times but as it was performed in the Elizabethan age. To historicize Shakespeare's history plays is to change nothing about them, leaving the plays as modern approximations of Elizabethan versions of medieval stories. Paradoxically, properly historicizing Shakespeare's history plays in the theater means stepping away from—not toward—historical authenticity in setting and narrative. At the end of the nineteenth century, one could strive for the historical Richard III or for Shakespeare's, but it was no longer reasonable to strive for history through Shakespeare because Shakespeare was already anathema to history. Shakespearean drama was not the means to the end of history but an impediment.

Theatrical historicism grew from a quest for continuity between art and history. It resulted in an internally contradictory artwork and had to be done away with to preserve aesthetic quality. Shakespeare's history plays were now seen not as history plays dependent on some external, historical frame of reference for their coherence but as fictional narratives whose coherence is internal: *Is it a good story?* replaced *Is it a true story?* Since the end of the nineteenth century, Shakespeare's history plays have been presented as Shakespearean plays, not history plays. They have been self-consciously mythologized history—good stories—worthy to be told because Shakespeare wrote them. They do not advance claims for historical accuracy: consider the overtly artificial set of Olivier's *Richard III* or the fade-in from the Elizabethan playhouse in Olivier's *Henry V*.

This transformation had to occur—Shakespeare's history plays had to become autonomous narratives independent of their historical referents—for them to join the twentieth-century phenomenon of resetting Shakespearean plays in modern dress. Setting a comedy like *Much Ado about Nothing* in 1960s Cuba isn't conceptually troubling, but putting a history play like *Richard III* in 1930s Germany is. A history play ought to be, by definition, specific to its original setting. After Shakespeare's history plays became detached from their external referents in the second half of the nineteenth century, however, the path was clear to reset them in other times and places. Thus, the most recent mainstream trend in staging *Richard III*—dating back to German productions by Leopold Jessner (1920) and Jürgen Fehling (1937); glimpsed in older English productions featuring Richard Whorf (1949), José Ferrer (1953),

Marius Goring (1953), and Ian Richardson (1975); but only fully realized in more recent productions from Ramaz Chkhikvadze (1980), Michael Moriarty (1980), Antony Sher (1984), Andrew Jarvis (1988), Anton Lesser (1988), Ian McKellen (1990), Simon Russell Beale (1992), Kenneth Branagh (2002), Peter Dinklage (2004), Jonathan Slinger (2006), Kevin Spacey (2011), Martin Freeman (2014), Lars Eidinger (2015), Ralph Fiennes (2016), and L. Peter Callender (2018)—is to make Richard a modern man in modern clothes in a modern world.

II. Intersectional Richards from the Nineteenth Century to the Twenty First

"There are three toxic plays that resist rehabilitation," Shakespeare scholar Ayanna Thompson said on NPR's *Code Switch* in 2019. "With *Merchant*, it is kind of some deep anti-Semitism. With *Othello*, it is deep racism. And with *Taming of the Shrew*, it's deep misogyny."[47] Does *Richard III*, with its deep ableism, belong on this list? All four plays present socially stigmatized characters, explore their experiences, even empower them, disrupting traditions of discrimination, yet eventually contain them within a retrograde ideology of social legitimacy. Thompson illustrates intersectional solidarity against oppression based on different identity categories—religion, race, gender—while showing how disability can be overlooked in the politics of solidarity. As A. J. Withers and Liat Ben-Moshe note, "Disability issues have often been ignored or marginalised within (other) radical theory."[48]

The intersectionality in Shakespeare's different sites of stigma surfaces within *Richard III* itself. As Urvashi Chakravarty discusses, when Henry Tudor, the play's able-bodied answer to disabled villain Richard III, is blessed to "beget a happy race of kings" (*R3*, 5.3.156), ableism shows its allegiances to racism and heteronormativity.[49] Conceived thus, the Tudor dynasty exhibits an ideology of normality expressed through opposition to any identity different from the straight, White, wealthy, Christian, able-bodied, cisgender, middle-aged Englishman embodied in Henry Tudor—what Rosemarie Garland-Thomson calls a "normate," an imagined embodiment of a culture's corporeal ideals.[50] The intersectionality of stigma—the interlocking structures of exclusion extended to identities different from an avouched norm—opens *Richard III* up to historically marked identities other than disability. "One might think of disability as the master trope of human disqualification," David T. Mitchell and Sharon L. Snyder argue, with Tobin Siebers adding, "Not because disability theory is superior to race, class, or sex/gender theory, but because all oppressive systems function by reducing human variation to deviancy and inferiority defined on the mental and physical plane."[51] What happens to Richard's body when the actor playing him is not disabled yet has a body that has historically been stigmatized in other ways? What forms of stigma carry over from one identity category, such as ability, to others, such as race, gender, religion, sexuality, age, and class? What disability experiences don't carry over? What are the particularities, the parallels, and the overlaps of disability experience in light of other socially marked identities? What connects Richard III, Aaron the Moor, Shylock the Jew, and Caliban the savage, and what distinguishes them?[52] How do the nationalism, racism, ableism, elitism, misogyny, bigotry, and heteronormativity of Shakespeare's plays overlap?[53] How are those traditions of stigma encountered—resisted, reinscribed—in modern performance? How does, for example, an actor's racialized body relate to a character's disabled body?

On September 17, 1821, *Richard III* became the first play produced by an African American theater company.[54] The African Grove opened in 1816 in the backyard of 38 Thomas Street in New York City, created by William Henry Brown, a sailor from the West Indies who turned his talents crewing a ship to managing a Black community space, at first somewhere to get tea and ice cream. After a few years, neighbors complained of noise, and police shut the African Grove down. Brown and company decided to mount a play in the upstairs apartment on Thomas Street—theater of, by, and for Black folk. *Richard III* was perfect for the debut: such a popular play would draw an audience and invite comparison with the Park Theatre, a segregated theater facing City Hall Park that only allowed Black people in the upper galleries.

Richard was played by Charles Taft, alias Charles Beers, a formerly enslaved, now free Black man. New York sheriff Mordecai Noah, who fancied himself a theater critic, and whose racist reviews provide much of the surviving evidence of the beginnings of the African Grove Theatre, described Taft thusly: "A little dapper wooly-headed waiter at the City-Hotel personated the royal Plantagenet."[55] Stigmatized because of his race and class, creating an opportunity to consider intersectionality at the inception of African American theater, Taft played Richard as disabled. "The person of Richard was on the whole not amiss," Noah wrote, comparing Taft's Richard (it seems) to either the consensus of historians or the precedent of earlier actors. "Yet the actor had made the King hump backed, instead of crooked backed, having literally a hump behind his neck little less than a camels. Shaping 'the legs of an unequal size' was also difficult but was overcome by placing false calves before, and wearing a high heeled shoe." For Taft's royal garments, "King Richard had some robes made up from discarded merino curtains of the ball rooms." Taft's first lines Americanized *Richard III* to thunderous applause from the African Grove: "Now is de vinter of our discontent made glorus summer by de son of New-York."

While disability was part of the character's body, not the actor's, and Blackness part of the actor's, not the character's, for the audience—especially for any disabled Black folks present—Taft's Richard III was one step closer to authentic theatrical representation of the human condition. This Richard also exhibited what Frances Beal calls "double jeopardy," vulnerable to ableism and racism, although on the different levels of dramatic illusion and theatrical reality.[56] Richard the character in the imagined story and Taft the actor on the actual stage were "outsiders within," to use Patricia Hill Collins's phrase, adding disability to "the interlocking nature of race, gender, and class oppression."[57] At times there will be analogies, but experiences and histories of ableism are qualitatively different than those of racism, as Deborah K. King discusses, and moments of "multiple jeopardy" involve different systems of discrimination with different internal structures and histories.[58] Adapting a line from Kimberlé Crenshaw, who coined the term *intersectionality*, Taft's Richard showed "the need to account for multiple identity when considering how the [theatrical] world is constructed."[59]

With a little imagination, Taft's embodiment of Richard may show, to quote Robert McRuer, "what it means, for the purposes of solidarity, to come out as something you are—at least in some ways—not."[60] To the extent that Taft, by performing Richard, was "claiming crip," to use Alison Kafer's phrase, his Richard III suggested that "such claims might be more available, more imaginable, to some people than others."[61] From this angle, Taft's Richard illustrates Sami Schalk's theory of "disidentification": "This kind of disidentifying process among/across/between minoritarian subjects can allow for coalitional theory and political solidarity."[62]

Taft only played Richard once. The day after his premier, he was arrested for stealing $100 and some cravats from a private house. During the trial, Noah wrote that "this fellow belonged to the black corps dramatique; it seems he wanted clothes to dress in the character of Richard the 3rd, and therefore stole them."[63] The parallel between Taft and Richard—willing to commit crime to surmount social barriers and achieve professional ambitions—is suggestive. While someone looking at the character may say, *That's disability*, and someone looking at the actor, *That's race*, the fate of Taft's Richard invites the analysis of Nirmala Erevelles and Andrea Minear: "Individuals located perilously at the interstices of race, class, gender, and disability are constituted as non-citizens and (no) bodies by the very social institutions (legal,

FIGURE 6.10 TCS 44 (Hewlett, James, as Richard the Third in imitation of Mr. Kean). Houghton Library, Harvard University (Cambridge, Massachusetts).

educational, and rehabilitational) that are designed to protect, nurture, and empower them."[64] For instance, the *New-York City Hall Recorder* read Richard into Taft by punctuating its account of his crime with quotes from the play: "I am determined to prove a villain."[65]

The African Grove needed more space. For the next week's performance, on September 24, the company converted a house in a more remote part of town into a theater. The role of Richard III went to James Hewlett, a native to the West Indies who possibly worked for English actor George Frederick Cooke when the Park Theatre brought him to New York. Hewlett played Richard with no visible disability "in imitation of Mr. Kean," as seen in an engraving from the 1820s (see Figure 6.10). Where Taft's Richard added layers of stigma, Hewlett's erased disability, a version of what McRuer calls "compulsory able-bodiedness," mirroring the able-bodiedness of actors who have played the role of Richard III for most of its history.[66]

Hewlett played the role again on October 1. On October 5, the Park staged *Richard III* featuring Junius Brutus Booth, yet White audiences wanted to see the African Grove's Shakespeare. In late October, the African Grove "graciously made a partition at the back of their house, for the accommodation of the whites."[67] With market demand high, the theater moved again in early January 1822, renting Hampton's Hotel for performances—right next door to the Park. With ticket sales threatened, the Park's jealous manager, Stephen Price, hired some White hecklers to harass the African Grove company and create disturbances. Police ordered the shows at the African Grove to stop and, during a January 7 performance of *Richard III*, infiltrated the audience, storming the stage during one of Hewlett's soliloquies. He defiantly quoted Richard: "Fellow begone—I'm not at leisure."[68] Police arrested and jailed the whole cast. "To de tower?" Hewlett quipped. They were only released when they "promised never to act Shakespeare again," so the African Grove Theater turned to original plays. The company's final performance in June 1823 was Brown's play about a Black revolution against the British government in the Caribbean, *The Drama of King Shotaway*, the first play on record authored by an African American. In 1826, Hewlett traveled to London, but records of him soon disappear. He died in 1831, having adopted Richard's line "I am myself alone" as his motto.

A London caricature of Richard III as a baboon from around this time, titled *Richard's Himself Again*, may be a racist slander of Hewlett.[69] The connection is uncertain (the motive is as unknown as the date), but racism may be filling the stigma-shaped gap created by the erasure of disability in Hewlett's performance. Meanwhile, in the United States, the racism that created the stereotyped character Jim Crow added an overlapping ableism, citing *Richard III*: "I been born wid sharp set grinders jis like dey say in de play King Dick hab."[70] As Dennis Tyler Jr. writes, "Blackness became intimately tethered to disability in the Jim Crow era."[71]

After starting his career at the African Grove, the African American actor Ira Aldridge played Richard when he reached England—select scenes starting in 1829 and the full play in 1848—in whiteface.[72] To my knowledge, reviews of Black Richards, such as Samuel Morgan Smith in 1866, B. J. Ford in 1878, and Paul Molyneaux in 1883, do not discuss disability. In 1886, J. A. Arneaux "lacked the silent dragging of the foot of the generally translated morose and cruel Gloster."[73] Whether disability was erased in these performances or simply not mentioned in the commentaries on them, missing is an opportunity to consider what it might have meant to be Black and disabled or to be Black and play disabled in the nineteenth century. The examples that emerge—like

FIGURE 6.11 *Miss Ellen Bateman as Richard 3rd; Miss Kate Bateman as Richmond* (London, England: London Printing Company, mid-19th c.), line engraving, 7 × 4 ½ in. each, at the Folger Shakespeare Library (Washington, DC). Image from Folger Digital Image Collection.

a Black man in whiteface playing a disabled character whose disability was erased from the performance—do not easily fall into what King calls the "merely additive" vision of multiple jeopardy (racism plus ableism plus classism).[74] As King would observe, these examples point to different traditions of discrimination and privilege overlapping in nineteenth-century theater.

Similarly played without disabilities, child Richards in London, including twelve-year-old William Henry West Betty in 1804, twelve-year-old Jane Fisher in 1805, and six-year-old Clara Fisher in 1817, allowed audiences, to quote Marlis Schweitzer, "to take delight in Richard's monstrous plasticity."[75] In the United States in 1849, child prodigies Kate and Ellen Bateman encountered the simultaneous intrigue and revulsion that characterizes prodigality as Richard experiences it. The engraving of four-year-old Ellen as Richard and six-year-old Kate as Richmond suggests no disability (see Figure 6.11), but the Batemans encountered resistance because of their bodies, mirroring Richard's experience with disability and in keeping with nineteenth-century resistance to new actorly bodies playing the role of Richard: "The announcement of the coming of these infantile Thespians was not favorably received by the habitués of the Broadway: the appearance of prodigies of any kind being a departure from the ways of that traditional home of the legitimate drama, and there was against these young stars formed a prejudice which only the absolute cleverness of their performances was able to overcome."[76]

In Philadelphia in 1836, Elizabeth Morton Woodson, known as Mrs. Henry Lewis, played Richard III, among other male parts, described by the theater manager as "monstrosities, such as have ever been objects of disgust to me,—male characters performed by a female."[77] No reviews survive of Australian actress Eliza Winstanley's scandalous performance as Richard at Sydney's Australian Olympic Theatre in 1842, perhaps a sign of critics boycotting. One who refused to attend declared in disgust: "That the interests of any company of performers would be advanced, by such an exhibition, appears to us to be a most preposterous notion. . . . Such an attempt is unsexly and indelicate."[78]

Richard III's disability invites intersectional analysis when performed by actors who hold identities historically stigmatized on the basis of race, gender, religion, or class. Yet the mid-nineteenth-century performance history of *Richard III* is filled with missed opportunities to consider intersectionality because Richard's disability was often erased. At the same time, nineteenth-century productions featuring actors stigmatized because of race, gender, age, and class often encountered exclusions reminiscent of Richard's experiences in Shakespeare's play, as registered in allusions to Richard—by both stigmatizers and stigmatized. As the identities of actors in the English-speaking world expanded, *Richard III* provided a venue for thinking about the process of coming into power, barriers encountered, and responses to them. While that dynamic is inextricably linked to Richard's disability in Shakespeare's text, the nineteenth-century erasure of that disability may have allowed actors and audiences to locate differently stigmatized identities in the story of Richard III. As Garland-Thomson observes, "the ability/disability system"—who has the privilege to do certain things in society, and who faces barriers—surfaces across different identity categories.[79] When looking at the new identities of actors in the nineteenth century, "integrating disability clarifies how this aggregate of systems operates together, yet distinctly, to support an imaginary norm and structure the relations that grant power, privilege, and status to that norm."[80] With nineteenth-century Richards, "the body, bodily variety, and normalization," to quote Kim Q. Hall, are "central to analyses of all forms of oppression"—whether looking at the character or the actor.[81] The stage history of *Richard III* in the nineteenth century illustrates "the vexed dynamics of difference and the solidarities of sameness" in identity politics and identity-conscious theatrical casting.[82]

Understanding the intersectionalities of different kinds of stigma is complex, and these issues persist. In his 1963 "I Have a Dream" speech, Martin Luther King Jr. wrote Richard's struggle with disability into the African American fight for racial justice. Just after identifying "the fierce urgency of now," and then four sentences starting with "Now is the time . . ."—echoing the "now . . . now . . . now" repeated in Richard's opening soliloquy—King vows, "This sweltering summer of the Negro's legitimate discontent will not pass until there is an invigorating autumn of freedom and equality."[83] The added qualifier "legitimate" may suggest that Richard's "discontent" is illegitimate; alternately, the legitimacy of the civil rights movement may lead to recuperations of Richard's villainy. King's point was that anger over racial injustice should not be cooled but embraced, positioning Shakespeare's disabled Richard III as a model for civil rights activism that doesn't shy away from what Audre Lorde calls "the uses of anger."[84]

Richard's disability was almost entirely ignored in Carlyle Brown's play *The African Company Presents Richard III* (1994), until near the end. Telling the story of William Brown, James Hewlett, and their *Richard III*, the play is keenly alert to questions of intersectionality as the character Ann Johnson—playing Lady Anne—negotiates the racism outside the theater and Hewlett's misogyny inside it. The gender dynamics of Anne and Richard in act 1, scene 2 of *Richard III* are the centerpiece of Brown's engagement with Shakespeare. It starts to feel like a missed opportunity to bring disability into the exploration of gender and race intersectionality until, near the end, Hewlett's delivery of Richard's opening soliloquy asks audiences to compare the disability stigma that is Shakespeare's focus and the racial stigma that is Brown's. That intersectionality then informs the new soliloquy that opens the new play—*King Shotaway*—that William Henry Brown writes, which James Hewlett recites:

> Behold these chains we wear. The shakles of our enslavers, the despotic English, who mend these merry garments with the thread of your labor and your dreams. And your children hunger for those dreams. They are weak for want of desire. Frail from wanting to see a face of a hero they could be. Blush in your shame and break with these vestments of disgrace. Spurn them with your burning indignation. Rise up naked and extirpate these despots from your world. Restore yourselves,

your wives and your children to the inheritance of your ancestors, who inspire your fury and who show you the way. Those marvelous, struggling spirits who suffered to you the air you breath; who knit time for you to walk on; who give you stars to cover your body.[85]

While it parallels Black liberation to Richard's disability experience, Carlyle Brown's ending is a stark change of genre from Shakespeare's. Both plays are filled with hatred, violence, and oppression, but, in the creation of autonomous Black art, Carlyle Brown finds hope for the future amid Shakespeare's purely tragic exploration of stigma.

Two years later, Barbara Gaines cast Brendan Corbalis as Richard III, plus Black actors for two of his henchmen. In Lisa Anderson's reading, "A black Richard III in the context of an otherwise all-white cast displaces our revulsion at Richard's physical deformity—his hump—onto his racial difference."[86] In critiquing Gaines's racism, Anderson conveys an ableist sentiment ("our revulsion") that may be difficult for Black folks with disabilities to read. Yet Anderson's critique could extend to the *Richard III* of *The Show Must Go Online* (2020), where the only three Black actors in the show play the York brothers, each horrible in his own way, all dead by the end. With these trials and errors in mind, I believe that one of the most successfully intersectional *Richard III*s may be Denzel Washington's from 1990, a disabled Black man who, like the many other Black actors in this production, has felt the horrors of racism yet is ostracized within that racial community because of his disability.

While films such as *That Most Important Thing: Love* (1975) and *The Goodbye Girl* (1977) show continued parallels between disability and sexuality stigma in readings of *Richard III*, Ian McKellen's performance in Richard Loncraine's 1995 film points toward intersectionality, at least in McRuer's 2011 reading. "Queer pleasures" and "crip pleasures" intersect as the gay actor plays the disabled character, which, McRuer argues, appeals to audiences through its desire to burn down "the marriage of compulsory heterosexuality and compulsory able-bodiedness."[87] Evan Choate (looking at Shakespeare's play) and Lauren Coker (looking at McKellen's film) observe that ability and disability are thoroughly sexualized throughout *Richard III*, as figured in things that stand erect, or don't, or that can perform at the right time, or can't, or that have power, or are impotent.[88] Alternately, a de- and re-stigmatized Richard appears in *Requiem of the Rose King* (2013–), a Japanese manga series in which Richard is not disabled but intersexual, "neither man nor woman."[89] Replacing disability with a differently stigmatized identity that carries a different experience and history will always raise questions about particularities that do not transcend identity categories and create opportunities to consider parallels. Thus, recent theatrical Richards by female actors—including Lisa Wolpe (1996), Kathryn Hunter (2003), Emily Carding (2014), Kate Mulvany (2017), Sarah Harlett (2018), and Sophie Russell (2019)—ask audiences to see the character as female and disabled, drawing attention to (1) intersectional oppressions disabled women experience that disabled men do not and (2) solidarities that recognize the shared goals of feminism and disability justice.

The concept of intersectionality grows specifically out of American Black feminist thought and "center[s] Black women," to quote Crenshaw's coining of the term.[90] One illustration of the thesis of intersectionality is that, prior to 2022, there had not been a Black woman in the role of Richard III on a major stage. Where Crenshaw shows "how Black women are theoretically erased" under the law (139), the example of Richard III shows how Black women can be theatrically erased. Theater-makers and audiences who enthusiastically embrace race- and gender-conscious Richards show that "dominant conceptions of discrimination condition us to think about subordination as disadvantage occurring along a single categorical axis" (140). As gender-conscious casting tends to privilege White women, and race-conscious casting Black men, and ability-conscious casting White men, there emerges a matrix of disadvantages and privileges to play Richard III in English and American theater. The stage history of Richard III bears out Crenshaw's point that "any analysis that does not take intersectionality into account cannot sufficiently address the particular manner in which Black women are subordinated" (140). Danai Gurira playing Richard III at the Public Theater in 2022 is the most authentically intersectional embodiment in the history of the role, given intersectionality's origins in African American feminism.[91]

In the end, the example of Richard III invites us to adapt the ideas of Crenshaw and other critical race theorists into a notion of *theatrical intersectionality*. This term addresses the interlocking systems of disadvantages and privileges that emerge when an identity draws from the imagined dramatic world of the character and the real theatrical world of the actor. An able-bodied actor may bring social privilege to their performance of a disabled character. Audiences may read an actor's racialized or gendered body in relation to a character's disabled body. When actor and character are differently stigmatized, different formulations will occur. There may be an analogy suggested between two discrete traditions of the stigma or two experiences of stigmatization. There may be multiple jeopardies suggested in which identities held by the actor are added into identities held by the character. The privileges and prejudices of the audience may mirror or sharply depart from those of the characters on stage. Above all, it will be impossible to conduct single-issue analysis. Matrix analysis will be needed.

III. The Erasure of Richard's Disability in Political, Global, and Digital Appropriations

In the main, there are two ways to politicize Shakespeare's *Richard III*.[92] The first emphasizes Richard's impairment, drawing a parallel to the body of some political figure to degrade him. As discussed in Chapter 5, Richard III's disability was used to mock Robert Cecil; as mentioned in this chapter, some mid-twentieth-century productions costumed Richard to look like Nazi Minister of Propaganda Joseph Goebbels, born with a clubfoot. Such efforts are older, less prominent, and less interesting than the second model, in which the central feature of Shakespeare's character—disability—is ignored to draw an analogy between Shakespeare's play and modern politics. This second model itself has two versions.

The first parallels Shakespeare's character—his villainy, ambition, hypocrisy, tyranny—to a political figure. Writing in 1649, John Milton used Richard, "a deep dissembler, not of his affections onely, but of Religion," to impugn the false piety of Charles I.[93] From the other side of the ideological spectrum, a Restoration-era performance of *Richard III* included a prologue analogizing Richard to Oliver Cromwell, both presented as "Usurpers" and "Tyrants" who "Puft up with pride, still vanish in despair. / But lawful Monarchs are preserv'd by Heaven."[94] During World War II, Wolfit's productions of *Richard III* went after Adolf Hitler rather than Goebbels—after someone's actions rather than someone's body. While Wolfit depicted Richard's disability, it wasn't the source of his political analogy: "My wig of long red hair with a cowlick across the forehead gave a more curious resemblance, in an impressionistic way, to the Fuhrer."[95] A 1963 Russian Richard's disability was similarly de-emphasized so the production could draw a connection to Joseph Stalin, described by one critic as "the real, bloody 'Richard' of recent Soviet history."[96]

The second version compares cultures rather than characters: by emphasizing the supporting cast surrounding Richard and suggesting a modern political analogy, authors critique those who enable the rise of a charismatic villain. In 1920, Jessner's production at the National Theater of Berlin eschewed a realistic representation of character psychology in favor of an expressionist account of the play's politics, relating the play to recent efforts to overthrow the Weimar republic.⁹⁷ Focused on social situation rather than individual character, Jessner's production influenced Bertolt Brecht's *The Resistible Rise of Arturo Ui* (1941), an allegory for Hitler's rise that compares its main character to Richard III, but only to analogize the cultures of complicity around these figures.⁹⁸ Margaret Webster's 1953 production of *Richard III*, starring José Ferrer, set the stage with a hodge-podge of totalitarian symbols (swastikas, sickles, hammers).⁹⁹ In the next generation, productions starring Al Pacino (1973, 1974), Michael Moriarty (1974, 1980), and Brian Bedford (1977) staged widespread government corruption with a nod to the Watergate scandal.¹⁰⁰

This model of politicizing *Richard III* through analogous characters or cultures—rather than analogous bodies—culminated in Richard Eyre's 1990 Nazi-themed production starring McKellen, which Loncraine made into a film in 1995.¹⁰¹ In a 2001 staging from avant-garde Chinese director Lin Zhaohua, "with the Machiavellian Richard looking distinctly like Chairman Mao and sporting an identical cropped half-bald hairstyle, Lin's *Richard III* drew attention to the 'cross-cultural' villainous qualities of political players."¹⁰² After the Iraq War, Sulayman Al-Bassam rewrote *Richard III* as an allegory for Saddam Hussein, though Al-Bassam later modified his production to point less to an individual and more to Arab dictators in general. His first draft retained Shakespeare's lines about Richard's disability, but the final version excised and reimagined them:

> But I, whose chest is weighed with a weather-proof heart,
> Shorn of a mug to lock the lusty female eye;
> I, born to the mother with the narrow pelvis,
> spat into this world so beaten, buckled and battered that even maids
>   start at me.
> No lover I.¹⁰³

Graham Holderness reports that, ultimately, "Al-Bassam's Richard has neither hump nor limp. . . . Reviewers and spectators saw him as charismatically handsome rather than hideously deformed."¹⁰⁴

While this second model of politicizing *Richard III* is newer, more prominent, and more interesting than the first, the elements emphasized in the second model—Richard's personality and actions, plus the response to him by surrounding characters—are inextricably bound up with his disability in Shakespeare's play. The story of Richard III, as told by Shakespeare, does not exist without disability. Richard's disability inaugurates the social and mental tensions that drive the play. Yet the story of Richard III is often retold in the modern world without disability. The social and mental tensions of Shakespeare's play are staged absent the disability that motivates them.

A text like *House of Cards* erases Richard's disability when turning him into a charmingly ambitious modern politician, first in the British novels, then in the BBC show, then in the U.S. series on Netflix.[105] Cultural commentators appropriated Richard III sans disability to gloss political machinations during national debates like "Libspill" in Australia in 2015 and "Brexit" in the UK in 2016.[106] Hamid-Reza Naeemi's *Richard* (2018) preserved Richard's "hunchback" but threw much more emphasis behind "a political critique of dictatorship that has caused the preservation of the oppressive social order in modern Iran."[107] And the tendency to retain Richard's personality and plot while eliminating his disability extends beyond overtly political appropriations. The film *King Rikki* (2002) erased Richard's disability when making him a hunky Latin American gang lord in East Los Angeles. Richard has no disability when he becomes a cut-throat Hollywood executive in the low-budget flop *Richard III* (2007), or when he time-travels into the comic *Batman: Knight and Squire* (2011).[108] At the 2012 Globe to Globe festival in London, Chinese director Wang Xiaoying and actor Zhang Dongyu staged "Richard with no deformity but driven by a desire to prove his abilities and hold absolute power."[109] That same year, Polish director Grzegorz Wiśniewski's *Richard III* in Łódź had no deformity.[110] Started in 2012, the gag Twitter account @Richard_Third—filled with jokes about kingdoms for horses, happenings around Leicester, and years-long rivalries with @KngHnryVIII and @Wwm_Shakespeare—only mentions "disability" in 4 of its 9,617 tweets (as of this writing).[111] In Thomas Ostermeier's 2015 production featuring Lars Eidinger, Richard's disability was a forgery, prosthetics and appendages worn to manipulate his public image but stripped off during the wooing of Anne.[112]

Both versions of the second model of politicizing Richard appear in Stephen Greenblatt's 2016 op-ed for the *New York Times*, "Shakespeare Explains the 2016 Election."[113] On the one hand, Donald Trump as a person is analogous to Richard as a character: in Greenblatt's reading, both are "loathsome, perverse" "sociopaths," "inwardly tormented by insecurity and rage," "haunted by self-loathing," finding "refuge in a feeling of entitlement, blustering overconfidence, misogyny and a merciless penchant for bullying," with a "weird, obsessive determination to reach a goal that look[s] impossibly far off, a position for which he ha[s] no reasonable expectation, no proper qualification and absolutely no aptitude," and offering "no glimpse of anything redeemable in him and no reason to believe that he could govern the country effectively." On the other hand, Greenblatt shifts from character criticism to cultural criticism, listing five ways in which Richard's England is "a nation of enablers": some do not recognize the fragility of the political order, some do not believe that Richard is as bad as he seems to be, some feel helpless in the face of bullying, some exploit Richard's rise for their own gain, and some take a perverse pleasure in Richard's giddy destruction of the nation. "Shakespeare evidently wanted to emphasize the element of consent in Richard's rise," Greenblatt concludes.

Citing Greenblatt in promotional material, Anton Juan and Ricardo Abad's play *RD3RD* (2018) erased Richard's disability to analogize him to the president of the Philippines, Rodrigo Duterte.[114] Will Power's *Seize the King* (2018) erased disability in its hip-hop adaptation of *Richard III*.[115] Meanwhile, Trump-era scholars Kai Wiegandt and Richard Ashby have developed theories—of mediated history, of post-truth politics—based on *Richard III* that don't say much about the disability that is central to the narrative they're theorizing.[116] As Marina Gerzić's research shows, there are many examples where Richard's disability is sheepishly preserved (in children's literature and comics), uncomfortably exaggerated (the raven on the hump in *Manga Shakespeare: Richard III* [2007]), or partially revised (withered arm but no hunchback in *Kill Shakespeare* [2010]).[117] But trends in twentieth- and twenty-first-century political, global, and digital Richards point to a key question: What are the implications of modern appropriations of *Richard III* that erase the motivating feature—disability—of Richard III?

The story and themes that Shakespeare's *Richard III* develops specifically in response to disability are often applicable to modern life even when disability is not in play, allowing modern writers to adapt *Richard III* but leave the disability behind. In these adaptations, Richard represents the universal disability that comes with human embodiment in modern life—the restrictions placed upon humans by the natural and social conditions into which we are born. Bolstered by the valorization of individuality in modern thought, we tend to resist and try to circumvent those restrictions but, because the circumstances we seek to outmaneuver are largely permanent, at least at the level of an individual's life-span, efforts to overcome our limitations almost always falter. From this angle, the modern condition is defined by tragedy, including not only fear of what we cannot control and pity for those who have no control but also ambition to achieve goals denied to us and revenge against the world when our aspirations are thwarted. As *Richard III* shows, an individual committed to ambition and revenge can attract large groups of people—characters within the dramatic illusion and people out in the audience—who share similar desires and admire the individuality of the person who pursues them against all odds, shifting tragic catastrophe from the level of the individual to the level of the society. In other words, modern society, like the modern individual, has a disposition toward tragedy, which can find artistic expression in stories of disability.

If Lennard Davis is right in arguing that disability is the default condition of the modern human being—which he calls "dismodernism"—then Richard III may be the quintessential modern character, and the first (Hamlet, who spends three acts disabled—unable to do anything—came a few years later).[118] That's partly why Katherine Schaap Williams invokes Davis to see Richard, "with deliberate anachronism," as a "dismodern subject."[119] It's also why Sigmund Freud thought that "Richard is an enormous magnification of something we find in ourselves as well."[120] *Richard III* remains central because it captures the tragedy of identity in modernity. "Disability can be seen as the postmodern subject position," Davis writes (14) when developing dismodernism: "The dismodern era ushers in the concept that difference is what we all have in common" (26). Like Shakespeare's Richard III, modern life is a viscerally creatural, material embodiment and a negotiation of centuries of deeply ingrained social meanings made of our bodies. Like *Hamlet* and *King Lear*, *Richard III* is a key text for modernity because the experiences surrounding disability are widely felt in our time, even when impairment is not present. Many are, to quote the Americans with Disabilities Act of 1990, "a discrete and insular minority who have been faced with restrictions and limitations, subjected to a history of purposeful unequal treatment, and relegated to a position of political powerlessness in our society, based on characteristics that are beyond the control of such individuals and resulting from stereotypic assumptions not truly indicative of the individual ability of such individuals to participate in, and contribute to, society."[121] Like *Othello*, *Richard III* centers life experienced from the periphery of a society. Disability isn't universal. "It is too easy to say, 'We are all disabled,'" Davis writes (31). You know who doesn't think that everyone is disabled? Most disabled people. Carrie Sandahl notes that Davis's metaphor works against political activism fighting for a fairer world.[122] Kafer aptly describes the notion that "we are *all* disabled" as "well-intentioned but deeply ableist."[123] Disability isn't the postmodern condition, nor is it tragic. But when disability meets tragedy, as in *Richard III*, it provides a lexicon of social and psychological experience that resonates in modern life far beyond the specifics of physical impairment. For most of us, life in the modern age is more *Richard III* than *Henry V*. We are, like Shakespeare's

Richard III, heavily influenced by history in our composition and obsessively interpreted in our social reception. *Richard III* is universal only insofar as the dance between the particularity of embodiment and the burden of historically codified interpretations of our identities is experienced by all of us, some more acutely than others. Richard's disability is the mechanism by which his mythologized story of good and evil, heroes and villains is accessible to us.

IV. Cripping Richard: Aesthetics and Politics in Disability Theater

In October 2001, the Nouveau Theatre Experimental in Montreal, Quebec, staged *Dave Wants to Play Richard III* in the basement of the Sainte-Justine Children's Hospital.[124] With the patients upstairs in mind, audiences saw Dave Richer, an actor with cerebral palsy who uses a wheelchair, adapt Shakespeare's play into a reflection on the relationship between a disabled actor's body and the English language's most famous disabled character. The play's fictionalized casting director ultimately refuses to offer Dave the role of Richard, worried that it would make a spectacle of Dave's disability, or that it's tokenizing or exploitative, or that the physical requirements are insensitive to Dave's needs. A frustrated Dave then speaks Richard's lines—the disabled actor's experience with exclusion in the theater industry illuminating the disabled character's experience in medieval England. In one account, "the focus for the spectator is not so much what the lines are saying but how they are made to read on Dave's body."[125]

Despite its liabilities, Shakespeare's *Richard III* has been a venue for the exploration of disabled subjectivity. The very same Shakespearean irony—the openness of interpretation—that has allowed *Richard III* to be a tool in ableist culture has also allowed *Richard III* to be reclaimed for disability activism. The most intriguing Richard IIIs of recent years are those played by disabled actors, including Jan Potměšil (2000), Dave Richer (2001), Kathryn Hunter (2003), Peter Dinklage (2004), Henry Holden (2005), Rene Moreno (2008), Stephen Madigan (2015), Debbie Paterson (2016), Michael Patrick Thornton (2016), Kate Mulvany (2017), and Mat Fraser (2017). This section looks at the motives behind these performances and the meanings given to them—by the actors themselves, the directors who cast them, and audiences. I ask why the phenomenon of disabled actors playing Richard III emerged when it did. Why didn't it emerge earlier? Or later? What was happening at the start of the twenty-first century that led a series of theater organizations to start doing the same thing?

An anthropology of audience can help: the rise of disabled actors playing Richard allows us to use a phenomenon from the Shakesphere to identify and analyze a non-Shakespearean cultural trend. The goal is not to generate a reception history for Shakespeare scholars but to exploit the infusion of Shakespeare in modern culture to generate observations about society that illuminate the world for people whose primary concerns in life are not related to Shakespeare (*how dare they!*). Shakespeare is not the target of analysis but an opportunity, an instrument, even a methodology making cultural studies possible.

Specifically, these productions of *Richard III* illuminate the logic of "cripping," a term of empowerment indicating efforts to reclaim and reconfigure the stigmas associated with disability based on knowledge gained from disability activism and disability studies.[126] Positioned against theatrical traditions of disability from the nineteenth and twentieth centuries—the freak show parading people with deformities out on stage for the abject fascination of "normals," and able-bodied actors "cripping up" to play disabled characters (often to critical praise)[127]—"cripping" has become increasingly popular in England and America since the establishment of the Graeae Theatre Company in 1980, which describes itself as "a force for change in world-class theatre, boldly placing D/deaf and disabled actors centre stage and challenging preconceptions."[128] The year 1986 brought the Alliance for Inclusion in the Arts, "America's leading advocate for full diversity as a key to the vitality and dynamism of American theatre, film, and television."[129] Yet, as Petra Kuppers points out in a 2001 article, disabled actors have largely remained both invisible ("relegated to borderlands, far outside the central arc of cultural activity") and hypervisible ("instantly defined in their physicality").[130] Siebers explains that "the disabled body, when it appears on the stage, stands out as a spectacle in and of itself, one that threatens to draw attention to itself and away from the other performances on the stage."[131] Thus, Kirsty Johnston concludes, "Realist and naturalist aesthetics pose the strongest challenges for disabled actors who seek to embody non-disabled characters or for non-disabled actors who seek to portray disabled characters."[132] The aesthetic problem of hypervisibility creates the political problem of invisibility.

Disability theater—defined by Thomas Fahy in 2002 as "drama written and performed by disabled artists, and/or staged works about disability and the social constructions of physical difference"[133]—responds to both problems. Often avant-garde, disability theater takes its theoretical cue from "the sense that disability in daily life is already performance," as Carrie Sandahl and Philip Auslander put it in 2005.[134] Working against traditions of "cripping up," scholars such as Kuppers have emphasized "disabled people as artists and originators of artistic social texts and practices," shifting attention "from non-disabled certainties about disability to disabled perspectives on these certainties."[135] Disabled performers continue to encounter structural inaccessibility in the workplace, as Sandahl has repeatedly documented. In a 2005 essay, she builds from the connection between invisibility and hypervisibility ("Because disability always signifies in representation, the trained disabled actor is rarely given the opportunity to play nondisabled characters") to illustrate the ableist bias of actor-training programs and theater spaces.[136] In a 2007 work, she develops, along with Terry Galloway and Donna Nudd, an "ethic of accommodation" for disability in the theater world, "often necessitating that the majority make difficult changes in its practices and environment" (a political concern related to invisibility), including "letting go of preconceived notions of perfectability" (an aesthetic concern related to hypervisibility).[137] Writing in 2008, Sandahl synthesizes these concerns to examine "disability identity at work on two primary levels: the level of the play and the level of production."[138] The first level ("how disability functions dramaturgically in new disability plays" [227]) is aesthetic: "Disabled actors argue that non-disabled actors, no matter how good their technical skill at imitating the physicality of a disabled character . . . lack the lived experience of disability necessary to bring these characters fully to life" (236). The second level ("apparent at the level of production, particularly around issues of casting" [235]) is political: "Disabled actors rarely make a living in their profession because so few roles are available to them" (236).

Sandahl's terms help us see that the main motive behind the cripping of Richard III in recent years is not simply that a disabled actor can connect with and portray Shakespeare's disabled king better than an able-bodied actor. If we see this attitude as the *aesthetic* motivation behind the cripping of Richard, the *political* motivation has exerted more force: a disabled actor playing Richard III exemplifies the recent push for fair hiring practices in the English-speaking world. Every time an able-bodied actor plays Richard, that's one less role available for a disabled actor. Since disabled actors are less likely to be cast in roles for able-bodied characters, employment opportunities are limited. This dynamic has the look and feel of structural discrimination on the basis of disability, which laws and standards since the 1990s have sought to curb. In the main, having disabled actors play Richard III isn't about offering a radically new interpretation of the play or even a better, more realistic performance; it's about enhancing the visibility and status of disabled actors in the hopes that they will secure more roles, including roles for characters that don't have disability as a centerpiece. The political goal of disabled actors is to bring the way the world looks and feels on stage closer into line with the way it is in reality. This means having disabled actors portraying characters in stories about disability as well as disabled actors playing characters in stories having nothing to do with disability.

As Leslie C. Dunn illustrates, "Shakespearean disability theatre" includes a spectrum of experiences, with vibrant community spaces for artistic disability visibility navigating ableist performance histories, inaccessible stages, offensive directorial visions, and regressive audience expectations.[139] Richard Burbage, David Garrick, Edmund Kean, Henry Irving, and Laurence Olivier are only the most famous actors to "crip up" for Richard. These performers, though costumed in disability, have tended to bound around the stage with an energetic athleticism, rarely suggesting mobility impairments. Kean, Irving, and Olivier limped intermittently. Olivier fell to one side when dropping to his knee in front of Lady Anne. Irving, Goring, and Holm wore a raised boot as a prosthetic for Richard's "legs of an unequal size" (*3H6*, 3.2.159). But Richard only really became disabled in the 1980s with the rise of disability activism and disability studies as an academic discipline.

The beginning of the disability rights movement is usually traced to the Union of the Physically Impaired Against Segregation (UPIAS), an English group whose 1974 policy statement draws a distinction between "impairment" residing in the human body and "disability" hoisted upon an impaired person from the outside. Bodies don't disable people, UPIAS argued: "In our view, it is society which disable[s] physically impaired people. Disability is something imposed on top of our impairments by the way we are unnecessarily isolated and excluded from full participation in society."[140] This attitude was theorized as "the social model of disability" and given academic credibility in Mike Oliver's book *Social Work with Disabled People* (1983).[141] Since then, disability studies has taken off and become its own academic field in the hands of scholars such as Henri-Jacques Stiker, Lennard Davis, Rosemarie Garland-Thompson, Simi Linton, David Mitchell, and Sharon Snyder.[142]

The rise of disability as a political and academic concern provides the backdrop for the first major disabled Richard III, played by Antony Sher in the early 1980s in a Royal Shakespeare Company tour in England.[143] As recounted in Sher's memoir of the performance, *Year of the King* (1985), a few years before playing Richard, his Achilles tendon snapped during an accident on stage.[144] His leg placed in a plaster cast for six months, Sher used arm crutches to walk, finding the experience frustrating: "My temporary disability made any journey from my home in Islington difficult and vaguely humiliating" (13). Those emotions came rushing back when he was cast to play Richard. He envisioned a costume indicating massive deformity, though he worried about the toll a tour in that costume might take on his body, as he wrote in his diary: "Play him on crutches perhaps? They would take a lot of the strain off the danger areas: lower back, pelvis and legs. And my arms are quite strong after months at the gym. Also I was on crutches for months after the operation so they have a personal association for me of being disabled" (30). Nearly one-third of Sher's book is devoted to designing the proper costume for Richard, since "everything comes from his deformity, his pain" (58). Sher researched physical deformities in medical libraries and visited medical hospitals. He sketched the movement of disabled people he saw on the street. Reasoning that scoliosis, spastic movement, or a disability stemming from poliomyelitis wasn't quite right, Sher landed on a Richard exhibiting severe kyphosis (a large upward curvature of the spine). He played Richard with his arm crutches, emphasizing the sense of a "bottled spider" (*R3*, 1.3.241). In consultation with his therapist, Sher saw an Oedipal complex at work, though in his diary he was embarrassed about that reading: "An absence of love. Caused by a hating mother. This is what I will base my performance on. But I will have to be quite secretive about it, because it sounds so corny—his mother didn't love him" (130). Drawing the distinction between the deformity that characterizes Richard in the early-modern age and the disability of the twenty-first century, Sher concludes: "I had set out to look for a physical shape, but maybe what I found is something about *being* disabled" (117).

Although Sher had experience with disability before his run as Richard, his casting still involved an able-bodied actor cripping up to play disabled. It took a second wave of disability activism—marked in the United States by the passage of the Americans with Disabilities Act in 1990 and in the United Kingdom by the Disability Discrimination Act in 1995—to inaugurate a new age in the casting of Richard III. Where the first wave of disability advocacy in the 1970s and 1980s focused on de-stigmatization, with a somewhat nebulous emphasis on amending cultural attitudes, the second wave that began in the 1990s focused on fair employment, with a laserlike emphasis on legislation. Similarly, there were two waves of disabled actors cast as Richard III, the first motivated largely by aesthetics, the second by politics. The paragraphs that follow address each production in turn, discussing what made each unique, and then step back to consider the trend in general.

The Czech star Jan Potměšil played Richard in a wildly popular production by the Divadelní Spolek Kašpar company, opening in September 2000 at the Divadlo v Celetné (Theatre in Celerna Street) in Prague.[145] Formerly a hot, young, rising actor in Czech theater and film, Potměšil was injured in a 1989 car accident during the Velvet Revolution while engaged in dissident activities to oppose the Communist government. Paralyzed from the waist down, he began using a wheelchair and shifted from heartthrob roles like Romeo to characters with physical and mental disabilities. His *Richard III* juxtaposed historically specific medieval costumes and sets with his modern wheelchair, swapped at times for a palanquin throne or a horse moved by an able-bodied actor hidden under the saddle. In Marcela Kostihova's analysis of the production, two points stand out (which often apply to later disabled Richards).[146] First, promotional materials and critical reviews focused on Potměšil rather than on Richard: the actor's disability experience eclipsed the character's. Thus, second, the production unintentionally re-created the dynamic of the freak show, as Kostihova argues: "It is Potměšil's non-normative body that is the heart of this sought-after spectacle that provides an audience with the unprecedented ability to indulge the otherwise forbidden (yet difficult to resist) urge to stare at the disabled body" (146).

There was a very different vibe when Kathryn Hunter played Richard in 2003 at the Globe.[147] With a woman playing a man, the intersection of disability-based stigma and gender-based stigma was on display. In her daily life, Hunter walks with a limp, her right arm askew because it was once reset improperly after a break. She was motivated by a sympathetic reading of Richard's disability: "By finding his heart and his mind and what drives him, I hope we'll begin to see how the disabled person can be unreasonably maligned and marginalized and then begin to see Richard as a complex human being rather than a cursed person whose external deformities explain his inner evil."[148] As Charles Spencer described Hunter's Richard in the *Telegraph*, "The character's physical disability is superbly caught, with Hunter's body twisted at awkward angles, her hand a grotesque claw, while her damaged right foot forces her to hobble painfully on tiptoe."[149] Yet this facet of Hunter's performance was overshadowed, Elizabeth Klett points out, because reviews focused on director Barry Kyle's decision to stage the play with an all-female cast; critics complained that the casting didn't add or reveal anything new about *Richard III*.[150] There are two possible readings. On the one hand, it could be another instance of disability overlooked and unacknowledged. Hunter's performance as Richard suggests that, when someone holds multiple stigmatized identities, the recognition of one stigmatized identity can preclude the recognition of others, obscuring intersectionality. On the other, the response to Hunter's disability could be ideal because not much fuss was made about it: disability was just a regular part of the world, not anything terribly remarkable. Disabled actors usually want to portray a banker, a teacher, or a heartbroken lover, not a disabled banker, a disabled teacher, or a disabled heartbroken lover. Yet this latter position rings hollow because disability is such a central part of who Richard is as a character and Hunter's portrayal of him.

In contrast, reviews of Peter Dinklage's 2004 performance as Richard at the Public Theater in New York were all about his disability: his casting saved an otherwise flat production.[151] Born with achondroplasia, a form of dwarfism, Dinklage stands 4 feet 5 inches tall. Like Shakespeare's Richard, Dinklage's disability is congenital, in contrast to Potměšil's and Hunter's disabilities acquired later in life. Dinklage channeled the experience of growing up in a world not built for him, as he said to Charles McNulty: "With me being a dwarf, the difference is already there. There's no need to play up the deformity. I can experience it from the inside."[152] Dinklage explained to director Peter DuBois that society's impulse not to stare at people with disabilities—to turn away, to pretend one doesn't see them—allows someone like Richard III to get away with things when people aren't looking. As *New York Times* theater critic Ben Brantley pointed out, Dinklage's body brought new meaning to Shakespeare's play in unexpected moments, such as Richard climbing the throne upon his ascension: "For this Richard, physically placing himself in the seat of power requires strenuous and gymnastic exertions, made more difficult by the oversize royal cape that enfolds and thwarts him."[153] Here, Richard's principle opposition in life comes not from his body, nor from the stigmatizing venom other characters hurl at him, but—in keeping with the social model of disability—from a social environment designed for able-bodied people. That social model of disability was publicized, as it were, through Dinklage's celebrity. Well-known for his leading role in *The Station Agent* (2003), Dinklage was the most famous disabled actor in the world at the time and, as Allison Hobgood has remarked—contrasting the invisibility of Richard as described by Dinklage with the prominence of the actor himself—Dinklage's performance "forced audiences to grapple with their own contemporary relationship to disability and, moreover, to the visibility—or lack thereof—of disabled persons in modern, Western culture."[154]

The invisibility of people with disabilities in everyday life was also a central concern for Henry Holden, who played Richard III in 2005 at the Spoon Theatre in New York.[155] Disabled by polio in 1952, Holden had an artificial left leg and used arm crutches, invoking the image of Antony Sher. The Spoon Theatre is the first fully inclusive theater in New York, and artistic director Stephanie Barton-Farcas sought out Holden because she saw Richard as "just a normal guy who has had enough," thinking that he could be "any disabled member of our society even today."¹⁵⁶ Holden's Richard was an exhausted employee in the workplace who grows increasingly frustrated with day-to-day discrimination. As Holden noted in a 2013 op-ed for the *New York Times*, describing challenges he faced in careers ranging from teaching to sales to acting, "The unemployment rate for Americans with disabilities is 75 percent higher than for those with no disabilities."¹⁵⁷ Just as gender overshadowed Hunter's disability, however, Holden's had to compete with another unconventional aspect of the production. With results that were uninspiring to many reviewers, Richard's lines were split between two actors: Holden delivered the asides and soliloquies, while Richard's interactions with other characters were ventriloquized by another actor (Andrew Hutchinson) from a lectern at the back of the stage as Holden pantomimed. Reviewers read this directorial choice as an underwhelming attempt to emphasize the difference between the public and private Richards, but it was actually an accommodation designed for Holden, as Barton-Farcas would discuss years later in her book *Disability and Theatre: A Practical Manual for Inclusion in the Arts* (2017):

> About halfway through the rehearsal process I was let in on a problem that was happening. Henry couldn't memorize some of his lines. . . . I set forth to figure this out as he had starred in many other things in the past and didn't seem to have issues with lines. After watching rehearsals and talking with him I realized he was having what I termed a "physical disconnect." If he stood still (as Richard does when he "monologues" to the audience and lets them in on his plans) he remembered all his lines. However, if he started moving around the stage in complicated scenes his body demanded his attention and his brain lost his lines. This is a three-act play with a lot of dialogue and about half (the monologues to the audience) he had memorized, but no matter what we worked on, the minute he moved he lost the lines.¹⁵⁸

Holden's Richard captures the challenge of the "reasonable accommodations" instituted by the Americans with Disabilities Act: Barton-Farcas's accommodation for Holden was entirely reasonable, even inspired, but the results were uninspiring to outside observers not aware of a disability accommodation being made. There's a tension between a purely performance-based view of labor and efforts to provide disability accommodation in the workplace.

There's also a tension between wanting to preserve the privacy and dignity of a disabled worker and wanting to acknowledge the presence of disability accommodation. Those critiquing Barton-Farcas's production would have probably felt awful if they had learned of the accommodation. Insider knowledge that an accommodation is in place recalibrates a purely performance-based assessment of a worker's productivity and merits.

Holden's crutches were swapped for Rene Moreno's wheelchair in a 2008 *Richard III* directed by Ian Leson at the Kitchen Dog Theatre in Dallas, Texas.[159] Using a wheelchair since an accident in 1991, Moreno became a successful actor and director in the Dallas theater scene, with most of his projects having nothing to do with disability. After his accident, Moreno longed to play Richard III, though Leson didn't know that and fretted about offering Moreno the role for fear of offending the actor. Leson's vision for Richard was not of a villain taking revenge on a society that had mistreated him but of a disabled man weighed down by monotony: "He seemed bored. I'm bored therefore I'll do this. And I think there's a lot to Rene bringing to the table every day what he deals with as a man in a wheelchair and what that must do over time. And I think there's a point where Richard says, enough is enough."[160] Moreno's only requirement for the role was that the set be ADA-compliant, except for a small staircase that Moreno couldn't climb, meant to indicate Richard's sense of exclusion. Like Dinklage, Moreno brought the frustration of moving through a world that wasn't built for people with disabilities. As a professional actor, Moreno's frustrations came largely from navigating an ableist theater industry: "One particular time I lost it and went off," Moreno said about a tense exchange with fellow actors during rehearsal. "I realized that I was trying very passionately to explain to them what sometimes my life is like moving in the world in the chair—and I realized that's exactly what's going on with Richard." Like Holden, Moreno's performance was informed—in his portrayal of the character and in press coverage of the production—by his experience working in an industry often unwelcoming to people with disabilities.

Stephen Madigan performed Richard, also in a wheelchair, in an amateur 2015 production directed by Sally Wood at the Portland Stage Company in Maine.[161] Madigan had used a wheelchair since being disabled by an auto accident early in life. Unlike the other Richards I have discussed, Madigan was not a professional actor. After his accident, he went to medical school and became a successful radiologist. In interviews about the production, Madigan eagerly thematized the "overcoming adversity" story of his life.[162] He first wanted to play Richard III after reading about the discovery of Richard's skeleton. The play presented a challenge that Madigan wanted to take on to demonstrate to himself and others that he was perfectly capable of doing things usually thought to be prohibited from disabled people. He wanted to inspire people with disadvantages to achieve success. Perhaps he did not produce earth-shattering theater, but it was life-affirming for him and many in his audience. What's most remarkable about Madigan's performance is that it has almost nothing to do with the story of Richard and almost everything to do with the story of Madigan. Attention was thrown from disabled character to disabled actor.

The tone was not triumphant but indignant in a 2016 *Richard III* in Winnipeg, advertised as "a disability revenge play."[163] It starred Debbie Patterson, diagnosed with multiple sclerosis in 1999. Using a pair of canes, she walked with a limp and had a weak left hand. Like Dinklage and Moreno, she drew upon her experience as a disabled person in the theater industry. She often felt excluded, Patterson told the *Winnipeg Free Press*, critiquing able-bodied actors "cripping up," drawing an analogy to blackface.[164] Not only have disabled actors been barred from roles even though there are many disabled characters, Patterson pointed out, but disabled actors can play any role, not just disabled characters. She only came to the role of Richard III by doing one of his soliloquies during an audition for a nondisabled character in *Antony and Cleopatra*. Her Richard was not sinister but "justifiably resentful."[165] It wasn't the slander and hostility that Richard receives from his social enemies that motivated his resentment. Instead, it was the more mundane frustration that comes from having to navigate an ableist world.

Years before playing Richard, Michael Patrick Thornton had a spinal stroke that left him paralyzed from the neck down. He could use a walker but preferred a wheelchair, which is how Thornton's Richard appeared on stage in a 2016 production at the Steppenwolf Theatre in Chicago, Illinois.[166] In the scene of Anne's wooing, Richard trapped Anne in his walker, symbolizing his willingness to use disability to gain leverage over his enemies. Then, in the scene of his coronation, Richard employed a ReWalk exoskeleton procured from a partnership with the Rehabilitation Institute of Chicago—a robotic suit allowing Richard to stand and walk—physical ability representing Richard coming into power.[167] Thornton drew inspiration for his juxtaposition of disability and power from his own career. Like Richard, he was an actor who achieved some level of success, power, and notoriety (a beloved member of the Chicago theater scene, Thornton had a successful career as an actor playing roles usually unrelated to disability). Like Holden, Moreno, and Patterson, Thornton used his experience of clawing for success in an entertainment industry that often overlooks people with disabilities as a model for Richard's pursuit of power. Even for disabled actors emphasizing their ability to tell the story of Richard III in a new way, their performances ultimately point to the situation of the disabled actor at the start of the twenty-first century more than Shakespeare's fifteenth-century king. The dramatic mode is more representational than presentational, drawing attention to how the play is being staged rather than the story being told. Even if a production of *Richard III* with a disabled actor does not emphasize the actor's identity, that issue becomes central by virtue of its departure from four centuries of performance.

Big-budget productions, such as *The Hollow Crown* (2016) on the BBC, featuring Benedict Cumberbatch as Richard III, have continued casting well-known able-bodied actors for the role.[168] In Sonya Freeman Loftis's reading, "*The Hollow Crown*, instead of undermining or avoiding disability stereotypes, leans into them with a campy and self-aware directness."[169] After being informed by the University of Leicester that he was Richard's third cousin sixteen times removed, Cumberbatch read Carol Ann Duffy's poem "Richard" at the reburial service in Leicester Cathedral in 2015.[170] Capturing history's constant reinvention of Richard, Duffy wrote that he was "lost long, forever found."[171]

The discovery of Richard's skeleton led Australian actor Kate Mulvany to play the role for the Bell Shakespeare Company in 2017.[172] "I saw his skeleton on TV and it was like looking at an X-ray of my own spine," Mulvany said, referring to cancer treatments she underwent in childhood. "I have the same condition as Richard, severe scoliosis. I know exactly the kind of pain he suffered."[173] Publicity featured images of Mulvany's spine and emphasized that she could be herself on stage for the first time ever:

> For my entire life, I've been told "You must present this way. If you can, try to lift that shoulder and even though it feels strange, drop that hip, keep your back straight, as straight as you can. Wear certain clothes to disguise this." . . . But with Richard, I get to follow my own curve. My spine kicks off to the left in a certain way, I rest my hand on my hip in a certain way when I'm just at home in my pyjamas, and basically what I'm doing is just taking those idiosyncrasies of myself and presenting them to an audience who are used to seeing a much straighter actor—they're going to get closer to the real me.[174]

Mulvany's Richard snickered naughtily with audiences when Queen Margaret listed out his villainies. When Margaret slandered Richard's body, however, he was crushed. Also the dramaturg for the production, Mulvany changed one word: "Behold, my *body* is like a blasted sapling," a line she delivered with her back naked to the audience. Many reviewers found Mulvany's performance refreshingly human, but Caitlin Mary West warned of "the potentially problematic consequences of following implied stage directions": adding a degree of realism by putting an actor with the body of the historical Richard in Shakespeare's obviously embellished play could have the unintended effect of legitimating Shakespeare's stereotypes of disability.[175]

All these issues culminated in Mat Fraser's *Richard III* at the Hull Truck Theatre in 2017.[176] After his mother was prescribed the morning-sickness drug Thalidomide during pregnancy, Fraser was born with phocomelia, a condition in which the hands are attached close to the shoulders. Like several other Richards discussed, Fraser has had a long and eclectic career. He was a drummer with several punk bands between 1980 and 1995. He wrote and starred in *Thalidomide! A Musical* in 2005. Beginning in 2001, he performed in retro Coney Island freak shows, studying the history of disability in theater from the nineteenth century to now. He played drums with the band Coldplay at the closing ceremonies of the 2012 Paralympics in London. Given his success, Fraser saw himself as an ambassador for disabled actors, and press coverage of his *Richard III* was filled with his calculated anger over the lack of disabled actors in mainstream media: "Every single theatre in Britain should be able to answer yes to the question: Have you employed one disabled actor in the last year? If the answer to that question is no, then the theatre should hang its head in shame and know that it is a relic of the past."[177] From this angle, the most inspired casting in *Richard III* at Hull wasn't Fraser as Richard; it was Dean Whatton, an actor with dwarfism who doubled as one of the young princes and one of Richard's murderers—roles that don't call for disability. "Disabled people are where black people were in the '80s," Fraser said in an interview. "They can't be baddies. People [in the TV industry] are too politically correct. But they're not ready to give us the hero role yet. So we get no role."[178] Fraser even wrote an opinion piece for *The Stage* calling out the "cliches of impairment—sticks, straps, eye patches, humps, leg braces etc." being used by another able-bodied actor playing Richard III at the same time at the Arcola Theatre in London, calling it backward to have nondisabled actors playing disabled characters.[179]

Drawing upon his background in Coney Island vaudevillian shows, Fraser brought an erotic edge to his performance as Richard. He found the unmitigated stigma of a less enlightened age oddly refreshing in our time when disability representations are done with the utmost sensitivity. Fraser thought Richard almost certainly had issues with body hatred: he is bitterly aware he will never fit in. Drawing from his own experience to play Richard, Fraser told Alfred Hickling of the *Guardian* that disabled people often must adopt a "by-any-means-necessary attitude towards life."[180] Since the normal rules of social advancement aren't available to him, Fraser said, he's learned to improvise, like Richard.

In these performances, the specifics of Richard's "deformity" have fallen away: the hunchback, crooked spine, withered arm, unequal legs, and teeth at birth in Shakespeare's text are transformed into any number of impairments, ranging from paralysis acquired in an accident to congenital phocomelia. Emphasis is on disability, stigma, and inaccessibility rather than "deformity." Thanks to the breadth of disability as an identity, many different actors with many different disabilities are able to play the same character.

These examples also allow us to see how Sandahl's two models of disability theater, the aesthetic model and the political model, surface in Shakespearean performance. These models are not mutually exclusive, but, in the productions I have examined, one or the other tends to emerge as dominant. In the case of *Richard III*, when the motive for casting a disabled actor as a disabled character is aesthetic, the idea is usually associated with a director who (1) comes from Shakespeare World and (2) is not disabled. Hoping that a disabled actor can draw upon their personal experience to perform a disabled character authentically, the director primarily emphasizes the character's identity and story. All energy and movement is toward the text: *How can we best tell this story?* With disabled Richards, this attention to accurate character portrayal appeared most clearly in earlier productions, with Hunter in 2003 and Dinklage in 2004. Note that these were big, well-financed productions in major cities, London and New York. The aesthetic model offers upper-class disability theater moving from Shakespeare to disability: the goal remains the best possible performance of Shakespeare's text. Thus, when the Royal Shakespeare Company cast Arthur Hughes in 2022, the headline in the *Guardian* was "'There's a Truth to It': RSC Casts Disabled Actor as Richard III."[181]

In contrast, the political model of disability theater is middle class, associated with smaller, less moneyed productions in remote locales: the second wave of disabled Richards—Holden, Moreno, Madigan, Paterson, Thornton, and Fraser—was largely staged in provincial places, such as Dallas, Chicago, and Hull. The energy and movement of the performance flows away from the text and toward society: the point is not to tell Shakespeare's story, *per se*, but to shine a light on issues of disability in the twenty-first century, most especially the lack of disabled actors in the theater industry. Where the aesthetic model focuses on accurate character portraits, the political model attends to fair employment practices. The emphasis shifts from the identity and story of the character to the identity and story of the actor. The political model arises from Disability World: the effort to have a disabled actor play a disabled character is mounted by someone, whether an actor or a director, who is themself disabled. The movement in the political model is from disability to Shakespeare: the goal remains the promotion of awareness about disability issues. Shakespeare is the means to that end. Thus, when HamletScenen's *Richard III* at Kronborg Castle in 2019 cast able-bodied actor Casper Crump as Richard, with disabled actors in other roles, director Lars Romann Engel consulted closely with disability organizations, such as the Graeae Theatre Company in London, Enactlab in Copenhagen, and the Danish Association for Disabled People. For dramaturg Nila Parly, "The fundamental premise of this production was to establish an inclusive theatre practice which would work with disabled actors and make itself accessible to disabled audiences, actively seeking diverse representation on the stage and in the audience."[182]

If those models address the deliberate motives behind cripping Richard, there are also larger social forces in play. A study of theatrical cripping can illuminate more general efforts to reclaim historically stigmatized identities in dramatic representation and public discourse at large. It is not true that theatrical producers and audiences are demanding identity-accurate casting. The rise of color-blind casting in recent years shows that producers and audiences are willing to suspend disbelief, use their imaginations, and recognize that a Black actor need not signify a Black character. Casting is not becoming more exactly mimetic; it is becoming more explicitly inclusive. This inclusivity manifests in seemingly opposed ways: in the case of color-blind casting, there is a separation between the identity of the actor and the identity of the character, whereas the casting of disabled actors for Richard III involves a union of actor's and character's identities.

Resistance to White actors using blackface is well known, but controversies involving the identity of actors playing stigmatized characters has recently extended from race to other facets. "Are Straight Actors in Gay Roles the New Blackface?" asked one 2013 headline in *Salon*.[183] "We Wouldn't Accept Actors Blacking Up, So Why Applaud 'Cripping Up'?" asked a 2015 article in the *Guardian*.[184] "Is It Ever OK to Cast a Cisgender Actor in a Transgender Role?" asked a 2016 headline in *Slate*.[185] The basis of these controversies is not that actors are constitutionally incapable of accurately portraying stigmatized characters in performance. Actors pretend: that's what they do. The critique is that casting so-called "normals" as stigmatized characters takes roles away from actors who hold those identities and therefore face discrimination in the workplace (in this case, the theater and film industries). The examples mentioned here—the decline of blackface (in waves) in the wake of the Emancipation Proclamation of 1863 and the Civil Rights Act of 1964, the rise of disability theater in the wake of the Americans with Disabilities Act of 1990 and the Disability Discrimination Act of 1995, and the controversies about gayface and transface that have arisen in the wake of the Matthew Shepard Act of 2009—suggest that nondiscrimination legislation creates a cultural awareness of the possibility of structural bias in the workplace, which manifests in the theater world in attention on the relationship between an actor's and a character's identities.

"Though [Mat Fraser's Richard III] made headlines, it does not yet appear to have become the norm as other examples of iconic casting have done," Roberta Barker notes. "The established cultural image of the character, rather than the individual body of the actor, appears to be the final arbiter of iconicity."[186] Indeed, the political motives behind the cripping of *Richard III* are most fully present not in performances of Shakespeare's play but in adaptations, which then activate the aesthetic motives for cripping Richard by infusing a "nothing about us without us" disability sensibility into the artwork from its inception. Starting with its un-Google-able title, Mike Lew's *Teenage Dick* is rebellious and relentlessly hilarious, with moments of vulnerability that sneak up on you, capturing Shakespeare's mixture of comedy, villainy, and tragedy. In 2012, Gregg Mozgala—founder and artistic director of the Apothetae, a New York theater company exploring the disabled experience—commissioned Lew to write an adaptation of *Richard III* set in an American high school. A proponent of Asian American theater, the able-bodied Lew saw parallels between barriers to disability in the theater world and racist exclusions he had experienced himself. A note at the start of the play doesn't mince words: "Cast disabled actors for Richard and Buck. They exist and they are out there. Also cast diverse actors."[187] Lee's Richard Gloucester has cerebral palsy and is "not one who is shaped for sports" (3), in contrast to the quarterback class president, Eddie. Damaged by years of disability discrimination, and a student of Machiavelli, Richard recruits his sardonic friend Buck, who uses a wheelchair, to help him slash through the ranks of the student council. Another of Richard's allies, the teacher Elizabeth York, whose brother had Down's syndrome, invites questions about disability accommodation and allyship:

CLARISSA How come Richard gets to show up late but when I'm late you read me the riot act?
ELIZABETH Richard is different.
EDDIE Differently abled? As in retarded?
ELIZABETH Eddie don't use that word. What I mean is that Richard is . . . well look at him Clarissa, he's got totally differing needs.
CLARISSA Buck has differing needs.
BUCK Please don't involve me. (6)

Hostilities from able-bodied people traumatize Lew's Richard, like Shakespeare's, but Lew explores social facets of the twenty-first-century disability experience that Shakespeare's play simply can't touch—the pity, the patronizing acts of charity, suspicion that all achievements are really just affirmative action, disability in-group solidarity, the particularities of different disabilities that challenge that solidarity, connection and mutual understanding between disabled and nondisabled people, hate crimes against people with disabilities, and love and hate within and beyond the disability community. Exploring how disability relates to teen culture, sports culture, Internet culture, and liberal culture, Lew Americanizes Shakespeare's portrait of a disabled man with a looking-glass self-image; an internalized ableism; a suspicion of others' motives; and the self-doubt, the thrills, and fears of flirting, romance, and love. The moral center of the play is Buck, who just wants to mind her own business and live her own life, although she is not present in the conclusion, having been pushed away by a Richard who, like Shakespeare's character, turns to vengeful violence. I'll admit that Lew's ending does not sit well with me. I suppose that's the point. Richard runs over Eddie with a car, "severing his spinal cord between the L1 and L2 vertebrae, never to walk again" (60). Richard survives the play, unlike Shakespeare's version, but in presenting disability as the ultimate punishment ("Now who's the cripple?" [60]), *Teenage Dick* presents disability as tragedy without much hope for social progress. I can't help but long for an adaptation of *Richard III* in which, instead of becoming a violent criminal, the protagonist organizes an intersectional community that passes unprecedented disability-rights legislation—and absolutely crushes the careers of any retrograde politicians who try to stop him.

A fitting text to end with is *richard III redux* (2018), written by Kaite O'Reilly and Phillip Zarrilli and first performed by Sara Beer, "a one woman show about Richard III from a disability perspective, performed by someone with the same physicality as the historical Richard."[188] O'Reilly's political motives are strategic, precise, and explicit: "As a counter to the tradition of 'cripping up' in Shakespeare's *Richard III*, we offer the rights to this text solely to the atypical performer: those who identify as disabled" (78). In a series of vignettes, the play scrolls through the history of Richard's bodies—from the rediscovered skeleton to Garrick and Hogarth, from Olivier to Sher and McKellen, from Spacey to Cumberbatch and Eidinger—interspersed with scenes juxtaposing a "National Treasure" preparing to play Richard with a disabled actor's approach to the role: "A body like mine can't play a body like mine. / A body like this can't play Richard" (129). There is a clear contrast between the big National Treasure actors who crip up for a wide audience and the smaller local theaters that pursue disability visibility. Ultimately, *richard iii redux* reveals the inseparability of the political and aesthetic motives of cripping and the priority of the political: casting people with disabilities is necessary for an accurate dramatic representation of the disability experience. In many ways, *richard iii redux* is the culmination of the cultural history of Richard's body: it is scholarly and artistic, historicist and presentist, a commitment to fair hiring practices for people with disabilities in the workplace and an exploration of the disability experience, rigorously researched and deeply personal, by and for the disability community, irreverent, feminist, showing that any interaction with *Richard III* is mediated by a history of changing bodies over time, and concluding with a request for interpretation from the audience: "'To be . . . or not to be,' Richard . . . that is my question" (82).

Conclusion

The Anthropology of Audience

Historical Presentism in
Shakespeare Studies

In 2004, Stephen Greenblatt's biography showed, as the subtitle said, "how Shakespeare became Shakespeare."[1] In 2007, Jack Lynch's reception history explained, as the introduction said, "how Shakespeare became Shakespeare."[2] If Shakespeare became Shakespeare in Greenblatt's biography, how could he become Shakespeare in Lynch's reception history? Both claim an origin story; clearly, "Shakespeare" invokes both man and myth. The story of Shakespearean becoming involves the life and times of the author as manifested in his text as well as the text as interpreted by audiences across time and space.

How to remember Shakespeare? As the person beneath the humble, flat gravestone in Holy Trinity Church at Stratford-upon-Avon? That calls for historicist scholarship of Shakespeare's life and times. Or as the writer memorialized by the lofty monument watching over Poet's Corner in Westminster Abbey? That calls for philosophical criticism of his insights on human nature. Should we heed the words he wrote for his gravestone—"cvrst be he y^t moves my bones"—and keep him contextualized in Elizabethan and Jacobean England, a scholarly mandate issued first by the new historicists and now by the "new materialists"? Or follow Ben Jonson's maxim that he is "for all time" and reanimate Shakespeare in the idiom of our own day, a time-honored theatrical tradition increasingly popular in scholarship, dubbed "presentism"?

In concert with these questions, Shakespeare studies exploded in the late 1980s with interest in his reception during the centuries between then and now. After Jan Kott's *Shakespeare Our Contemporary* (1964) knocked the field off its axis, reception studies such as Samuel Schoenbaum's *Shakespeare's Lives* (1970), Terence Hawkes's *That Shakespeherian Rag* (1986), Graham Holderness's *The Shakespeare Myth* (1988), and Gary Taylor's *Reinventing Shakespeare* (1989) grew into concerns with *The Appropriation of Shakespeare*, the title of the 1991 collection edited by Jean Marsden.[3] This field was cemented in 2005 with the creation of a dedicated journal, *Borrowers and Lenders: A Journal of Shakespeare and Appropriation*, edited by Christy Desmet and Sujata Iyengar.[4] In 2006, Douglas Lanier dubbed this field "Shakespearean cultural studies."[5] In 2014, he theorized "Shakespearean rhizomatics," which opposes the obsession with fidelity in the "arboreal conception of adaptation" (think of Shakespeare as the tall oak tree and his modern manifestations as the branches and leaves) in favor of an analogy to rhizomatic plants (think of Shakespeare as ground thatch that subterraneously throws off buds to create new stocks that aren't physically connected to the source but remain part of the same system).[6]

I'm slightly averse to Shakespearean rhizomatics for a highly non-academic reason: Japanese knotweed. It's one of the worst invasive species in the world. I've been fighting it in my backyard for five years. In my experience, rhizomes are malicious, and the human agency involved is about containing and eliminating the invasive system. That doesn't sound much like the Shakesphere, which expands through deliberate human industry and produces much joy. That's why I'm compelled by Valerie Fazel and Louise Geddes's effort to account for the variety of Shakespearean engagement—reading, watching, enjoying, studying, adapting, appropriating, translating, and so forth—by identifying "a theoretical shift from 'reader' to 'user' currently underway."[7] Building off this work, this methodological manifesto theorizes our efforts to understand Shakespeare's presence in modernity. To be clear, I'm not advocating for a new approach but trying to describe what's been going on for the past forty years. What are we doing when unearthing the reception of Shakespeare throughout time and across the globe? Why do we care about the uses and abuses of Shakespeare? What should we do with Shakespearean texts like *Richard III* whose meanings seem to change over time?

In response to these questions, I invoke the discipline of anthropology to theorize the "anthropology of audience" that has arisen in Shakespeare studies. In the 1980s, new historicism brought anthropology to bear on Shakespeare's text and context; the anthropology of audience redirects new historicism to reception. The simplest way to describe the anthropology of audience is to say that it is the objective study of the subjective experience of art. It is the scientific study of the political use of art. Collapsing together the central tension in Shakespeare studies at the moment, the anthropology of audience does historicist readings of presentist renderings of Shakespeare. It addresses the origins, motives, commitments, development, organization, networks, and institutions of audience behavior to create a body of knowledge about interpretive difference, consensus, disagreement, negotiation, and change. As the study of artistic experience in the context of cultural engagement, the anthropology of audience marries the philosophy of phenomenology with the social science of cultural materialism for a new kind of Shakespearean reception history and cultural studies.

I. Literary Theory: Meaning and Use

There are two central questions asked in the name of literary theory: (1) *How is sense communicated in a text?* (2) *What is the function of literature in society?*

These two questions—the one of *meaning*, the other of *use*—are connected. One's theory on how sense is communicated will influence one's belief on the social role of literature; what one thinks we should do with texts shapes one's notion of how they make sense. A third (and fourth) possible question could be *How do (or should) we determine what makes literature good?* So far, for me, that always dead-ends in a "we just do." Suffice it to say, for the purposes of what follows, these are the two key questions of literary theory: (1) *What's the meaning?* (2) *What's the use?*

II. The Literary Event: Text, Author, Audience, Universe

Literary theory in the classical age emphasized affect. To what degree can an author ensure a given response from an audience, and how much agency does the audience have in the construction of sense? The Greek sophist Gorgias thought that a powerful text might exert an almost magical influence upon the actions of its audience, the theory of literary sense making Plato had in mind when banishing poetry from his ideal society.[8] Aristotle responded forcefully with a theory of literary audition, returning agency in the making of sense to the receiving end of the text, the audience.[9] Because audiences are responsible for making sense of literature (an answer to the question of *meaning*), Aristotle argued, *contra* Plato, literature plays a positive role in society (an answer to the question of *use*): it helps us think about life.

M. H. Abrams called the collection of these concerns "the total situation of a work of art," which comprises four "elements": the Work, the Artist, the Audience, and the Universe.[10] With his famous triangle, Abrams set the terms for twentieth-century debates about professional correctness in literary studies—the various answers to the question *How should we study literature?* Rather, *What should we study?* The Work, the thing itself, its form and features? The Artist, the one who made the thing, what kind of a person might create such a thing, what they are trying to accomplish (i.e., the author's intent)? The Audience, those who read the Work, how they make sense of it, the feelings and thoughts they have (i.e., the reader's experience)? Or the Universe, the situation of the thing in history, whether that's the world of the Artist (the culture conditioning the composition of the Work) or the situation of the Audience (the culture conditioning the reception of the Work)?

Four prominent models of U.S. literary studies in the second half of the twentieth century correspond with the four elements in Abrams's diagram: new criticism addressed the literary work, psychoanalytic theory the literary artist, reader-response theory the literary audience, and new historicism the literary universe. We can even imagine ourselves at Yale University in 1962, casting roles for an allegorical dramatization of Abrams's diagram. The role of the Work would go to someone who thinks that the proper concern of literary studies is the form and features of the textual object itself. At Yale in 1962, that would be the revered professor Cleanth Brooks, whose mantra was "the formalist critic is concerned primarily with the work itself."[11] For the role of the Artist, someone would have to believe that a text signifies the unconscious psychological state and the fully conscious authorial intent of its composer. Harold Bloom, an assistant professor at Yale in 1962 who would go on to argue that "a poem is always a person," would be perfect to play the Artist.[12] The Audience would have to think that a text produces a subjective response in its readers and that this response ought to be the object of literary interpretation instead of the text, *per se*. The role of the Audience would go to Stanley Fish, who filed his dissertation at Yale in 1962 before going on to argue that "there are no fixed texts, but only interpretive strategies making them."[13] Finally, the role of the Universe would go to someone believing that the proper object of literary interpretation is the relationship between a text and the culture that shapes and is shaped by it. The Universe could be played by Stephen Greenblatt, in the sophomore year of his undergraduate career at Yale in 1962, long before he would write that "there can be no art without social energy."[14]

III. The Rise of Audience-Oriented Criticism and Theory

While Bloom, Fish, and Greenblatt developed their literary theories organically out of criticism on canonical English authors (primarily Shakespeare and Milton), those theories quickly came into contact with the wave of European philosophy that hit the United States in the 1960s and 1970s. Drawing upon an "anti-foundationalism" in the tradition of phenomenology (the philosophy of how the world *appears* to us in contrast to how the world actually *is*, the latter being metaphysics or ontology), this European philosophy argued, in part, that all knowledge is necessarily and unavoidably filtered through—conditioned or constructed by—one's subjective situation in the world.[15] In 1967, Roland Barthes declared "the death of the author": the relative insignificance of authorial intent in light of cultural influences on a work of art and, in any event, the inaccessibility of authorial intent via the artwork.[16] Intent came to be understood as a construction of the audience's experience, as articulated in Michel Foucault's notion of an "author-function" in his 1969 essay, "What Is an Author?"[17] The implication was that the audience needed to become more central to (if not the exclusive concern of) literary studies. Previously diminished as "subjective experience" and the "affective fallacy" in a discourse seeking "objective truth," the reader was recuperated in the 1960s and 1970s in concert with the mounting sentiment that truth is actually subjective.[18] In the hands of Fish and others, literary criticism and theory started attending to "reader response" (how readers make sense of texts[19]) and "interpretive communities" (groups of like-minded readers who make sense of texts in similar ways[20]).

In Shakespeare studies, the rise of the audience led American critic Stephen Booth to complain in 1969 that critics "would rather talk about what a work says or shows (both of which suggest the hidden essence bared of the dross of physicality) than talk about what it does." Booth's reading of *Hamlet* argues that "it is reasonable to talk about what the play does do and to test the suggestion that in a valued play what it does do is what we value."[21] Booth's essay appeared in a collection edited by Norman Rabkin, who situated the book amid reader-response criticism, and who himself argued in a 1981 reading of *The Merchant of Venice* that "a thesis about what the play means denies to Shakespeare's intention or the play's virtue what the comedy actually *does* to us."[22] Writing in 1992, the British critic Terence Hawkes similarly argued that "the point of Shakespeare and his plays lies in their capacity to serve as instruments by which we make cultural meanings for ourselves. . . . They don't, in themselves, 'mean.' It is *we* who mean *by* them."[23] This audience-oriented criticism and theory even started drawing from the social science of anthropology. If there were "communities" of readers, they could be studied as we study actual communities of humans (i.e., societies, cultures, and sub-cultures). The German critic Wolfgang Iser's book *Prospecting: From Reader Response to Literary Anthropology* (1993) reprinted his 1983 reader's-response interpretation of *As You Like It*, which suggests that we can learn about how humans function—an anthropological concern—by studying how we make sense and make use of literature.[24]

As Iser was theorizing this "literary anthropology," American critic Steven Mailloux was taking audience-oriented literary theory in a different direction. Like Hans Robert Jauss's 1967 essay "Literary History as a Challenge to Literary Theory," Mailloux's 1985 essay "Rhetorical Hermeneutics" called for reader-oriented critics to "provide histories of how particular theoretical and critical discourses have evolved" (the activity I'm currently doing):

> Why? Because acts of persuasion always take place against an ever-changing background of shared and disputed assumptions, questions, assertions, and so forth. Any full rhetorical analysis of interpretation must therefore describe this tradition of discursive practices in which acts of interpretive persuasion are embedded. Thus rhetorical hermeneutics leads inevitably to rhetorical histories.[25]

If it's true that meaning is made, not discovered, then we need—if we're going to lay claim to the meaning of a text—reception histories of the various ways meaning has been made of literary texts. If truth is subjective and perspectival—and I, constrained as I am by my situation in the world, can therefore make no claim to have discovered the absolute meaning of a text—then we need interpretations of the interpretations of the text, especially as they pertain to the specific historical contexts in which those interpretations take place. In his book *Reception Histories* (1998), Mailloux extended the audience-oriented language and logic of reader response, interpretive communities, rhetorical hermeneutics, and reception histories to cultural studies, and specifically to a "rhetorically oriented cultural studies" that "describes and explains past and present configurations of rhetorical practices as they affect each other and as they extend and manipulate the social practices, political structures, and material circumstances in which they are embedded at particular historical moments."[26] By the time he wrote *Disciplinary Identities*

(2006), Mailloux was able to say, forcefully, that "the only hermeneutic theory passing rhetorical muster in the present antifoundationalist moment involves persuasive descriptions of historical acts of interpretation."[27]

IV. The Meaning of the Use

What's surprising about the origins of Shakespearean cultural studies is its utter independence from the theoretical basis of the practice. After Booth and Rabkin brought Fish's reader-response theory into Shakespeare studies, the next logical steps would have been to import Fish's theory of interpretive communities, Mailloux's method of reception histories, Iser's ideas about literary anthropology, and the field of cultural studies as theorized by the likes of Stuart Hall.[28] Those ideas were in the air in the late 1980s, but they weren't cited in the earliest books establishing Shakespearean reception histories and cultural studies as a distinct field: Arthur Sherbo's *The Birth of Shakespeare Studies* (1986), Terence Hawkes's *That Shakespeherian Rag* (1986), Graham Holderness's *The Shakespeare Myth* (1988), Lawrence Levine's *Highbrow/Lowbrow* (1988), Gary Taylor's *Reinventing Shakespeare* (1989), Jonathan Bate's *Shakespearean Constitutions* (1989), Péter Dávidházi's *The Romantic Cult of Shakespeare* (1989), Margreta de Grazia's *Shakespeare Verbatim* (1991), Hugh Grady's *The Modernist Shakespeare* (1991), Jean Marsden's *The Appropriation of Shakespeare* (1991), and Michael Dobson's *The Making of the National Poet* (1992). To my knowledge, the first Shakespearean reception history to invoke cultural studies explicitly is Peter Stallybrass's "Shakespeare, the Individual, and the Text," published in the collection *Cultural Studies* in 1992.[29] The field has ballooned since the 1990s—hundreds of books, thousands of articles, *Borrowers and Lenders*—but Shakespearean reception histories and cultural studies have rarely been situated among the audience-oriented literary theory and criticism that reached its zenith in the 1970s and then evolved into theories of interpretive communities and such fields as cultural studies. Thus, the anthropology of audience brings together two discourses that belong to the same "interpretive community" yet have never met: the Shakespearean cultural studies epitomized by *Borrowers and Lenders* and the audience-oriented literary theories of Fish, Iser, and Mailloux.

Where Iser pursued a "literary anthropology" attempting to understand the human experience by examining how we read literature, an anthropology of audience aims to understand the literary experience by examining its historical manifestations. Like other audience-oriented literary criticism and theory—reader response, interpretive communities, reception history, cultural studies—the anthropology of audience exhibits a phenomenological as opposed to metaphysical approach to meaning: it is concerned not with what the meaning *is* but with what it *appears* to be. What it appears to be *is* what it is. Like anthropology itself, however, the anthropology of audience is ultimately more scientific than philosophical. It looks to give a descriptive rather than prescriptive answer to the question *What's the use?* It seeks not a normative answer to the ethical question *How should we read Shakespeare?* but a positive answer to the historical question *What do we do with Shakespeare?* Describing why audiences think what they think and do what they do requires a narrative of how the objective realities of a text come into contact with the objective realities of an audience's culture to produce a subjective interpretive experience. The anthropology of audience asks *What's the meaning of the use of literature?*

V. The Return of Culture-Oriented Criticism and Theory: Historicisms and Presentisms

The rise and consolidation of science in the early twentieth century brought about attempts to create a scientific study of literature, commonly called "formalism," seeking to study the literary artwork objectively, as well as a scientific study of history, what we now think of as "old historicism," seeking to study history objectively.[30] The science of literature and the science of history were both upended in the third quarter of the twentieth century by one of the central insights of poststructuralism: the situatedness of everything. On the one hand, it became difficult to deliver an objective science of either literature or history due to our situatedness as analysts. On the other hand, the meaning of the things we sought to describe was to be found in their situatedness in culture and history.

In Shakespeare studies in the 1980s, the situatedness of everything led to a renewed interest in the universe—culture—as an element in the literary event, but this interest surfaced in different ways. In the United Kingdom, the cultural materialism practiced by Jonathan Dollimore and Alan Sinfield emphasized the situatedness of the literary audience, and specifically the political currents at the time of the critic who could potentially sway them with a politicized form of literary criticism inspired by the "dialectical materialism" of Marx.[31] Culture-oriented Shakespeare studies in the United States were less activist.[32] As theorized by Greenblatt and others, "cultural poetics," also called "new historicism," emphasized the situatedness of the literary author, drawing upon the field of anthropology to give "thick descriptions" of how the author was influenced by, and influenced, the social conditions of their time and place.[33] Both of these culture-oriented approaches to criticism and theory—British cultural materialism and American new historicism—were *decentering* in that they (1) examined in detail marginal texts often left out of big-picture histories of canonical authors and (2) called into question the central concern of history—specifically, the historian's ability to step outside the present to accurately depict the past. Thus, coining the term *new historicism*, Greenblatt wrote that "the new historicism erodes the firm ground of both criticism and literature": both the literary critic and the literary author are situated in culture.[34]

With the end of the age of high theory in Anglophone literary criticism, roughly around the turn of the twenty-first century, new historicism in the United States ossified into a movement called "new materialism," while cultural materialism in the United Kingdom evolved into one dubbed "presentism."[35] First, inaugurating new materialism, David Scott Kastan argued in *Shakespeare after Theory* (1999) that "theory has now brought us to the point where we must begin to respond to its significant challenges, not by producing more theory but more facts, however value-laden they will necessarily be."[36] This new materialism was not—indeed, was sharply opposed to—the politicized cultural materialism of British Shakespeare scholars. In his quest for historical particulars uninhibited by a political polemic, Kastan wryly called his version of materialism "the new boredom" (18).

Turning to presentism, the most vocal advocate was Hawkes, who simultaneously recuperated the term *presentism* (previously a pejorative for anachronistic historical analysis) and distinguished it from new historicism in his book *Shakespeare in the Present* (2002):

> Paying the present that degree of respect might more profitably be judged, not as a "mistake," egregious and insouciant, blandly imposing a tritely modern perspective on whatever texts confront it, but rather as the basis of a critical stance whose engagement with the text is of a particular character. A Shakespeare criticism that takes that on board will not yearn to speak with the dead. It will aim, in the end, to talk to the living.[37]

The line about "speak[ing] with the dead" is a rebuke of Greenblatt's well-known new historicist desire to "speak with the dead."[38] But Hawkes later realized that he also needed to confront new materialism in a revised version of the same "Introduction" for *Presentist Shakespeares* (2007), now saying, less aggressively, that he "will not *only* yearn to speak with the dead" (emphasis mine):

> Maybe a resolute insistence on the concrete, on objects and their material production and use in daily life, carries with it its own anti-traditional, anti-idealistic values. But if this materialism is "new," it is so precisely because of its indifference to any engagement with the politics and way of life of our own day on which an older materialism insisted.[39]

Like the new historicism and cultural materialism that spawned them, these newer forms of materialism and presentism were about the universe in which a literary text exists, but historicism in all its forms is about the author's universe, while presentism is about the audience's universe.

In brief, new materialism is a discourse of truth: it is nostalgic for objectivity. It is about the *meaning* of literature. Presentism is purposefully subjective: it is a discourse of virtue. It is about the *use* of literature. At their core, what the historicist and the presentist are really saying is *I want to be scientific* versus *I want to be political*. Marrying these concerns, the anthropology of audience is the scientific study of the political use of literature.

VI. Historical Presentism

What's the meaning? Historicism locates it in the relationship between the work and the universe of the author. *What's the use?* Presentism locates it in the relationship between the work and the universe of the audience. These approaches can combine into a historical presentism that uses Shakespeare to do history, not to mention sociology, anthropology, and cultural studies. The massive phenomenon Bryan Reynolds terms "Shakespace"—"the territory within discourses, adaptations, and uses of Shakespeare"[40]—offers a unique opportunity to do historicist readings of presentist renderings of Shakespeare. Like other forms of presentism, historical presentism attends to the use of literature. Like other forms of historicism, historical presentism is concerned with the past—with past presentisms—focusing on objective reality and aiming for objectivity. A historical presentism is the objective study of the subjective experience of art, uncovering not only how *I* interpret as an individual but also how *we* interpret as humans and how *they* interpret as cultures.

There's a pretty obvious reason Shakespeare studies never needed the theories of reader response, interpretive communities, reception histories, and cultural studies. Shakespearean reception histories and cultural studies grew not out of a movement affiliated with a surge in twentieth-century European philosophy but, instead, organically out of the facts that (1) Shakespeare wrote drama, so his plays have been repeatedly performed as the centuries have passed, resulting in a text with a wayward temporality; (2) Shakespeare was canonized in the early nineteenth century as the greatest English writer of all time and grew to be regarded as the best in the West in the twentieth century and a global superstar in the twenty-first; thus (3) there is a massive cultural knowledge of Shakespeare, resulting in a constant stream of art and ideas working off and away from his texts. Even more basically, as dramatic poetry, which is poetic (literary, written, printed, permanent, material) and dramatic (theatrical, acted, live, mutable, temporal), Shakespeare's art constitutionally requires attention to the form of the work itself and the experiences of its audiences. Shakespeare studies requires a historical presentism because its object of study—Shakespeare—is both very historical (conditioned by his life, times, and works) and very present with us (in our performances, appropriations, and criticism). As Julia Lupton observes, "Drama in particular builds self-renewal over time into its very being as an art form, and thus invites thoughtful movement between the past and its manifold futures."[41] A historical presentism is not an importation of a theoretical model to Shakespeare criticism; it is the form of inquiry appropriate to the object of study. The tension between historicism and presentism in Shakespeare studies is a false choice, coaxing us to pledge allegiance to fabricated factions, obscuring the best historicism (concerned with social problems ongoing today) and the best presentism (deeply informed by the past). Shakespeare's works—as very old printed texts and plays often performed today—constitutionally call for both historicism and presentism. A historicism that doesn't presentize is as limited as a presentism that doesn't historicize. Both historicism and presentism, in isolation, are deeply un-Shakespearean in spirit. If we work up from the Shakespearean text—rather than down upon it, importing outside methodologies—every study would be historicist and presentist. Every Shakespeare scholar would be too.

VII. Literature as Second Nature

The greatest statement of literary theory from the Renaissance, Philip Sidney's *The Defense of Poesy* (1595), makes four points (among many others) that, taken together, provide the basis for an anthropological approach to literary experience.[42] First, Sidney writes that poetry "hath the more force in teaching" than either history or philosophy (91)—he is thinking here about moral education. That's an answer to the question *What's the use?* History is all particulars, no universals: it only says what has been, not what is or should be. Philosophy is all universals, no particulars: it only deals with ideas and therefore is boring. In contrast to both, Sidney thinks, poetry packages universals in particulars: the poet "coupleth the general notion with the particular example" (90). We can now envision two triangles: Abrams's triangle in which the Artwork is at the center of the Author/Audience/Universe triad and Sidney's triangle in which the Good Life is at the center of the Philosophy/History/Poetry triad.

But—and this is a big *but*—Sidney's second point is that poetry does not make truth claims. He is responding to Stephen Gosson, who, like Plato, fears poets create a false image of reality, deceiving audiences into false beliefs. Like Aristotle, Sidney denies that poets are dangerous. Poets are not liars because they don't present themselves as truth tellers: "For the Poet, he nothing affirms, and therefore never lieth" (103). Sidney is unflinching and unambiguous: poetry, he thinks, is constitutionally incapable of laying claim to truth whether—we must infer—it be historical truth concerned with the question *What happened?*; metaphysical truth responding to the question *What is real?*; or ethical truth related to the question *What is right?* Poetry affirms nothing.

That's a radical idea but, in reiterating and developing it, Sidney makes a third and even more radical suggestion. He claims that poetry creates something like a second nature:

> The Poet . . . lifted up with the vigour of his own invention, doth grow in effect into another nature, in making things either better than Nature bringeth forth, or quite anew, forms such as never were in Nature, as the Heroes, Demigods, Cyclops, Chimeras, Furies, and such like: so as he goeth hand in hand with Nature, not enclosed within the narrow warrant of her gifts, but freely ranging only within the Zodiack of his own wit. (85)

Poetry presents things that are patently not real—centaurs, monsters, ghosts, aliens, magic, what have you—but, because it does not present them as real, it is not a discourse of deception, as Plato and Gosson think. No one is so dense as to believe that such things are real just because they appear in a poem. Poetry is not an imitation of nature but the invention of a "second nature," although the second nature of literature has a practical purpose for the first nature of life. We use literature to think and talk about life. That's not a profound or controversial idea: anyone who has identified with the story told in a work of literature and gained insight from thinking or talking about their own life in the context of the situation represented in the literary work knows this to be true. Book clubs know this to be true. But Sidney draws a profound analogy—Milton Nahm calls it "the great analogy"[43]—between the poet and God, who "having made man to His own likeness, set him beyond and over all the works of that second nature" (86). Collapsing together a number of early-modern and modern, theological and scientific beliefs, the analogy runs something like this: just as God created a nature that is inhabited and experienced by humans who form together into societies that can be studied through the social science of anthropology, a discourse attending to the form and meaning of the subjective experience of objective reality, the literary author creates a "second nature" that is inhabited and experienced by readers who form together into interpretive communities that can be studied scientifically through an anthropology of audience, a method of literary criticism attending to the form and meaning of the subjective experience of literature. Just as humans live within and make sense of nature, readers live within and make sense of the second nature of poetry.

In synthesizing these ideas, Sidney lands upon his fourth and final point. Poetry offers a good opportunity for readers to develop ideas about the world:

> Though he recount things not true, yet because he telleth them not for true, he lieth not. . . . The poet's persons and doings are but pictures, what should be, and not stories what have been, they will never give the lie to things not affirmatively, but allegorically and figuratively written. And therefore, as in History looking for truth, they go away full fraught with falsehood, so in Poesy looking but for fiction, they shall use the narration but as an imaginative ground-plot of a profitable invention. (136)

Poetry does not make claims about the world; it creates an imaginative space for thinking about the world. Sidney's analogy to history is complicated, but also profound. In history, a person looking for truth may find falsehood, an unfortunate transaction; in poetry, a person looking for fiction may find truth, a happy accident.

Taking a cue from Sidney's statement that literature is a "second nature," representing not the world as it *is* but the world as it *seems* or as it *ought to be*, I want to note something viscerally obvious to all lovers of literature but hard-won by literary theorists: literature gives writers and readers a conceptual space in which to consider the problems of culture. Literature is equipment for thinking, not giving answers to the great *hows* and *whys* of life but helping us ask those questions in the first place.[44] And the interpretations of a text that emerge over time due to shifting contexts of interpretation allow us to study, in an anthropological manner, what it's like to live within the literary world created by the text—in the space for thought, communication, and debate opened up by the text.

VIII. The Anthropology of Audience

The anthropology of audience is an attempt to study objectively the way we experience literature subjectively—"we" as individuals, but also "we" as cultures and communities. It is a method of literary criticism involving speculative explanations of historically specific habits and customs of *making sense* and *making use* of literature. It aims to understand the interpretations of a text on their own terms, whatever their conditions may be and regardless of whether their claims are justified. In an effort to understand how literature is experienced, the anthropology of audience studies the behavior of readers within interpretive communities and the interactions among interpretive communities across space and throughout time. It is a return to the audience-oriented criticism and theory that was the immediate consequence of the "death of the author" in poststructuralism, but a return that envelops the attention to the social contexts of reading (also a consequence of poststructuralism) that are emphasized, in different ways, in historicism and presentism. The difference between reception history and the anthropology of audience is the same as the difference between history and anthropology as such: reception history is a collection of particulars from the past, while the anthropology of audience involves an attempt to explain how meaning is ascribed to literature and how interpretations interact with each other. In the anthropology of audience, an analyst tries to make sense of the ongoing interpretive space created by a literary text by becoming immersed in different interpretive communities of the past and then returning to the present to report and analyze observations.

The anthropology of audience is scientific as opposed to philosophical and materialistic as opposed to metaphysical, keeping in mind that subjective experience is a part of the material world. It is an empirical approach to subjective literary experience: knowledge is based on observation, both of the text (conceived of here as nature, i.e., second nature) and of the readers who live within the interpretive space created by the text, as well as the societies of readers formed within that space. In anthropology, an account of an indigenous society might give us a thick description of the place: the names of the mountains and the valleys, which villages produce corn for tortillas, which produce charcoal, who wears shoes and who doesn't. Likewise, the anthropology of audience involves systematic observation of the second nature of literature, not only the thick description of the features of the text that condition and generate meaning but also an attention to what it's like to experience and make sense of those features. A critic conducts embedded research of a kind (i.e., fieldwork) in the societies of readers formed in response to a text. The immersed critic observes how readers interact with texts and how readers interact with each other through discussion, debate, negotiation, friendship, and so forth. The analyst studies the meanings readers give to texts and the uses readers make of texts, regardless of whether those meanings and uses are encouraged or supported by them. There is an interest in collecting massive amounts of data—interpretations—that are the material manifestations of readerly experience. Quantitative data can be collected about a society of readers, enhancing the qualitative analysis more common in the humanities. More likely, there can be an ethnography of sorts, a narrative describing in detail an interpretive community. This is not merely history, a record of particulars; it is a social science providing explanations and generalizations about how things work in certain cultures of reading (the concern of sociology) and across cultures of reading (the concern of anthropology).

The anthropology of audience identifies themes and exemplars in the reception of a text; it creates schemes, models, and metaphors to describe and explain them. It is inductive, working up from particulars methodically collected to abstractions carefully considered. Hunches form hypotheses; hypotheses are tested through experimentation; results should be replicable and verifiable; laws (descriptions of phenomena repeatedly observed) and theories (explanations of repeated phenomena) can be articulated and tested against additional experience. Thus, the anthropology of audience uses the scientific method to study readerly behavior as it occurs within the second nature of the literary text that allows people from different spaces and times to live and interact with each other, as interpretations, in the same space. This is not a facile scientism that acts as if all readerly phenomena can be accurately measured and optimized with the new truth revealed through science. But it is an attempt to provide an objective way of looking at subjective literary experience. Just as the reason to do anthropology and sociology *per se* is to better understand one's own lived experience, the reason for doing the anthropology of audience is to better understand one's own experience as a reader and as an inhabitant of the second nature of literature.

Notes

INTRODUCTION

1. References to Shakespeare's plays are to Stephen Greenblatt, ed., *The Norton Shakespeare*, 3rd ed. (New York: Norton, 2016), and are cited parenthetically by abbreviated play titles.

2. John Simpson and Edmund Weiner, ed., "Hunch, v.," in the *Oxford English Dictionary*, 2nd ed. (Oxford: Clarendon Press, 1989).

3. Tobin Siebers, "Shakespeare Differently Disabled," in *The Oxford Handbook of Shakespeare and Embodiment: Gender, Sexuality, and Race*, ed. Valerie Traub (Oxford: Oxford University Press, 2016), 435.

4. Grey Friars Research Team, *The Bones of a King: Richard III Rediscovered* (Chichester: Wiley Blackwell, 2015).

5. These books range from early character criticism—the anonymous *Remarks on the Character of Richard the Third; as played by Cooke and Kemble* (London: Parsons and Son, 1801) and John Phillip Kemble, *Macbeth and King Richard the Third: An Essay in Answer to Remarks on Some of the Characters of Shakespeare* (London: John Murray, 1817)—to more recent scholarship, such as Wolfgang Clemen, *A Commentary on Shakespeare's Richard III*, trans. Jean Bonheim (London: Methuen, 1968); Antony Sher, *Year of the King: An Actor's Diary and Sketchbook* (London: Chatto and Windus, 1985); Charles A. Hallett and Elaine S. Hallett, *The Artistic Links between William Shakespeare and Sir Thomas More: Radically Different Richards* (New York: Palgrave Macmillan, 2011); and Philip Schwyzer, *Shakespeare and the Remains of Richard III* (Oxford: Oxford University Press, 2013).

6. Walter Murray and Thomas Kean, dir., *Richard III*, Nassau Street (New York, 1749).

7. William Henry Brown, dir., *Richard III*, African Grove Theatre (New York, 1821).

8. Al Pacino, dir., *Looking for Richard* (Fox Searchlight Pictures, 1996), and Jeremy Whelehan, dir., *NOW: In the Wings on a World Stage* (Treetops Productions, 2014).

9. Jeffrey R. Wilson, "Shakestats: Writing about Shakespeare between the Humanities and the Social Sciences," *Early Modern Literary Studies* 20, no. 2 (2018): 15, 17.

10. Beau Willimon, *House of Cards* (Netflix, 2013–2019); Stephen Greenblatt, "Shakespeare Explains the 2016 Election," *New York Times Sunday Review* (Oct. 8, 2016).

11. James Siemon, "Halting Modernity: Richard III's Preposterous Body and History," in *Shakespeare in Europe: History and Memory*, ed. Marta Gibinska (Krakow: Jagiellonian University Press, 2008), 114.

12. Katherine Schaap Williams, "Performing Disability and Theorizing Deformity," *English Studies* 94, no. 7 (2013): 769.

13. Alice Wong, ed., *Disability Visibility: First-Person Stories from the Twenty-First Century* (New York: Vintage, 2020).

14. Shakespeare described these posters in *Macbeth* when he had Macduff threaten, "We'll have thee, as our rarer monsters are, / Painted on a pole, and underwrit, / 'Here you may see the tyrant'" (5.8.25–27).

15. "monster, *n.*, *adv.*, and *adj.*," in *Oxford English Dictionary*, etymology.

16. Anna Dunthorne, "How to Approach a Monster: A Comparison of Different Approaches to the Historiography of Early Modern Monster Literature," *History Compass* 6, no. 4 (2008): 1116.

17. Alan W. Bates, *Emblematic Monsters: Unnatural Conceptions and Deformed Births in Early Modern Europe* (New York: Rodopi, 2005), 12.

18. Lindsey Row-Heyveld, "'Known and Feeling Sorrows': Disabled Knowledge and *King Lear*," *Early Theatre* 22, no. 2 (2019): 158.

19. Elizabeth B. Bearden, *Monstrous Kinds: Body, Space, and Narrative in Renaissance Representations of Disability* (Ann Arbor: University of Michigan Press, 2019), 5; Richard H. Godden and Asa Simon Mittman, ed., *Monstrosity, Disability, and the Posthuman in the Medieval and Early Modern World* (New York: Palgrave Macmillan, 2019), 11.

20. David Houston Wood, "'Some Tardy Cripple': Timing Disability in *Richard III*," in *Richard III: A Critical Reader*, ed. Annaliese Connolly (London: Bloomsbury, 2013), 144.

21. Stanley Fish, "Literature in the Reader: Affective Stylistics," in *Is There a Text in This Class? The Authority of Interpretive Communities* (Cambridge: Harvard University Press, 1980), 27.

22. William Jefferson Clinton, "Presidential Grand Jury Testimony," *CSPAN* (Aug. 17, 1998).

23. Bearden, *Monstrous Kinds*, 5.

24. "Mean," in *Oxford English Dictionary*, def. I.

25. Norman Rabkin, *Shakespeare and the Problem of Meaning* (Chicago: University of Chicago Press, 1981), 13.

26. Fish, "Literature in the Reader," 32.
27. Walter Benjamin, *The Origin of German Tragic Drama* (1928), trans. John Osborne (London: Verso, 1977), 228.
28. Richard Farrant, *The Warres of Cyrus King of Persia* (London: Edward Allde, 1594), D2.
29. Allison P. Hobgood, "Teeth before Eyes: Impairment and Invisibility in Shakespeare's *Richard III*," in *Disability, Health, and Happiness in the Shakespearean Body*, ed. Sujata Iyengar (New York: Routledge, 2015), 23.
30. Susan Neiman, *Evil in Modern Thought: An Alternative History of Philosophy* (Princeton: Princeton University Press, 2002).
31. Genesis, in the Geneva Bible, i.e., *The Bible and Holy Scriptures* (Geneva: Rouland Hall, 1560), 19.4.
32. Saint Augustine, *Enchiridion* (ca. 420), anonymous trans. (London: Humfrey Lownes for Thomas Clarke, 1607), 61.
33. Immanuel Kant, *Werke*, ed. Komiglich Preussische, vol. 1 (Berlin: Akademie der Wissenschaften, 1902), 417–472.
34. Voltaire, "Poem on the Lisbon Disaster," in *Selected Works of Voltaire*, ed. and trans. Joseph McCabe (London: Watts, 1911), 1–5.
35. Joseph Hall, *The Genealogie of Vertve*, in *Two Guides to a Good Life* (London: W. Iaggard, 1604), B6.
36. Katharine Park and Lorraine J. Daston, "Unnatural Conceptions: The Study of Monsters in Sixteenth- and Seventeenth-Century France and England," *Past and Present* 92 (1981): 25.
37. Stanley Fish, "Interpreting the *Variorum*," in *Is There a Text in this Class?*, 150.
38. Jean E. Howard, introduction to *Richard Duke of York (3 Henry VI)*, in *The Norton Shakespeare*, ed. Walter Cohen, Stephen Greenblatt, Jean E. Howard, and Katharine Eisaman Maus, 2nd ed. (New York: Norton, 1997), 291.
39. Genevieve Love, "Richard's 'Giddy Footing': Degree of Difference and Cyclical Movement in Shakespeare's *Richard III*," in *Early Modern Theatre and the Figure of Disability* (London: Bloomsbury, 2019), 144, 139.
40. Fish, "Interpreting the *Variorum*," 164.
41. Fish, "Literature in the Reader," 49.
42. Siebers, "Shakespeare Differently Disabled," 451.
43. Paul K. Longmore, *Why I Burned My Book and Other Essays on Disability* (Philadelphia: Temple University Press, 2003), 10.
44. Union of the Physically Impaired Against Segregation, *Policy Statement* (1974), available at www.leeds.ac.uk/disability-studies/archiveuk/UPIAS/UPIAS.pdf.
45. See, for example, Lennard J. Davis, *Enforcing Normalcy: Disability, Deafness, and the Body* (London: Verso, 1995), and James I. Charlton, *Nothing about Us without Us: Disability Oppression and Empowerment* (Berkeley: University of California Press, 1998).
46. Henri-Jacques Stiker, introduction to *A History of Disability* (1982), trans. William Sayers (Ann Arbor: University of Michigan Press, 1999), 14. See also Henri-Jacques Stiker, "Using Historical Anthropology to Think Disability," in *Disability in*

Different Cultures, ed. Brigitte Holzer, Arthur Vreede, and Gabriele Weigt (Bielefeld: Transcript-Verlag, 1999), 352–380; and Henri-Jacques Stiker, "Disability History for the Twenty-First Century," in *The Imperfect Historian: Disability Histories in Europe*, ed. Sebastian Barsch, Anne Klein, and Pieter Verstraete (Frankfurt am Main: Peter Lang, 2013), 271–274.

47. David Mitchell and Sharon Snyder, *Narrative Prosthesis: Disability and the Dependencies of Discourse* (Ann Arbor: University of Michigan Press, 2000), 25.

48. Paul K. Longmore and Lauri Umansky, "Disability History: From the Margins to the Mainstream," in *The New Disability History: American Perspectives*, ed. Paul K. Longmore and Lauri Umansky (New York: New York University Press, 2001), 1–32.

49. See Douglas C. Baynton, "Disability: A Useful Category of Historical Analysis," *Disability Studies Quarterly* 17 (1997); B. J. Gleeson, "Disability Studies: A Historical Materialist View," *Disability and Society* 12 (1997): 179–202; Catherine J. Kudlick, "Disability History: Why We Need Another 'Other,'" *American Historical Review* 108, no. 3 (June 2003): 763–793.

50. See Christopher Bell, "Is Disability Studies Actually White Disability Studies?" in *The Disability Studies Reader*, ed. Lennard J. Davis, 3rd ed. (New York: Routledge, 2010), 374–382; Nirmala Erevelles and Andrea Minear, "Unspeakable Offenses: Untangling Race and Disability in Discourses of Intersectionality," *Journal of Literary and Cultural Disability Studies* 4, no. 2 (2010): 127–145; and Alison Kafer and Eunjung Kim, "Disability and the Edges of Intersectionality," in *The Cambridge Companion to Literature and Disability*, ed. Clare Barker and Stuart Murray (Cambridge: Cambridge University Press, 2018), 123–138.

51. See Elizabeth Bredberg, "Writing Disability History: Problems, Perspectives and Sources," *Disability and Society* 14, no. 2 (1999): 189–201; David L. Braddock and Susan L. Parish, "An Institutional History of Disability," in *Handbook of Disability Studies*, ed. Gary L. Albrecht, Katherine D. Seelman, and Michael Bury (Thousand Oaks, CA: Sage, 2001), 11–68; and Catherine J. Kudlick, "Disability History, Power, and Rethinking the Idea of 'the Other,'" *PMLA* 102, no. 2 (2005): 557–561.

52. See Rosemarie Garland-Thomson, *Extraordinary Bodies: Figuring Physical Disability in American Culture and Literature* (New York: Columbia University Press, 1997); Sharon L. Snyder, Brenda Jo Brueggemann, Rosemarie Garland-Thomson, and Michael Bérubé, ed., *Disability Studies: Enabling the Humanities* (New York: Modern Language Association of America, 2002).

53. Allison P. Hobgood and David Houston Wood, "Introduction," in *Disabled Shakespeares*, a special section of *Disability Studies Quarterly* 29, no. 4 (2009); Susan Anderson, "Introduction: Disability in Early Modern Theatre," *Early Theatre* 22, no. 2 (2019): 144.

54. Landmark books addressing earlier periods include Robert Garland, *The Eye of the Beholder: Deformity and Disability in the Graeco-Roman World* (Ithaca, NY: Cornell University Press, 1995); Hector Avalos, Sarah J. Melcher, and Jeremy Schipper, ed., *This Abled Body: Rethinking Disabilities in Biblical Studies* (Atlanta: Society of Biblical Literature, 2007); and Irina Metzler, *Disability in Medieval Europe: Thinking about Physical Impairment in the High Middle Ages, c.1100–c.1400* (Abingdon: Routledge, 2006). On

the early-modern age, see especially Susan Anderson and Liam Haydon, ed., *A Cultural History of Disability in the Renaissance* (London: Bloomsbury, 2020).

55. See Joshua R. Eyler, ed., "Breaking Boundaries, Building Bridges," in *Disability in the Middle Ages: Reconsiderations and Reverberations* (Abingdon: Routledge, 2010), 1–10; Jeffrey R. Wilson, "The Trouble with Disability in Shakespeare Studies," *Disability Studies Quarterly* 37, no. 2 (2017). Productive critiques of terminology and arguments advanced in my article (which needlessly presented a false choice between vocabularies of *disability* and *stigma*) have come from Katherine Schaap Williams, "Demonstrable Disability," *Early Theatre* 22, no. 2 (2019): 190–191; and Sonya Freeman Loftis, "Cripping (and Re-Cripping) Richard: Was Richard III Disabled?" in *Shakespeare and Disability Studies* (Oxford: Oxford University Press, 2021), 25–30.

56. See Allison P. Hobgood, "Caesar Hath the Falling Sickness: The Legibility of Early Modern Disability in Shakespearean Drama"; Lindsey Row-Heyveld, "'The Lying'st Knave in Christendom': The Development of Disability in the False Miracle of St. Alban's"; and David Houston Wood, "'Fluster'd with Flowing Cups': Alcoholism, Humoralism, and the Prosthetic Narrative in *Othello*," all in *Disability Studies Quarterly* 29, no. 4 (2009); David Houston Wood, "Shakespeare and Disability Studies," *Literature Compass* 8, no. 5 (2011); Lindsey Row-Heyveld, "Antic Dispositions: Mental and Intellectual Disabilities in Early Modern Revenge Tragedy," in *Recovering Disability in Early Modern England*, ed. Allison P. Hobgood and David Houston Wood (Columbus: Ohio State University Press, 2013), 73–87; Simone Chess, "Performing Blindness: Representing Disability in Early Modern Popular Performance and Print," in *Recovering Disability in Early Modern England*, 105–122; Angela Heetderks, "'Better a Witty Fool Than a Foolish Wit': Song, Fooling, and Intellectual Disability in Shakespearean Drama," in *Gender and Song in Early Modern England*, ed. Leslie C. Dunn and Katherine R. Larson (Farnham: Ashgate, 2014), 63–75; Amrita Dhar, "Seeing Feelingly: Sight and Service in *King Lear*," *Disability, Health, and Happiness in the Shakespearean Body*, ed. Sujata Iyengar (New York: Routledge, 2015), 76–92; Catherine E. Doubler, "'Gambol Faculties' and 'Halting Bravery': Falstaff, Will Kemp, and Impaired Masculinity," in *Disability, Health, and Happiness in the Shakespearean Body*, 142–157; David Houston Wood, "Shakespeare and Variant Embodiment," in *Shakespeare in Our Time: A Shakespeare Association of America Collection*, ed. Dympna Callaghan and Suzanne Gossett (London: Bloomsbury, 2016), 189–193; Michael Schoenfeldt, "Lessons from the Body: Moralizing Disability," in *The Cambridge Guide to the Worlds of Shakespeare*, ed. Bruce R. Smith (Cambridge: Cambridge University Press, 2016), 1:795–802; Avi Mendelson, "Enabling Rabies in King Lear," in *Performing Disability in Early Modern English Drama*, ed. Leslie C. Dunn (New York: Palgrave Macmillan, 2020), 161–183.

57. See Sujata Iyengar, "Shakespeare's 'Discourse of Disability,'" in *Disability, Health, and Happiness in the Shakespearean Body*, 1–19; Vin Nardizzi, "Disability Figures in Shakespeare," in *The Oxford Handbook of Shakespeare and Embodiment: Gender, Sexuality, and Race*, ed. Valerie Traub (Oxford: Oxford University Press, 2016), 455–467; and Williams, "Demonstrable Disability."

58. See Mary K. Nelson, "Shakespeare's *Henry VIII*: Stigmatizing the 'Disabled' Womb," *Disability Studies Quarterly* 29, no. 4 (2009); Abigail Elizabeth Comber, "A

Medieval King 'Disabled' by an Early Modern Construct: A Contextual Examination of Richard III," in *Disability in the Middle Ages: Reconsiderations and Reverberations*, ed. Joshua Eyler (Burlington, VT: Ashgate, 2010), 183–196.

59. See Robert McRuer, "Richard III: Fuck the Disabled: The Prequel," in *Shakesqueer: A Queer Companion to the Complete Works of Shakespeare*, ed. Madhavi Menon (Durham, NC: Duke University Press, 2011), 294–301; Katherine Schaap Williams, "Performing Disability and Theorizing Deformity," *English Studies* 94, no. 7 (2013): 757–772; Chloe Owen, "'It's the Opheliac in Me': Ophelia, Emilie Autumn, and the Role of Hamlet in Discussing Mental Disability," in *Shakespeare's Hamlet in an Era of Textual Exhaustion*, ed. Sonya Freeman Loftis, Allison Kellar, and Lisa Ulevich (Abingdon: Routledge, 2017), 59–72; Royce Best, "Making Obesity Fat: Crip Estrangement in Shakespeare's *Henry IV, Part 1*," *Disability Studies Quarterly* 39, no. 4 (2019); and Justin Shaw, "'Rub Him about the Temples': Othello, Disability, and the Failures of Care," *Early Theatre* 22, no. 2 (2019).

60. See Peter Novak, "Signing Shakespeare (ASL)," in *The Cambridge Guide to the Worlds of Shakespeare*, ed. Bruce R. Smith (Cambridge: Cambridge University Press, 2016), 2:1357–1362; Maura Michelle Tarnoff, "Diversely Abled Audiences," in *The Cambridge Guide to the Worlds of Shakespeare*, 2:1533–1538; Sid Ray, "Staging Epilepsy in *Othello*," in *Stage Matters: Props, Bodies, and Space in Shakespearean Performance*, ed. Annalisa Castaldo and Rhonda Knight (Lanham, MD: Fairleigh Dickinson University Press, 2018), 57–71; Sonya Freeman Loftis, "Autistic Culture, Shakespeare Therapy and the Hunter Heartbeat Method," *Shakespeare Survey* 72 (2019): 256–267; Jill Marie Bradbury et al., "ProTactile Shakespeare: Inclusive Theater by/for the DeafBlind," *Shakespeare Studies* (2019): 81–99; Jennifer L. Nelson, "Sign Gain to Deaf Gain: Deafness in Early Modern Manual Rhetoric and Modern Shakespeare Performances," in *Performing Disability in Early Modern English Drama*, 253–270; Sarah Olive, "'This Is Miching Mallecho. It Means Mischief': Problematizing Representations of Actors with Down's Syndrome in *Growing Up Down's*," in *Performing Disability in Early Modern English Drama*, 271–295; and Leslie C. Dunn, "Shakespearean Disability Theatre," in *Performing Disability in Early Modern English Drama*, 297–318.

61. See Jeff Blair, "Using Shakespeare to Debunk Myths about Disability," *English Journal* 107, no. 2 (2017): 78–80; David Houston Wood and Allison Hobgood, "Shakespearean Disability Pedagogy," in *Recovering Disability in Early Modern England*, 187–192; Allison P. Hobgood, "Shakespeare in Japan: Disability and a Pedagogy of Disorientation," in *Teaching Social Justice through Shakespeare: Why Renaissance Literature Matters Now*, ed. Hillary Eklund and Wendy Beth Hyman (Edinburgh: Edinburgh University Press, 2019), 46–54.

62. Lindsey Row-Heyveld, *Dissembling Disability in Early Modern English Drama* (New York: Palgrave Macmillan, 2018).

63. Genevieve Love, *Early Modern Theatre and the Figure of Disability* (London: Bloomsbury, 2019); Katherine Schaap Williams, *Unfixable Forms: Disability, Performance, and the Early Modern English Theater* (Ithaca, NY: Cornell University Press, 2021).

64. Allison Hobgood, *Beholding Disability in Renaissance England* (Ann Arbor: University of Michigan Press, 2021).

65. Alice Equestri, *Literature and Intellectual Disability in Early Modern England: Folly, Law and Medicine, 1500–1640* (Abingdon: Routledge, 2021).

66. Grace McCarthy, *Shakespearean Drama, Disability, and the Filmic Stare* (Abingdon: Routledge, 2021).

67. Loftis, *Shakespeare and Disability Studies.*

68. Anderson, "Introduction," 146.

69. Linda Charnes, *Notorious Identity: Materializing the Subject in Shakespeare* (Cambridge, MA: Harvard University Press, 1993).

70. Peter Sellers, "A Hard Day's Night," on *The Music of Lennon and McCartney* (Granada, December 16, 1965); *The Muppet Show*, 219 (Associated TeleVision, January 1, 1977).

71. William Steig, Ted Elliott, Terry Rossio, Joe Stillman, and Roger S. H. Schulman, wr., and Andrew Adamson and Vicky Jenson, dir., *Shrek* (DreamWorks Animation, 2001).

72. David Lindsay-Abaire, wr., *Shrek the Musical*, 5th Avenue Theatre (Seattle, 2008).

CHAPTER 1

1. On Richard's teeth, see Bethany Packard, "Richard III's Baby Teeth," *Renaissance Drama* 1–2 (2013): 107–129; Allison P. Hobgood, "Teeth before Eyes: Impairment and Invisibility in Shakespeare's *Richard III*," in *Disability, Health, and Happiness in the Shakespearean Body*, ed. Sujata Iyengar (New York: Routledge, 2015), 23–40; and Emily Rebekah Huber, "*Richardus Tertius Dentatus*: Textual History and the King's Teeth," *Philological Quarterly* 94, no. 4 (2015): 313–334.

2. E.M.W. Tillyard, *Shakespeare's History Plays* (London: Chatto and Windus, 1944).

3. For the history of Richard's reputation, see George Bosworth Churchill, *Richard the Third up to Shakespeare* (Berlin: Mayer and Müller, 1900); Paul Murray Kendall, "Richard's Reputation," in *Richard the Third* (New York: Norton, 1955), 496–514; Alison Hanham, *Richard III and His Early Historians, 1483–1535* (Oxford: Clarendon Press, 1975); Roxane C. Murph, *Richard III: The Making of a Legend* (Metuchen: Scarecrow, 1977); Charles Ross, "The Historical Reputation of *Richard III*: Fact and Fiction," in *Richard III* (Berkeley: University of California Press, 1981), xix–liii; Desmond Steward, "Introduction: The Black Legend," in *Richard III: England's Black Legend* (London: Penguin, 1982), 1–10; Jeremy Potter, "The Posthumous Hunchback," in *Good King Richard? An Account of Richard III and His Reputation, 1483–1983* (London: Constable, 1983), 136–144; P. W. Hammond, "The Reputation of Richard III," in *Richard III: A Medieval Kingship*, ed. John Gillingham (New York: St. Martin's, 1993), 133–149; Paul Murray Kendall, "Richard's Reputation," in *Richard the Third* (New York: Norton, 1996), 496–514; and Andreas Hofele, "Making History Memorable: More, Shakespeare and *Richard III*," in *Literature, Literary History and Cultural Memory*, ed. Herbert Grabes, *REAL: Yearbook of Research in English and American Literature* 21 (Tubingen: Gunter Narr Verlag, 2005), 187–204.

4. On the discovery of Richard's skeleton, see Philippa Langley and Michael Jones, *The King's Grave: The Discovery of Richard III's Lost Burial Place and the Clues It Holds* (New York: St. Martin's, 2013); A. J. Carson, ed., *Finding Richard III: The Official Account of Research by the Retrieval and Reburial Project* (Horstead: Imprimis Imprimatur, 2014); and the Grey Friars Research Team, *The Bones of a King: Richard III Rediscovered* (Chichester: Wiley Blackwell, 2015). For some early reflections on Richard's disability in the wake of the rediscovery of his skeleton, see Sarah Knight and Mary Ann Lund, "Richard Crookback," *Times Literary Supplement* (Feb. 6, 2013); *Finding Richard: A Forum*, a special section on *Upstart: A Journal of English Renaissance Studies* (2013), especially contributions by Catherine Paul, "The Truth Is in There," and Jonathan Hsy, "Distemporality: Richard III's Body and the Car Park"; Philip Schwyzer, introduction to *Shakespeare and the Remains of Richard III* (Oxford: Oxford University Press, 2013); Mary Ann Lund, "Richard's Back: Death, Scoliosis and Myth Making," *Medical Humanities* 41, no. 2 (2015): 89–94; David Horspool, *Richard III: A Ruler and His Reputation* (London: Bloomsbury, 2015); and Fay Bound Alberti, "Getting It Straight: Spines, Scoliosis, and the Hunchback King," in *This Mortal Coil: The Human Body in History and Culture* (Oxford: Oxford University Press, 2016), 20–38.

5. Jo Appleby et al., "The Scoliosis of Richard III, Last Plantagenet King of England: Diagnosis and Clinical Significance," *The Lancet* 383, no. 9932 (May 2014): 1944.

6. Good biographies include Ross, *Richard III*; Horspool, *Richard III*; and Michael Hicks, *Richard III: The Self-Made King* (New Haven: Yale University Press, 2019).

7. The most historically informed recovery of Richard's disability experience in medieval England is Lund, "Richard's Back."

8. On experiences associated with scoliosis, see Elisabetta d'Agata, *Enjoy Life with Idiopathic Scoliosis during Adolescence: Psychology for Professionals of Scoliosis* (Barcelona: Junio, 2019).

9. Good guides to medieval medical and cultural conventions of disability come in two books from Irina Metzler, *Disability in Medieval Europe: Thinking about Physical Impairment in the High Middle Ages, c.1100–c.1400* (Abingdon: Routledge, 2006) and *A Social History of Disability in the Middle Ages: Cultural Considerations of Physical Impairment* (Abingdon: Routledge, 2013).

10. All these characters are represented in Richard's personal library; see A. F. Sutton and L. Visser-Fuchs, *Richard III's Books: Ideal and Reality in the Life of a Medieval Prince* (Stroud: Sutton, 1997).

11. See Gary Johnstone, dir., *Richard III: The New Evidence* (Channel 4, 2014).

12. Thomas Kuhn, *The Structure of Scientific Revolutions* (1962), 2nd ed. (Chicago: University of Chicago Press, 1970).

13. Archibald Whitelaw, "Address to King Richard III" (1484), trans. David Shotter, in *The North of England in the Age of Richard III*, ed. A. J. Pollard (New York: St. Martin's, 1996), 194. A foreign nobleman entertained at court, Nicholas von Poppelau, described Richard as "a little slimmer and not as bulky as him, also very much more lean; he had very fine-boned arms and legs, also a great heart"; quoted from Grey Friars Research Team, *Bones of a King*, 129.

14. *The Rous Roll* (1484), ed. Charles Ross (Gloucester: Alan Sutton, 1980), 63.

15. The image of Richard III and Anne in the Salisbury Roll (ca. 1483), in the British Library (London), Loan MS 90, fol. 154, is available in Grey Friars Research Team, *Bones of a King*, 20.

16. John Rous, *Historia Regum Angliae* (1486), trans. Alison Hanham, in *Richard III and his Early Historians*, ed. T. Hearne (Oxford: Sheldonian Theatre, 1716), 120–121.

17. See John Rous, *Historia Regum Anglie* (1486), Cotton MS Vespasian A XII, in the British Library (London, England), 135r.

18. Richard's deformity is not mentioned in Nicholas Pronay and John Cox, ed., *The Crowland Chronicle Continuations, 1459–1486* (London: Richard III and Yorkist History Trust, 1986); Dominic Mancini, *The Usurpation of Richard the Third* (1483), trans. C.A.J. Armstrong (Oxford: Clarendon Press, 1936); Bernard Andrè, *Vita Regis Henrici Septimi* (ca. 1500–1503), ed. James Gairdner (London: Longman, Brown, Green, Longmans, and Roberts, 1858), 3–77; Robert Fabyan, *Newe Cronycles of Englande and of Fraunce* (London: Richard Pynson, 1516); or two poems by Humphrey Brereton, "The Song of the Lady Bessy" (early sixteenth c.), in *The Most Pleasant Song of Lady Bessy; and How She Married King Henry the Seventh, of the House of Lancaster*, ed. James Orchard Halliwell (London: Percy Society, 1847), 14.56, and "The Ballad of Bosworth Field" (early sixteenth c.), in *Bishop Percy's Folio Manuscript, Ballads and Romances*, ed. J. W. Hales and F. J. Furnivall (London: N. Trubner, 1868), 3.233–259 and 2.6–8.

19. York Civic Record (1491), quoted from Robert Davies, ed., *Extracts from the Municipal Records of the City of York, during the Reigns of Edward IV, Edward V, and Richard III* (London: J. B. Nichols and Sons, 1843), 221.

20. See Pamela Tudor-Craig, *Richard III: National Portrait Gallery, 27 June–7 October 1973* (London: National Portrait Gallery, 1973), 93; and Roland Mushat Frye, "The 'Shakespearean' Portrait of Richard III in Edward Alleyn's Picture Collection," *Shakespeare Quarterly* 32, no. 3 (1981): 352–354.

21. Polydore Vergil, *English History* (1512–1513), anonymous trans., ed. Henry Ellis (London: Camden Society, 1844), 226–227.

22. Thomas More, *The History of King Richard the Thirde* (1513), in *Workes*, ed. William Rastall (London: John Cawod, John Waly, and Richarde Tottell, 1557), 37.

23. See Hanan Yoran, "Thomas More's *Richard III*: Probing the Limits of Humanism," *Renaissance Studies* 15 (2001): 514–536; Gillian Day, "Sceptical Historiography: Thomas More's *History of Richard III*," in *The Anatomy of Tudor Literature: Proceedings of the First International Conference of the Tudor Symposium*, ed. Mike Pincombe (Burlington: Ashgate, 2001), 24–33; and Dan Breen, "Thomas More's *History of Richard III*: Genre, Humanism, and Moral Education," *Studies in Philology* 107, no. 4 (2010): 465–492.

24. Phillipa Vincent Connolly, *Disability and the Tudors: All the King's Fools* (Yorkshire: Pen and Sword History, 2021), xvii.

25. Richard Grafton, *A Continuacion of the Chronicle of England*, in *The Chronicle of Ihon Hardyng* (London: Richard Grafton, 1543), cvi.

26. Edward Hall, *The Vnion of the Two Noble and Illustre Famelies of Lancastre Yorke* (London: Richard Grafton, 1548), Edward V, I; Richard Rainolde, "A Narracion

Historicall vpon Kyng Richard the Third, the Cruell Tiraunt," in *The Foundacion of Rhetorike* (London: Ihon Kingston, 1563), xiij.

27. George Buck, *The History of the Life and Reigne of Richard the Third* (London: W. Wilson, 1646), 79.

28. John Stow, *The Chronicles of England from Brute vnto this Present Yeare of Christ* (London: Ralphe Newberie, 1580), 755.

29. William Baldwin, ed., *A Myrroure for Magistrates* (London: Thomas Marshe, 1559), lxxx.

30. "Howe the Lord Hastynges was Betrayed by Trustyng to Much to his Evyl Consayler Catesby, and Vilanously Murdered in the Tower of London by Richarde Duke of Glocestre," in *A Myrroure for Magistrates*, ed. William Baldwin (London: Thomas Marshe, 1563), cxi.

31. Raphael Holinshed, *The Chronicles of England, Scotlande, and Irelande* (London: Henry Bynneman and Henry Denham, 1577), 2.79.

32. Richard is referred to as a monster in manuscript in *The Stanley Poem* (ca. 1562), in J. O. Halliwell-Phillipps, ed., *Palatine Anthology: A Collection of Ancient Poems Relating to Lancashire and Cheshire* (London: C and J Adlard, 1850): "Thus lo! Richard the usurper was made king / A mercilesse manne and a monstrous thinge, / A wretched body and a tyrante in harte, / A devill in his deedes, deformed in ech parte" (248).

33. *The True Discription of Two Monsterous Chyldren Borne at Herne in Kent* (London: Thomas Colwell, 1565).

34. *The Description of a Monstrous Pig the Which was Farrowed at Hamsted* (London: Alexander Lacy, 1562).

35. *The Forme and Shape of a Monstrous Child, Borne at Maydstone in Kent* (London: John Awdeley, 1568).

36. A. P. Rossiter, "Angel with Horns: The Unity of *Richard III*," in *Angel with Horns*, ed. Graham Storey (London: Longmans Green, 1961), 15.

37. *A Discription of a Monstrous Chylde, Borne at Chychester in Sussex* (London: Leonard Askel, 1562).

38. Ambroise Paré, *Of Monsters and Prodigies* (1573), in *The Workes of that Famous Chirurgion Ambrose Parey* (1585), trans. Thomas Johnson (London: Thomas Cotes and R. Young, 1634), 961–1026.

39. *The True Reporte of the Forme and Shape of a Monstrous Childe, Borne at Muche Horkesleye* (London: Thomas Marshe, 1562).

40. Thomas Legge, *Richardus Tertius* (ca. 1580), trans. Robert J. Lordi (New York: Garland, 1979), 396, 340, 440, and 457. George Whetstone's *The English Mirror* (London: I. Windet, 1586) also speaks of "the monstrous murders of king *Richard* the third" (9).

41. *The True Tragedie of Richard the Third* (London: Thomas Creede, 1594).

42. Giles Fletcher, *The Rising to the Crowne of Richard the Third*, in *Licia* (Cambridge: John Legat, 1593).

43. Anthony Chute, *Beawtie Dishonoured Written vnder the Title of Shores Wife* (London: John Wolfe, 1593), 46.

44. Hendrik Goltzius, *Edouard IV, Edouard V, Richard III, et Henri VII* (1585), in *The Illustrated Bartsch*, vol. 3 (New York: Abaris, 1978).

45. Hippocrates, *The History of Epidemics* (400–375 B.C.E.), trans. Samuel Farr (London: T. Cadell, 1780), which includes chapter titles "Physiognomy" (book 2.6, p. 60) and "Physiognomy, as an Index of the Mind" (book 2.6, p. 63); Plato, *Republic* (ca. 380 B.C.E.), trans. G.M.A. Grube, rev. C.D.C. Reeve, in *Plato: Complete Works*, ed. John M. Cooper and D.S. Hutchinson (Indianapolis: Hackett, 1997), 620a–d.

46. Aristotle, *Prior Analytics* (ca. 350 B.C.E.), trans. Robin Smith (Indianapolis: Hackett, 1989), 2.27.

47. *Physiognomonics* (ca. 300 B.C.E.), in Aristotle, *The Complete Works*, ed. J. Barnes (Princeton, NJ: Princeton University Press, 1984), 814a.

48. Elizabeth C. Evans, "Galen the Physician as Physiognomist," *Transactions and Proceedings of the American Philological Association* 76 (1945): 28–98; "The Physiognomy of Adamantius the Sophist," trans. Ian Reparth, in *Seeing the Face, Seeing the Soul: Polemon's Physiognomy from Classical Antiquity to Medieval Islam* (Oxford: Oxford University Press, 2006), 487–548.

49. Martin Henry Porter, "A Persistent Fisnomical Consciousness c. 400 B.C.E.–c. 1470 C.E.," in *Windows of the Soul: Physiognomy in European Culture, 1470–1780* (Oxford: Oxford University Press, 2005), 46–78.

50. Baldassarre Castiglione, *The Courtyer* (1528), trans. Thomas Hoby (London: Wyllyam Seres, 1561), Rb.i.

51. See Bartolomeo della Rocca (called Cocles), *The Rebirth of Chiromancy and Physiognomy* (1504), trans. Thomas Hill, in *The Whole Art of Phisiognomie* (London: John Waylande, 1556); Johannes Indagine, *The Arte of Phisiognomy*, in *Briefe Introductions, both Naturall, Pleasaunte, and also Delectable vnto the Art of Chiromancy, or Manuel Diuination, and Physiognomy* (1522), trans. Fabian Withers (London: Iohannis Day, 1558); Richard Roussat, *Of Physiognomie* (1542), trans. William Warde, in *The Most Excellent, Profitable, and Pleasant Booke of the Famous Doctour and Expert Astrologian Arcandam or Aleandrin* (London: Henry Denham, 1562).

52. See Thomas Hill, *The Contemplation of Mankinde* (London: Henry Denham, 1571).

53. Quoted from Zakiya Hanafi, *The Monster in the Machine: Magic, Medicine, and the Marvelous in the Time of the Scientific Revolution* (Durham, NC: Duke University Press, 2000), 100.

54. Erving Goffman, *Stigma: Notes on the Management of Spoiled Identity* (New York: Simon and Schuster, 1963), 5.

55. Michael Polanyi, *Personal Knowledge: Towards a Post-Critical Philosophy* (Chicago: Psychology Press, 1958), 172.

56. Erich Auerbach, *Mimesis: The Representation of Reality in Western Literature* (1946), trans. Willard R. Trask (Princeton, NJ: Princeton University Press, 1953), 433.

57. See Erich Auerbach, "Figura" (1938), trans. Ralph Manheim, in *Scenes from the Drama of European Literature: Six Essays* (New York: Meridian, 1959), 11–76.

58. For a more detailed discussion, see Jeffrey R. Wilson, "The Figure of Stigma in Shakespeare's Drama," *Genre* 51, no. 3 (2018): 237–266.

59. My approach to chronology and authorship in this book is based on Gary Taylor and Gabriel Egan, ed., *The New Oxford Shakespeare: Authorship Companion* (Oxford:

Oxford University Press, 2017), especially the summative chapter 25, Gary Taylor and Rory Loughnane's "The Canon and Chronology of Shakespeare's Works" (417–602), which, for example, credits Christopher Marlowe as a coauthor of the *Henry VI* trilogy.

60. "stigmatic, *adj.* and *n.*" in *Oxford English Dictionary*, ed. John Simpson and Edmund Weiner, 2nd ed. (Oxford: Clarendon Press, 1989), def. B2.

61. See C. P. Jones, "*Stigma:* Tattooing and Branding in Graeco-Roman Antiquity," *Journal of Roman Studies* 77 (1987): 139–155; Mark T. Gustafson, "*Inscripta in fronte:* Penal Tattooing in Late Antiquity," *Classical Antiquity* 16, no. 1 (1997): 79–105; and C. P. Jones, "Stigma and Tattoo," in *Written on the Body: The Tattoo in European and American History*, ed. Jane Caplan (Princeton: Princeton University Press, 2000), 1–16.

CHAPTER 2

1. Abigail Elizabeth Comber, "A Medieval King 'Disabled' by an Early Modern Construct: A Contextual Examination of *Richard III*," in *Disability in the Middle Ages: Reconsiderations and Reverberations*, ed. Joshua Eyler (Burlington: Ashgate, 2010), 183, 192.

2. Geoffrey A. Johns, "A 'Grievous Burthern': *Richard III* and the Legacy of Monstrous Birth," in *Disability, Health, and Happiness in the Shakespearean Body*, ed. Sujata Iyengar (New York: Routledge, 2015), 55.

3. Allison Hobgood, *Beholding Disability in Renaissance England* (Ann Arbor: University of Michigan Press, 2021), 3.

4. "prodigy, *n.*," in *Oxford English Dictionary*, ed. John Simpson and Edmund Weiner, 2nd ed. (Oxford: Clarendon Press, 1989), etymology.

5. Adam Max Cohen, "The Metaphorical Use of the Prodigious Birth Tradition," in *Wonder in Shakespeare* (New York: Palgrave Macmillan, 2012), 57.

6. John W. Ellis-Etchison, "Monstrous Sovereignty and the Corrupt Body Politic in *Richard III* and *The Duchess of Malfi*," in *Holy Monsters, Sacred Grotesques: Monstrosity and Religion in Europe and the United States*, ed. Michael E. Heyes (Lanham, MD: Lexington, 2018), 135–166.

7. John Milton, *Paradise Lost*, in *The Riverside Milton*, ed. Roy Flannagan (Boston: Houghton Mifflin, 1998), 2.654, 2.657–658.

8. Ovid, *Metamorphosis* (8), trans. Arthur Golding (London: Willyam Seres, 1567), 174.

9. Dante, *Inferno*, trans. Robert Hollander and Jean Hollander (New York: Anchor, 2002), 34.38.

10. Edward Burnett Tylor, *Primitive Culture: Researches into the Development of Mythology, Philosophy, Religion, Art, and Custom* (London: John Murray, 1871), 1.101–105; James Fraser, *The Golden Bough: A Study in Magic and Religion* (1890–1915), abridged ed. (New York: Macmillan, 1922), 11–12.

11. Tylor, *Primitive Culture*, 1.105; Sigmund Freud, *Totem and Taboo; Some Points of Agreement between the Mental Lives of Savages and Neurotics* (1930), trans. James Strachey (New York: Norton, 1950), 108.

12. Ato Quayson, *Aesthetic Nervousness: Disability and the Crisis of Representation* (New York: Columbia University Press, 2007), 15.

13. Erich Auerbach, *Mimesis: The Representation of Reality in Western Literature* (1946), trans. Willard R. Trask (1953), 50th anniv. ed. (Princeton, NJ: Princeton University Press, 2003), 73–74.

14. Erich Auerbach, "Typological Symbolism in Medieval Literature," *Yale French Studies* 9 (1952): 5.

15. Francis Bacon, "Of Deformity," in *The Essayes* (London: John Haviland, 1625), 254–255.

16. See Sigmund Freud, "On Narcissism: An Introduction" (1914), in *The Standard Edition of the Complete Psychological Works of Sigmund Freud*, ed. James Strachey, vol. 14 (London: Hogarth, 1958), 56–82.

17. Robert N. Watson, "Kinship and Kingship: Ambition in Shakespeare's Major Histories," in *Shakespeare and the Hazards of Ambition* (Cambridge, MA: Harvard University Press, 1984), 15–16; Linda Charnes, "Belaboring the Obvious: Reading the Monstrous Body in *King Richard III*," in *Notorious Identity: Materializing the Subject in Shakespeare* (Cambridge, MA: Harvard University Press, 1993), 32.

18. Freud, "Exceptions," in *Complete Psychological Works*, 314.

19. John Rous, *Historia Regum Angliae* (1486), ed. T. Hearne (Oxford: Sheldonian Theatre, 1716), trans. Alison Hanham, in *Richard III and His Early Historians, 1483–1535* (Oxford: Clarendon Press, 1975), 121.

20. Raphael Holinshed, *The Chronicles of England, Scotlande, and Irelande* (London: Henry Bynneman and Henry Denham, 1587), 3.703.

21. Freud, *Totem and Taboo*, 104.

22. Lindsey Row-Heyveld, "Rules of Charity: *Richard III* and the Counterfeit-Disability Tradition," in *Dissembling Disability in Early Modern English Drama* (New York: Palgrave Macmillan, 2018), 145.

23. August Wilhelm von Schlegel, "Respecting the Pieces Said to Be Falsely Attributed to Shakespeare" (1808), in *A Course of Lectures on Dramatic Art and Literature*, trans. John Black (London: Baldwin, Craddock, and Joy, 1815), 2:249–250.

24. E. W. Tullidge, "Characters of Shakespeare: Richard the Third," *American Phrenological Journal* 44, no. 6 (1866): 166; Henry Norman Hudson, *Shakespeare: His Life, Art, and Characters* (Boston: Ginn, 1872), 2.144; E.M.W. Tillyard, *Shakespeare's History Plays* (London: Chatto and Windus, 1944), 210; Bernard Spivack, *Shakespeare and the Allegory of Evil* (New York: Columbia University Press, 1958), 403–404; Robert B. Pierce, *Shakespeare's History Plays: The Family and the State* (Columbus: Ohio State University Press, 1971), 101; Robert Ornstein, *A Kingdom for a Stage: The Achievement of Shakespeare's Plays* (Cambridge, MA: Harvard University Press, 1972), 57; Coppélia Kahn, *Man's Estate: Masculine Identity in Shakespeare* (Berkeley: University of California Press, 1981), 63–64; Maurice Hunt, "Ordering Disorder in *Richard III*," *South Central Review* 6, no. 4 (1989): 14; E. Pearlman, "The Invention of Richard of Gloucester," *Shakespeare Quarterly* 43, no. 4 (1992): 423–424; Charnes, "Belaboring the Obvious," 29; Michael Hattaway, introduction to *The Third Part of King Henry VI* (Cambridge: Cambridge University Press, 1993), 13; James R. Siemon, "Sign, Cause, or General Habit? Toward a 'Historicist Ontology' of Character on the Early Modern Stage," *European Legacy* 2, no. 2 (1997): 221; and David Houston Wood, "'Some Tardy

Cripple': Timing Disability in *Richard III*," in *Richard III: A Critical Reader*, ed. Annaliese Connolly (London: Bloomsbury, 2013), 152.

25. Union of the Physically Impaired Against Segregation, *Policy Statement* (1974), available at www.leeds.ac.uk/disability-studies/archiveuk/UPIAS/UPIAS.pdf.

26. Rosemarie Garland-Thomson, *Extraordinary Bodies: Figuring Physical Disability in American Culture and Literature* (New York: Columbia University Press, 1997), 9.

27. Tobin Siebers, *Disability Theory* (Ann Arbor: University of Michigan Press, 2008), 53–54, 61, 68.

28. Katherine Schaap Williams, "Enabling Richard: The Rhetoric of Disability in *Richard III*," *Disability Studies Quarterly* 29, no. 4 (2009).

29. Allison P. Hobgood, "Teeth before Eyes: Impairment and Invisibility in Shakespeare's *Richard III*," in *Disability, Health, and Happiness in the Shakespearean Body*, ed. Sujata Iyengar (New York: Routledge, 2015), 31.

30. Erving Goffman, *Stigma: Notes on the Management of Spoiled Identity* (New York: Simon and Schuster, 1963), 3.

31. W. I. Thomas and D. S. Thomas, *The Child in America: Behavior Problems and Programs* (New York: Knopf, 1928), 571–572.

32. Robert McRuer, "Richard III: Fuck the Disabled: The Prequel," in *Shakesqueer: A Queer Companion to the Complete Works of Shakespeare*, ed. Madhavi Menon (Durham, NC: Duke University Press, 2011), 301.

CHAPTER 3

1. According to *Open Source Shakespeare* (http://www.opensourceshakespeare.org), the word *stand* and its cognates appear thirty-four times in *3 Henry VI*, the most of any of Shakespeare's plays other than *Julius Caesar* (thirty-eight instances) and *Coriolanus* (thirty-seven instances).

2. Michael Torrey, "'The Plain Devil and Dissembling Looks': Ambivalent Physiognomy and Shakespeare's *Richard III*," *English Literary Renaissance* 30 (2000): 139.

3. Thomas Hill, "The Preface to the Reader," in *The Whole Art of Phisiognomie* (London: John Waylande, 1556).

4. Aristotle, *Prior Analytics* (ca. 350 B.C.E.), trans. A. J. Jenkinson, in *The Complete Works of Aristotle*, ed. Jonathan Barnes, vol. 1 (Princeton, NJ: Princeton University Press, 1984), 70b.

5. Pseudo-Aristotle, *Physiognomonics* (ca. 300 B.C.E.), in Aristotle, *Complete Works*, 805a–b.

6. Desiderius Erasmus, *That Chyldren Oughte to be Taught and Brought Vp Gently in Vertue and Learnynge* (1529), trans. Richard Sherry, in *A Treatise of Schemes and Tropes* (London: John Day, 1550), K.iii; and *Apophthegmes* (1538), trans. Nicholas Udall (London: Ricardi Grafton, 1542), 33.

7. Hill, "Preface"; Hill, *The Contemplation of Mankind* (London: Henry Denham, 1571), ★iiii.

8. Richard Huloet, "Physiognomie," in *Huloets Dictionarie* (London: Thomas Marsh, 1572).

9. Thomas Hill, *The Contemplation of Mankind* (London: Henry Denham, 1571), 85, 90.

10. James Parsons, *Human Physiognomy Explain'd* (London: C. Davis, 1746), i; Georg Christoph Lichtenberg, *Über Physiognomik, wider die Physiognomen*, ed. Fritz Aerni (Waldshut-Tiengen: Aerni, 1996), 32 (translation mine).

11. Johann Caspar Lavater, *Essays on Physiognomy, Designed to Promote the Knowledge and the Love of Mankind*, trans. Henry Hunter (London: John Murray, H. Hunter, and T. Holloway, 1789–1798), 1.24.

12. Sibylle Baumbach, *Shakespeare and the Art of Physiognomy* (Tirril: Humanities-Ebooks, 2008), 8. See also Sibylle Baumbach, "Voice, Face and Fascination: The Art of Physiognomy in *A Midsummer Night's Dream*," *Shakespeare Survey* 65 (2012): 77–91; and Sibylle Baumbach, "'Thy Face Is Mine': Faces and Fascination in Shakespeare's Plays," in *Shakespeare and the Power of the Face*, ed. James A. Knapp (New York: Routledge, 2016), 15–29.

13. Baumbach, *Shakespeare and the Art of Physiognomy*, 179, playing off King Duncan's statement that "there's no art / To find the mind's construction in the face" (*Macbeth*, 1.4.11–12).

14. Joel Elliot Slotkin, "Honeyed Toads: Sinister Aesthetics in Shakespeare's *Richard III*," *Journal for Early Modern Cultural Studies* 7, no. 1 (2007): 11.

15. Katherine Schaap Williams, "Performing Disability and Theorizing Deformity," *English Studies* 94, no. 7 (2013): 764–765.

16. Katherine Schaap Williams, "Deformed: Wanting to See Richard III," in *Unfixable Forms: Disability, Performance, and the Early Modern English Theater* (Ithica: Cornell University Press, 2021), 28.

17. David Houston Wood, "'Some Tardy Cripple': Timing Disability in *Richard III*," in *Richard III: A Critical Reader*, ed. Annaliese Connolly (London: Bloomsbury, 2013), 129–154; Allison P. Hobgood, "Teeth before Eyes: Impairment and Invisibility in Shakespeare's *Richard III*," in *Disability, Health, and Happiness in the Shakespearean Body*, ed. Sujata Iyengar (New York: Routledge, 2015), 23–40; and Allison Hobgood, "Making Gains," in *Beholding Disability in Renaissance England* (Ann Arbor: University of Michigan Press, 2021), 49–78.

18. Katherine Schaap Williams, "Richard III and the Staging of Disability," in the *Discovering Literature: Shakespeare* section of the British Library website (2016), http://www.bl.uk/shakespeare/articles/richard-iii-and-the-staging-of-disability.

19. Linda Charnes, "Belaboring the Obvious: Reading the Monstrous Body in *King Richard III*," in *Notorious Identity: Materializing the Subject in Shakespeare* (Cambridge, MA: Harvard University Press, 1993), 31.

20. Lindsey Row-Heyveld, "Rules of Charity: *Richard III* and the Counterfeit-Disability Tradition," in *Dissembling Disability in Early Modern English Drama* (New York: Palgrave Macmillan, 2018), 144.

21. For the philology of "vice," see, for example, Cicero, *Those Fyue Questions, which Marke Tullye Cicero, Disputed in his Manor of Tusculanum* (ca. 45 B.C.E.), trans. John Doman (London: Thomas Marshe, 1561): "A faulte [*vitia*] is, when the limmes of the bodye are not equallye proporcioned: but some miss placed, and yll fauoured to see" (4.13).

22. See Wood, "Timing Disability in *Richard III*."

23. David T. Mitchell and Sharon L. Snyder, "Performing Deformity: The Making and Unmaking of Richard III," in *Narrative Prosthesis: Disability and the Dependencies of Discourse* (Ann Arbor: University of Michigan Press, 2000), 104.

24. For instance, Autolycus calls the Clown an "ape-bearer" in *The Winter's Tale* (4.3.95).

25. Ulpian Fulwell, *Like Wil to Like* (London: John Allde, 1568), F.

26. Dominic Cooke, dir., *Richard III*, in *The Hollow Crown* (BBC, 2016).

27. See Scott Colley, *Richard's Himself Again: A Stage History of* Richard III (Westport, CT: Greenwood Press, 1992), 136.

28. Thomas More, *The History of King Richard the Thirde* (1513), in *Workes*, ed. William Rastall (London: John Cawod, John Waly, and Richarde Tottell, 1557), 54.

29. Williams, "Deformed," 36.

30. See More, *History of King Richard the Thirde*, 67.

31. See Erving Goffman, *Stigma: Notes on the Management of Spoiled Identity* (New York: Simon and Schuster, 1963), 4–5.

32. Philip Schwyzer, *Shakespeare and the Remains of Richard III* (Oxford: Oxford University Press, 2013), 20.

33. John Speed, *The History of Great Britaine* (London: William Hall and John Beale, 1611), 725.

CHAPTER 4

1. Edward Hall, *The Vnion of the Two Noble and Illustre Fameliies of Lancastre Yorke* (London: Richard Grafton, 1548), clxxxiiij.

2. Nicholas Brooke, "Reflecting Gems and Dead Bones: Tragedy versus History in *Richard III*," *Critical Quarterly* 7 (1965): 134.

3. See Kristin M. Smith, "Martial Maids and Murdering Mothers: Women, Witchcraft and Motherly Transgression in *Henry VI* and *Richard III*," *Shakespeare* 3, no. 2 (2007): 143–160.

4. Thomas Heywood, "Of Witches," in *Gynaikeion* (London: Adam Islip, 1624), 399.

5. Maurice Charney, *Wrinkled Deep in Time: Aging in Shakespeare* (New York: Columbia University Press, 2009), 9.

6. Hall, *The Vnion of the Two Noble and Illustre Fameliies*, ccxxi.

7. "The Slaughter of the Innocents and the Death of Herod," in *The N-Town Play*, ed. Stephen Spector (Oxford: Oxford University Press, 1991), 272–273; *Everyman* (London: John Scot, 1528).

8. Christopher Marlowe, *Tamburlaine the Great* (London: Richard Jones, 1590), 5.6; *The Lamentable Tragedie of Locrine* (London: Thomas Creede, 1595), 1.2; Robert Yarington, *Two Lamentable Tragedies* (London: R. Read, 1601), F3.

9. See Scott Eaton, "Witchcraft and Deformity in Early Modern English Literature," *Seventeenth Century* 35, no. 6 (2020): 815–828.

10. Reginald Scot, *The Discouerie of Witchcraft* (London: Henry Denham, 1584), C4.

11. Edmund Spenser, *The Faerie Queene* (1590), ed. A. C. Hamilton (New York: Longman, 2001), I.viii.48.

12. *A Most Wicked Worke of a Wretched Witch* (London: R. Bourne, 1592).

13. *The Wonderful Discouerie of the Witchcrafts of Margaret and Phillip Flower* (London: G. Eld, 1619).

14. *A Most Wicked Worke of a Wretched Witch*; and *The Witch of Edmonton*, attributed to William Rowley, Thomas Dekker, and John Ford (London: J. Cottrel, 1658), 13.

15. *A Certaine Relation of the Hog-Faced Gentlewoman Called Mistris Tannakin Skinker* (London: John Okes, 1640).

16. See "The Weird Sisters," in Raphael Holinshed, *The Chronicles of England, Scotlande, and Irelande* (London: Henry Bynneman, 1577), 1.243; and Laura Shamas, "From Goddess to Witch," in *We Three: The Mythology of Shakespeare's Weird Sisters* (New York: Peter Lang, 2007), 9–33.

17. Holinshed, *Chronicles*, 1.243–244.

18. Ibid., 1.249, 1.251.

CHAPTER 5

1. See Chapter 1, note 3.

2. See Alice Ida Perry Wood, *The Stage History of Shakespeare's King Richard the Third* (New York: AMS, 1909); Chris R. Hassel Jr., *Songs of Death: Performance, Interpretation, and the Text of Richard III* (Lincoln: University of Nebraska Press, 1987); Scott Colley, *Richard's Himself Again: A Stage History of* Richard III (Westport, CT: Greenwood, 1992); Gillian Day, *Shakespeare at Stratford: King Richard III* (London: Arden Shakespeare, 2002); James R. Siemon, ed., "Upon Stages," in *Richard III* (London: Arden Shakespeare, 2009), 79–123; and Jim Casey, "'Richard's Himself Again': The Body of Richard III on Stage and Screen," in *Shakespeare and the Middle Ages: Essays on the Performance and Adaptation of the Plays with Medieval Sources or Settings*, ed. Martha W. Driver and Sid Ray (Jefferson, IA: McFarland, 2009), 27–48.

3. Exceptions to the elision of the seventeenth century include Jeremy Potter, *Good King Richard? An Account of Richard III and His Reputation, 1483–1983* (London: Constable, 1983), especially Chapter 16, "After the Tudors: Bacon and Buck"; and M. G. Aune, "The Uses of Richard III: From Robert Cecil to Richard Nixon," *Shakespeare Bulletin* 24, no. 3 (2006): 23–47.

4. Kuhn first uses the term "disciplinary matrix" in his "Postscript" to *The Structure of Scientific Revolutions*, 2nd ed. (Chicago: University of Chicago, 1970), 182. Fish develops the term "interpretive community" in essays such as "Interpreting the *Variorum*" (147–173), "Normal Circumstances and Other Special Cases" (268–292), and "Is There a Text in This Class?" (303–321), in *Is There a Text in This Class? The Authority of Interpretive Communities* (Cambridge, MA: Harvard University Press, 1980).

5. J. S. Bruner and Leo Postman, "On the Perception of Incongruity: A Paradigm," *Journal of Personality* 18 (1949): 207.

6. Norwood Russell Hanson, *Patterns of Discovery: An Inquiry into the Conceptual Foundations of Science* (Cambridge: Cambridge University Press, 1958), 19.

7. Kuhn is building on a suggestion from Max Planck, *Scientific Autobiography and Other Papers*, trans. F. Gaynor (New York: Philosophical Library, 1949), 33–34.

8. John Milton, *Eikonoklestes* (London: Matthew Simmons, 1649), 11.

9. Erving Goffman, *Stigma: Notes on the Management of Spoiled Identity* (New York: Simon and Schuster, 1963), 4–5.

10. Thomas Heywood, *The First and Second Partes of King Edward the Fourth* (London: F. K., 1600), H7.

11. *The Returne from Pernassus* (London: G. Eld, 1606), G4.

12. Richard Corbet, *Iter Boreale*, in *Certain Elegant Poems* (London: R. Cotes, 1647), 12.

13. Thomas Talbot, "Richardvs III," in *The True Portraiture of the Countenances and Attires of the Kings of England* (London: R. Field, 1597).

14. Michael Drayton, *Englands Heroicall Epistles* (London: James Roberts, 1597), 50.

15. Michael Drayton, *Poly-Olbion* (London: Humphrey Lownes, 1613), 263.

16. John Davies of Hereford, *Microcosmos* (London: Joseph Barnes, 1603), 141.

17. Richard Niccols, *A Winter Night's Vision* (London: Felix Kyngston, 1610).

18. "King Richard the Third," in ibid., 750.

19. Christopher Brooke, *The Ghost of Richard the Third* (London: G. Eld, 1614), B2. With Brooke, Richard's catalog of the "fatall *Signes* [that] raign'd at my fearefull Byrth" becomes even more extensive, with each physical deformity signifying a conceptually similar spiritual defect (B3).

20. See Aune, "Uses of Richard III," 26, citing P. M. Handover, *The Second Cecil: The Rise to Power 1563–1604* (London: Eyre and Spottiswood, 1959), 55, 34, 57; and Robert Naunton, *Fragmenta Regalia: Memoirs of Elizabeth, Her Court and Favorites* (London: Charles Baldwin, 1824), 139.

21. Quoted from Pauline Croft, "The Reputation of Robert Cecil: Libels, Political Opinion and Popular Awareness in the Early Seventeenth Century," in *Transactions of the Royal Historical Society*, 6th ser., no. 1 (1991), 47, citing Bodleian, MS Don c. 54f.

22. Quoted from Aune, "The Uses of Richard III," 29, citing "Early Stuart Libels: An Edition of Poetry from Manuscript Sources," in *Early Modern Literary Studies Text Series I*, ed. Alastair Bellany and Andrew McRae (2005), D4, available at https://www.earlystuartlibels.net.

23. Quoted from Aune, "Uses of Richard III," 29, citing "Early Stuart Libels," D5.

24. John Beaumont, *Bosworth-field* (London: Felix Kyngston, 1629), 1, 11.

25. Charles Aleyn, *The Historie of that Wise and Fortunate Prince, Henrie of that Name the Seventh* (London: Tho. Cotes, 1638), 2.

26. See Gerald Eades Bentley, *The Jacobean and Caroline Stage: Plays and Playwrights* (London: Clarendon Press, 1949), 5.1013.

27. "A Young Witty Lad Playing the Part of Richard the Third: At the Red Bull," in Thomas Heywood, *Pleasant Dialogues and Dramma's* (London: R. O., 1637), 247.

28. See Thomas Wincoll, *Plantagenets Tragicall Story* (London: M. F., 1649), 42.

29. Henry King, *Sermon Preached at White-Hall on the 29th of May Being the Happy Day of His Majesties Inauguration and Birth* (London: Henry Herringman, 1661), 15.

30. John Caryll, *The English Princess, or, the Death of Richard the III: A Tragedy* (London: Thomas Dring, 1667), 1.4.38.

31. John Crown, *The Misery of Civil-War, a Tragedy* (London: R. Bentley and M. Magnes, 1680), Epilougue.

32. Colley Cibber, *An Apology for the Life of Mr. Colley Cibber* (London: John Watts, 1740), 78.

33. William Camden, *Remaines of a Greater Worke, concerning Britaine* (London: George Eld, 1605), 216.

34. John Speed, *The History of Great Britaine* (London: William Hall and John Beale, 1611), 685.

35. John Trussell, *A Continuation of The Collection of the History of England* (London: M. D., 1636), 242.

36. Richard Baker, *Chronicle of the Kings of England* (London: Daniel Frere, 1643), 137. Baker is quoted later in the seventeenth century, for example, by Nathanial Wanley, *The Wonders of the Little World* (London: T. Basset et al., 1673) in his discussion "of the signal deformity, and very mean personage of some great persons and others," Richard being one of those exhibiting "distortions within and without" (29).

37. Henry Parker, *The True Portraiture of the Kings of England* (London: R. W., 1650), 35.

38. Anthony Weldon, *A Cat May Look upon a King* (London: William Roybould, 1652), 22.

39. William Assheton, *The Cry of Royal Innocent Blood* (London: Daniel Brown, 1683), 51.

40. William Cornwallis, "The Prayse of King Richard the Third," in *Essayes of Certaine Paradoxes* (London: George Purslowe, 1616), C3. For other sixteenth-century anti-figural readings, see Thomas Nash, *Quaternio or A Fourefold Way to a Happie Life* (London: John Dawson, 1633), in which a rustic asks, "Who [was] more deformed then *Richard* the third, King of *England*, yet who more Couragious?" (100); and Alexander Ross, *The History of the World* (London: John Saywell, 1652): "This Tyrant *Richard*, who in his life was monstrous, in his death courageous: He had a deformed body, but a cunning brain, an eloquent tongue, and a ready hand" (556).

41. George Buck, *The History of the Life and Reigne of Richard the Third* (London: W. Wilson, 1646), 79–80. Buck had personal stakes in this history. He was trying to delegitimize Henry VII, who had beheaded his grandfather (Sir John Buck) for fighting on the losing side at Bosworth.

42. See *Richard III* (ca. 1660), oil on canvas, 46.5 × 36 cm, at the National Trust (Bradford-upon-Avon, Wiltshire, England).

43. William Winstanley, *England's Worthies* (London: Nathaniel Brooke, 1660), 142.

44. John Dryden and Nathaniel Lee, *Oedipus a Tragedy* (London: R. Bentley and M. Magnes, 1679), 5–6.

45. *The First Folio of Shakespeare: A Transcript of Contemporary Marginalia in a Copy of the Kodama Memorial Library of Meisei University*, ed. Akihiro Yamada (Tokyo: Yushodo, 1998), 153.

46. James Siemon, "'The Power of Hope?' An Early Modern Reader of *Richard III*," in *A Companion to Shakespeare's Works*, ed. Richard Dutton and Jean E. Howard (London: Blackwell, 2003), 2:362.

47. See Paul Rapin, *The History of England, as well Ecclesiastical as Civil*, trans. Nicolas Tindal (London: James and John Knapton, 1725–1731), 6.240; John Oldmixon, *The Critical History of England* (London: J. Pemberton, 1726–1730), 1.101; Edmund Curll, "The Life and Prophesies of Merlin," in *The Rarities of Richmond* (London: E. Curll, 1736), 169; Guillaume Thomas François, abbé Raynal, "Seventh Epoch," in *The History of the Parliament of England*, anonymous trans. (London: T. Osborne, 1751), 144; Charlotte Lennox, *Shakespear Illustrated* (London: A. Millar, 1754), 3.163–164, 3.138; Ferdinando Warner, *The Ecclesiastical History of England* (London, 1756), 1.8.564; William Dodd, *The Beauties of Shakespear* (London: T. Waller, 1757), 188; and Tobias Smollett, "Richard III," in *A Complete History of England*, 2nd ed. (London: James Rivington, James Fletcher, and R. Baldwin, 1758), 5:199.

48. See Rapin, *History of England*, 6.240; Thomas Carte, *A General History of England from the Earliest Times* (London: Thomas Carte, 1750), iv; William Hay, *Deformity: An Essay* (London: R. and J. Dodsley, 1754), iv–v; and Thomas Mortimer, *A New History of England* (London: J. Wilson and J. Fell, 1764–1766), 2.132.

49. See Horace Walpole, *Historic Doubts on the Life and Reign of King Richard the Third* (London: J. Dodsley, 1768), 52–53.

50. *The Third Part of King Henry VI*, in *The Works of Shakespeare*, ed. Lewis Theobald (London: A. Bettesworth et al., 1733), 4:392n26.

51. *The Life and Death of Richard III*, in *The Works of Shakespeare*, ed. William Warburton (London: J. and P. Knapton et al., 1747), 5:234n7.

52. Voltaire, "Of Edward IV," in *The Works of M. de Voltaire*, ed. Tobias George Smollett and Thomas Francklin (London: J. Newbery, 1761), 243.

53. David Hume, "Richard III," in *The History of England, from the Invasion of Julius Caesar to the Accession of Henry VII* (London: A. Millar, 1762), 2:439.

54. See Colley Cibber, *The Tragical History of King Richard III as it is acted at the Theatre Royal* (London: B. Lintott and A. Bettesworth, 1700), 51.

55. See Francis Hayman, *David Garrick as Richard III* (1760), at the Royal National Theatre (London, England).

56. See Nathaniel Dance-Holland, *David Garrick as Richard III* (1771), at the Stratford-upon-Avon Town Hall (England).

57. Samuel Derrick, *A General View of the Stage. By Mr. Wilkes* (London: J. Coote and W. Whetstone, 1759), 236.

58. *The Third Part of King Henry the Sixth*, in *The Plays of William Shakespeare*, ed. Samuel Johnson (London: J. and R. Tonson et al., 1765), 5:173n3.

59. Samuel Johnson, *Mr. Johnson's Preface to his Edition of Shakespear's Plays* (London: J. and R. Tonson et al., 1765), viii.

60. See Sigmund Freud, "Some Character-Types Met with in Psycho-Analytic Work: The 'Exceptions'" (1916), in *Standard Edition of the Complete Psychological Works of Sigmund Freud*, ed. James Strachey (London: Hogarth, 1958), 14:311–315.

61. *The Life and Death of Richard the Third*, in *Plays*, ed. Johnson, 5:230n4.

62. *The First Part of King Henry the Fourth*, in *Plays*, ed. Johnson, 4:188n3.

63. Elizabeth Montagu, *An Essay on the Writings and Genius of Shakespear* (London: J. Dodsley et al., 1769), 58–59.

64. Francis Gentleman, *The Dramatic Censor; or, Critical Companion* (London: J. Bell and C. Etherington, 1770), 10; Thomas Whately, *Remarks on Some of the Characters of Shakespeare* (1770), ed. Joseph Whately (London: T. Payne and Son, 1785), 15.

65. George Steevens, in *General Evening Post* (March 14–17, 1772), in *Shakespeare: The Critical Heritage*, ed. Brian Vickers (London: Routledge, 1979), 5:494.

66. *The Life and Death of King Richard III*, in *The Plays of William Shakespeare*, ed. George Steevens (London: C. Bathurst et al., 1778), 7:31n8.

67. Elizabeth Griffith, *The Morality of Shakespeare's Drama Illustrated* (London: T. Cadell, 1775), 312.

68. See William Richardson, "On the Dramatic Character of King Richard the Third," in *Essays on Shakespeare's Dramatic Characters* (London: J. Murray, 1785), 14; August Wilhelm von Schlegel, "Respecting the Pieces Said to Be Falsely Attributed to Shakespeare" (1808), in *A Course of Lectures on Dramatic Art and Literature*, trans. John Black (London: Baldwin, Craddock, and Joy, 1815), 2:249–250; Samuel Taylor Coleridge, "The Twelfth Lecture" (1811), in *Seven Lectures on Shakespeare and Milton*, ed. John Payne Collier (London: Chapman and Hall, 1856), 127; and Søren Kierkegaard, *Fear and Trembling* (1843), trans. Howard V. Hong and Edna H. Hong (Princeton, NJ: Princeton University Press, 1983), 114.

69. See William Hazlitt, "Macbeth," in *Characters of Shakespear's Plays* (London: C. H. Reynell, 1817), 26.

70. William Hutton, *The Battle of Bosworth-Field* (Birmingham: Pearson and Rollasom, 1788), xvii; Sharon Turner, *History of England during the Middle Ages* (London: Longman, Hurst, Rees, Orme, and Brown, 1823), 3.477n44, 3.477, 3.371; Caroline Amelia Halsted, *Richard III. as Duke of Gloucester and King of England* (Philadelphia: Carey and Hart, 1844), 23, 414; John Heneage Jesse, *Memoirs of King Richard the Third and Some of His Contemporaries* (London: Richard Bentley, 1862), 76; James Gairdner, *History of the Life and Reign of Richard the Third* (London: Longmans, Green, 1879), 7; Alfred O. Legge, *The Unpopular King: The Life and Times of Richard III* (London: Ward and Downey, 1885), 2.265; Clements R. Markham, *Richard III: His Life and Character, Reviewed in the Light of Recent Research* (New York: E. P. Dutton, 1906), 187; Paul Murray Kendall, *Richard III* (London: Allen and Unwin, 1955), 537n26; and Charles Ross, *Richard III* (London: Eyre Methuen, 1981), 138.

71. Josephine Tey, *The Daughter of Time* (New York: Pocket Books, 1977); William H. Rehnquist, Susan Williams, and Randall Shepard, *The Trial of Richard III* (Bloomington: Indiana University School of Law, 1997); and Bertram Fields, *Royal Blood: Richard III and the Mystery of the Princes* (New York: HarperCollins, 2000), 276.

72. *Richard the Third*, ed. Johnson, 353n3.

73. Montagu, *Genius of Shakespear*, 149.

74. *King Richard III*, ed. Steevens, 150n3.

75. Griffith, *The Morality of Shakespeare's Drama*, 320.

76. Henry Fuseli, *Richard III, Asleep, Visited by Ghosts* (ca. 1769), at the Victoria and Albert Museum (London, England).

77. James Neagle after Henry Fuseli, *K. Richard III, Act 5. Sc. 3* (London: C. and F. Rivington, 1804), at the Folger Shakespeare Library (Washington, DC).

78. The Master of the Mallet, *King Appearing to a Seated Figure* (late eighteenth c.), at the Princeton University Art Museum (Princeton, NJ).

79. William Blake, *K. Richard III- Act 5. Sc. 3* (ca. 1806), at the British Museum (London, England).

80. Henry Fuseli, *Richard III Visited by Ghosts* (1777), at the British Museum.

81. Edward Capell, *Notes and Various Readings to Shakespeare* (London: Henry Hughs, 1779–1780), 2:190.

82. Nicolai Abildgaard, *Richard III Awakening from His Nightmare* (1787), at the Nasjonalgalleriet (Oslo, Norway).

83. Nicolai Abildgaard, *Richard III before the Battle of Bosworth* (ca. 1780–1789), at the Randers Kunstmuseum (Denmark).

84. William Hamilton, *John Phillip Kemble as Richard III* (ca. 1787), in the Raymond Mander and Joe Mitchenson Theatre Collection at the University of Bristol (England).

85. Thomas Stothard, *K. Richard III* (late eighteenth c.), at the Folger.

86. William Sharp, *Richard IIId., Act 5 Scene 3, in the Tent* (London: Mr. Woodmason, 1794), at the Folger.

87. "Shakespeare's Ghosts, and Lewis's Spectre," *Monthly Mirror* 5 (February 1798): 110.

88. Kemble's decision to remove Banquo's ghost was based on suggestions from Bonnell Thornton in 1752 and Robert Lloyd in 1760.

89. William Hazlitt, "Mr. Kean's Richard," *Morning Chronicle* (February 21, 1814), in *Dramatic Essays* (London: W. Scott, 1818), 9–10.

90. The *Times* (March 15, 1814), quoted from *Richard III*, ed. Julie Hankey (London: Junction, 1981), 234.

91. Charles Heath after Henry Howard, *Richard III* (London: Longman, 1816), at the Folger.

92. Alexandre Bida, *King Richard III, V, 3* (mid-nineteenth c.), at the Folger.

93. Frederick William Hawkins, "At the Zenith. 1814–1825," in *The Life of Edmund Kean* (London: Tinsley Brothers, 1869), 1:167

94. Jean Benedetti, *David Garrick and the Birth of Modern Theatre* (London: Methuen, 2001).

95. Many of Kuhn's examples in *The Structure of Scientific Revolutions* come from the eighteenth century, such as Newton's *Opticks* (1704), Franklin's *Electricity* (1750), and Lavoisier's *Chemistry* (1789).

96. Erich Auerbach, *Mimesis: The Representation of Reality in Western Literature* (1946), trans. Willard R. Trask (1953), 50th anniv. ed. (Princeton, NJ: Princeton University Press, 2003), 443.

97. Erich Auerbach, "Figura" (1938), trans. Ralph Manheim, in *Scenes from the Drama of European Literature* (New York: Meridian, 1959), 59.

98. Erich Auerbach, "Typological Symbolism in Medieval Literature," *Yale French Studies* 9 (1952): 5.

99. Michel Foucault, *Abnormal: Lectures at the Collège de France, 1974–1975*, trans. Graham Burchell (New York: Picador, 1999), 57; Henri-Jacques Stiker, *A History of Disability* (1982), trans. William Sayers (Ann Arbor: University of Michigan Press, 1999); Lennard J. Davis, *Enforcing Normalcy: Disability, Deafness, and the Body* (London: Verso, 1995), 24; Rosemarie Garland-Thomson, *Extraordinary Bodies: Figuring Physical Disability in American Culture and Literature* (New York: Columbia University Press, 1997), 57; David M. Turner, *Disability in Eighteenth-Century England: Imagining Physical Impairment* (Abingdon: Routledge, 2012); Essaka Joshua, *Physical Disability in British Romantic Literature* (Cambridge: Cambridge University Press, 2020).

100. See Michel de Montaigne, "Of Phisiognomy," in *Essays* (1571–1592), trans. John Florio (London: Melch. Bradwood, 1603); Joseph Addison, *Spectator* 86 (June 8, 1711).

101. See Giambattista della Porta, *On Human Physiognomy* (1586). On the number of editions, see Zakiya Hanafi, *The Monster in the Machine* (Durham, NC: Duke University Press, 2000), 101; Johann Caspar Lavater, *Essays on Physiognomy, Designed to Promote the Knowledge and the Love of Mankind* (1775–1778), trans. Henry Hunter (London: John Murray, H. Hunter, and T. Holloway, 1789–1798). On the number of editions, see Richard T. Grey, *About Face: German Physiognomic Thought from Lavater to Auschwitz* (Detroit: Wayne State University Press, 2004), xxx.

102. James Parsons, *Human Physiognomy Explain'd* (London: C. Davis, 1746).

103. John Clubbe, *Physiognomy* (London: R. and J. Dodsley, 1763).

104. Georg Christoph Lichtenberg, *Über Physiognomik, wider die Physiognomen* (1778), ed. Fritz Aerni (Waldshut-Tiengen: Aerni, 1996); Immanuel Kant, *Anthropology from a Pragmatic Point of View* (1798), trans. Robert B. Louden (Cambridge: Cambridge University Press, 2006), 195–202; and Georg Wilhelm Friedrich Hegel, *Phenomenology of Mind*, trans. J. B. Baillie (New York: Harper and Row, 1967), 181–183.

105. See Kevin Joel Berland, "'The Air of a Porter': Lichtenberg and Lavater Test Physiognomy by Looking at Dr. Johnson," *Age of Johnson* 10 (1999): 219–230.

106. Josef Warkany, "Congenital Malformations in the Past," *Journal of Chronic Diseases* 10, no. 2 (August 1959): 94.

107. See Shirley A. Roe, *Matter, Life, and Generation: Eighteenth-Century Embryology and the Haller-Wolff Debate* (Cambridge: Cambridge University Press, 2003), quote of Wolff from p. 126.

108. Isidore Geoffroy Saint-Hilaire, *Histoire Générale Et Particulière Des Anomalies De L'organisation Chez L'homme Et Les Animaux. Des Monstruosités, Des Varietés Et Vices De Conformation, Ou Traité De Tératologie* (Paris: J-B. Bailliere, 1823).

109. William John Little, "Hospital for the Cure of Deformities: Course of Lectures on the Deformities of the Human Frame," in *The Lancet* 41, no. 1049–1072 (October 7, 1843–March 16, 1844).

110. See P. J. Accardo, "Deformity and Character: Dr. Little's Diagnosis of Richard III," *Journal of the American Medical Association* 244, no. 24 (1980): 2746–2747.

111. Donald S. Miller and Ethel H. Davis, "Shakespeare and Orthopedics," *Surgery, Gynecology, and Obstetrics* 128 (1969): 361.

112. Mary Wortley Montagu and John Hervey, *Verses Address'd to the Imitator of the First Satire of the Second Book of Horace* (London: A. Dodd, 1733), 8.

113. Anodyne Tanner (i.e., John Dennis), *The Life of the Late Celebrated Mrs. Elizabeth Wisebourn* (London: A. Moore, 1721), 33; John Dennis, *A True Character of Mr. Pope* (London: S. Popping, 1716), 10.

114. John Hervey, *The Difference between Verbal and Practical Virtue* (London: J. Roberts, 1742), 6.

115. Alexander Pope, *An Essay on Man* (London: John Wright, 1734), 2.1–2.

116. "Deformity Not Always the Sign of an Ill Man," in *The History of Man: Displaying the Various Powers, Faculties, Capacities, Virtues, Vices, and Defects of the Human Mind* (London: M. Cooper, 1746), 1:178–179.

117. Hay, *Deformity*, 58.

118. Helen Deutsch, "The Body's Moments: Visible Disability, the Essay and the Limits of Sympathy," *Prose Studies* 27, no. 1 (2005): 11.

119. Randolph Bourne, "The Handicapped—By One of Them," *Atlantic Monthly* 108 (1911): 320–329; James I. Charleton, *Nothing about Us without Us: Disability Oppression and Empowerment* (Berkeley: University of California Press, 1998).

120. Samuel Johnson, *The Life of Pope*, in *The Lives of the English Poets* (Dublin: Whitestone, 1779), 382.

121. George Gordon, Lord Byron, "Letter 160. To Mr. Murray" (February 7, 1814), in *The Works of Lord Byron* (London: John Murray, 1832), 3:9–10, 3:40.

122. George Gordon, Lord Byron, *The Deformed Transformed* (London: J. and H. L. Hunt, 1824), 25–26.

123. See William E. Holladay and Stephen Watt, "Viewing the Elephant Man," *PMLA* 104, no. 5 (1989): 168–181.

124. See Victor Hugo, *The Hunchback of Notre Dame* (1831), trans. Catherine Liu (New York: Random House, 2002); Victor Hugo, *The Man Who Laughs* (1869), trans. Joseph L. Blamire (London: George Routledge and Sons, 1889); and Gaston Leroux, *The Phantom of the Opera* (1909–1910), trans. Leonard Wolf (New York: Plume, 1996).

125. See Alfred Adler, *Study of Organ Inferiority and Its Psychical Compensation* (1907), trans. Smith Ely Jelliffe (New York: Nervous and Mental Disease Publishing Company, 1917); Beatrice A. Wright, *Physical Disability: A Psychological Approach* (New York: Harper and Brothers, 1960); and Goffman, *Stigma*.

126. See Stiker, *History*; Davis, *Normalcy*; Garland-Thomson, *Bodies*; Simi Linton, *Claiming Disability: Knowledge and Identity* (New York: New York University Press, 1998); David Mitchell and Sharon Snyder, *Narrative Prosthesis: Disability and the Dependencies of Discourse* (Ann Arbor: University of Michigan Press, 2000); Ato Quayson, *Aesthetic Nervousness: Disability and the Crisis of Representation* (New York: Columbia University Press, 2007); and Tobin Siebers, *Disability Theory* (Ann Arbor: University of Michigan Press, 2008).

127. This is the view of modernization argued, for example, by Talcott Parsons, *The Evolution of Societies*, ed. Jackson Toby (Englewood Cliffs: Prentice-Hall, 1977). See also the helpful "General Commentary: The Meaning of Modernity," in *Modernity: Critical Concepts*, ed. Malcolm Waters (London: Routledge, 1999), 1:xi–xxiii.

128. See Chapter 2, notes 22–23.

129. Marcela Kostihova, "Digging for Perfection: Discourse of Deformity in Richard III's Excavation," *Palgrave Communications* 2, no. 16046 (2016): 2.

CHAPTER 6

1. See Chapter 5, note 2.

2. See, for instance, H. R. Coursen, "Filming Shakespeare's History: Three Films of *Richard III*," in *Shakespeare on Film*, ed. Russell Jackson (Cambridge: Cambridge University Press, 2000), 99–116; Barbara Freedman, "Critical Junctures in Shakespeare Screen History: The Case of *Richard III*," in *Shakespeare on Film*, ed. Russell Jackson (Cambridge: Cambridge University Press, 2000): 47–71; Saskia Kossak, *"Frame My Face to All Occasions": Shakespeare's* Richard III *on Screen* (Vienna: Braumüller, 2005); and for a full list, see Jose Ramon Diaz Fernandez, *"Richard III* on Screen: An Annotated Filmo-bibliography," in *Shakespeare on Screen: Richard III*, ed. Sarah Hatchuel and Nathalie Vienne-Guerrin (Rouen: Publications de l'Universite de Rouen, 2005), 281–322.

3. See Gilbert Stuart, *John Philip Kemble as Richard III* (1786), in a private collection; as well as John Thornthwaite after Gilbert Stuart, *Mr. Kemble as King Richard* (London: John Bell, 1798), in the National Portrait Gallery (London, England).

4. See Robert Thew after James Northcote, *King Richard the Third, Act III, Scene I* (London: John and Josiah Boydell, 1791), at the Folger Shakespeare Library (Washington, DC).

5. James Northcote, *The Meeting of Edward V, and His Brother Richard, Duke of York, Comtemplated by Richard III* (1799), at the National Trust (Petworth, West Sussex, England).

6. See N. C. Goodnight, *Mr. Holman as Richard* (ca. 1787), at the Folger.

7. Annabel Scratch, *Caricature of John Quick as Richard III in "Richard III"* (1790), in the University of Illinois Theatrical Print Collection (Urbana-Champaign, IL).

8. Henry Singleton and William Nutter, *King Richard III* (London: C. Taylor, 1792), at the Folger.

9. Unknown Artist, *John Bannister as Gloucester and John Pinder as Sir Richard Ratcliffe in "Richard III" by William Shakespeare* (ca. 1794), at the Theatre Royal (Bath, England).

10. Robert Dighton, *Mr. Cooke* (1800), at the Folger.

11. Charles Lamb, "Cooke's Richard the Third," *Morning Post* (Jan. 8, 1802), in *The Works of Charles and Mary Lamb*, ed. E. V. Lucas (London: Methuen, 1903), 1:37.

12. Anthony Cardon after J. T. Barber, *Mr. Cooke in the Character of Richard the 3rd* (London: John P. Thompson, 1805), at the Folger; C. R. Leslie and D. Edwin, *Cooke as Richard III* (nineteenth c.), in the UI Theatrical Print Collection; Samuel De Wilde, *The Late Mr. Cooke as Richard in Richard the 3rd* (London: Chapple, 1813), at the Folger; Samuel De Wilde and Cheesman, *Mr. Cooke as Richard III* (nineteenth c.), in the UI Theatrical Print Collection; James Thomson after C. R. Leslie, *The Late Mr. Cooke as Richard the Third* (London: Simpkin and Marshall, 1818), at the Folger; and *George Frederick Cooke as Gloucester in "Richard III" by William Shakespeare* (ca. 1805), at the Theatre Royal.

13. Leigh Hunt, *Examiner* 193 (February 25, 1815): 140.

14. John James Halls, *Edmund Kean as Richard in "Richard III" by William Shakespeare* (1814), at the Victoria and Albert Museum (London, England).

15. See London Green, "Edmund Kean's Richard III," *Theatre Journal* 36, no. 4 (December 1984): 505–524.

16. George Clint, *Edmund Kean as Gloucester in "Richard III" by William Shakespeare* (nineteenth c.), at the Theatre Royal.

17. *Mr. Cobham as Richard the Third* (Hoxton, New Town, England: I. Dyer, 1827), at the Folger.

18. C. Shoosmith and R. Cooper, *Junius Brutus Booth as Richard III* (1817), in the UI Theatrical Print Collection; William Bond after F. P. Stephanoff, *Junius Brutus Booth* (1817), at the Folger; and *Mr. Booth as Richard 3d* (early to mid-nineteenth c.), at the Folger.

19. Samuel De Wild, *William Charles Macready as Richard III* (1820), in the Somerset Maugham Collection at the Royal National Theatre (London, England); and W. H., *Mr. Macready as Duke of Gloucester, afterwards King Richard III* (London: Hodgson, nineteenth c.), at the Folger.

20. See London Green, "'The Gaiety of Meditated Success': The *Richard III* of William Charles Macready," *Theatre Research International* 10, no. 2 (June 1985): 107–128.

21. *King Richard IIIrd, Act 1, S. II* (early nineteenth c.), at the Folger.

22. *Mr. Edwin Forrest as Richard III* (1855), in the UI Theatrical Print Collection; *Mr. Freer as Richard the Third* (London: A. Park, nineteenth c.), at the Folger; *Mr. Wightman as Richard III* (London: W. West, early to mid-nineteenth c.), at the Folger; Bryan Edward Duppa, *J. P. Warde* (London: W. J. White, 1833), at the Folger; *Mr. Phelps as Richard III* (London: J. L. Marks, mid-nineteenth c.), at the Folger; and *Mr. Holloway as Richard the 3rd* (London: J. Redington, ca. 1850–1876), at the Folger.

23. In addition to the figures of Kean and Forrest reproduced here, see Victor Moblard, *J. B. Roberts as Richard III* (late nineteenth c.), at the Folger; Alexander Reid, *Mr. C. Kean as Gloster* (London Printing and Publishing Company, ca. 1857), in the Farnsworth Shakespeare Print Collection at Rhodes College (Memphis, TN); P. Haas, *Mr. J. W. Wallack as Gloucester* (London: J. Tallis, nineteenth c.), in the UI Theatrical Print Collection; and Mathew Brady Studio, *Edwin Forrest as "Richard III"* (ca. 1860), in the National Portrait Gallery, Smithsonian Institution (Washington, DC).

24. Charles F. Tomkins and James Robinson Planché, *Twelve Designs for the Costume of Shakespeare's Richard the Third* (London: Colnaghi and Son, 1830), 8.

25. Sharon Turner, *History of England during the Middle Ages* (London: Longman, Hurst, Rees, Orme, and Brown, 1823), 3.477n44.

26. Caroline Amelia Halsted, *Richard III. as Duke of Gloucester and King of England* (Philadelphia: Carey and Hart, 1844), 414.

27. *Richard III* (mid-nineteenth c.), at the Folger.

28. James Rees, *The Life of Edwin Forrest: With Reminiscences and Personal Recollections* (Philadelphia: T. B. Peterson, 1874), 254. The story of the Countess of Desmond remarking on Richard's beauty first appears in Horace Walpole's *Historic Doubts*.

29. Thomas Sherratt, *Mr. G. V. Brooke as the Duke of Gloster* (London: London Printing and Publishing Company, mid-nineteenth c.), at the Folger; McClees, Germon, and Hollis, *Mr. Couldock as Richard III* (nineteenth c.), in the UI Theatrical Print Collection.

30. John Gilbert, *Henry VI, Part 3- King Henry VI Is Murdered by Richard of Gloucester*, in *Shakespeare's Works* (London: Routledge, 1859); J. A. Wright, *Richard and Lady Anne* (London: Cassell, Petter, and Galpin, mid- to late nineteenth c.), at the Folger.

31. *Costume Worn by Edwin Booth in the Role of Richard III* (ca. 1870s), at the Folger.

32. John Galsworthy, "The Art of Edwin Booth," in *Loyalties: A Drama in Three Acts* (New York: Macmillan, 1894), 209.

33. Matt Stretch, *Mr. Barry Sullivan as Richard III* (1876), at the Folger.

34. J. Rogers, *John McCullough as Richard III in "Richard III"* (nineteenth c.), in the UI Theatrical Print Collection.

35. Dutton Cook, *Nights at the Play, a View of the English Stage* (London, 1883). According to the "Dramatic Notes," *Westminster Papers* 9 (February 1, 1877), Irving "gives us little or no deformity of body, and merely shows Richard's bodily drawbacks by a limp, as if the monarch had lately suffered from the gout" (198). According to "Music and the Drama," *Victoria Magazine* 28 (March 1877), "Irving's 'Richard' is slightly deformed, but only slightly, and halts, somewhat in these defects," in contrast to "all the hunch-backed ruffians that have played Richard III. up to the present time" (443).

36. *Boots Worn by Henry Irving in Richard III, 1877*, at the Victoria and Albert Museum (London, England).

37. Edwin Long, *Henry Irving as Richard, Duke of Gloucester* (1877), at Bob Jones University Museum and Gallery (Greenville, SC); Alfred Bryan, *Mr. Henry Irving as King Richard III* (London: Ben George Lith., 1878), at the Folger; and Harry Furniss, *Sir Henry Irving as Richard III* (after 1877), at the National Portrait Gallery (London, England).

38. After Macready's unsuccessful attempt to restore Shakespeare's text in 1836, Samuel Phelps tried with equally unsuccessful results in 1845 and 1849. After Irving's successful restoration in 1877, Cibber's *Richard III* largely disappeared from the London stage (though many of Cibber's cuts, such as excising Margaret, are made in more recent versions of *Richard III*, including those of Olivier and McKellen).

39. *Mr. Richard Mansfield as King Richard III* (London: Stereoscopic, 1889), at the Folger; John Ranken Towse, *Sixty Years of the Theatre: An Old Critic's Memories* (New York: Funk and Wagnalls, 1916), 326. Uneasy with the discrepancy between the historical Richard III and Shakespeare's, Mansfield says that he "preferred therefore to touch as lightly as possible ... upon the deformity of Richard's body" (see *King Richard III* [New York], "Nota"). This refusal to thematize Richard's deformity led one critic to write a letter to Mansfield complaining, "Give us more hump" (see Paul Wilstach, *Richard Mansfield: The Man and the Actor* [New York: Charles Scribner's Sons, 1908], 189).

40. Edwin Austin Abbey, *Richard, Duke of Gloucester, and the Lady Anne* (1896), in the Edwin Austin Abbey Memorial Collection at Yale University (New Haven, CT).

41. Benson, Warde, and Barrymore are notable for bringing Richard to film but don't do anything new with his disability. Barrymore, Holloway, and Williams are the first Richards influenced by Freud's psychoanalytic reading. Laurie and Wolfit suggest Hitler in their Richards. Olivier unites the psychological Richard of Barrymore, Hol-

loway, and Williams and the political Richard of Laurie and Wolfit. Rathbone and Price remake the story of Richard as a horror film, but, again, there is nothing new with respect to Richard's disability.

42. This account comes from John Newmark, quoted from Wilhelm Hortmann, *Shakespeare on the German Stage: Volume 2, The Twentieth Century* (Cambridge: Cambridge University Press, 1998), 137, citing " . . . so halb Totschlager und halb Gestapo," in *Frankfurter Rundschau* (October 31, 1987).

43. This argument is made by Casey, "Richard's Himself Again," 29–31.

44. See Day, *Shakespeare at Stratford*, on Holm (36–65), Goring (95–116), and Rodway (116–152).

45. George Bernard Shaw, "Richard Himself Again," *Saturday Review* 82, no. 2148 (December 26, 1896): 671.

46. Richard W. Schoch, *Shakespeare's Victorian Stage: Performing History in the Theatre of Charles Kean* (Cambridge: Cambridge University Press, 1998), 146.

47. "All That Glisters Is Not Gold," *Codeswitch* (NPR: August 21, 2019).

48. A. J. Withers and Liat Ben-Moshe, with Loree Erickson, Rachel da Silva Gorman, Talila A. Lewis, Lateef McLeod, and Mia Mingus, "Roundtable: Radical Disability Politics," in *The Routledge Handbook of Radical Politics*, ed. Ruth Kinna and Uri Gordon (Abingdon: Routledge, 2019), 178.

49. Urvashi Chakravarty, "'Live, and Beget a Happy Race of Kings': *Richard III*, Race and Homonationalism," in *Shakespeare/Sex: Contemporary Readings in Gender and Sexuality*, ed. Jennifer Drouin (London: Bloomsbury, 2020), 147–168.

50. Rosemarie Garland-Thomson, *Extraordinary Bodies: Figuring Physical Disability in American Culture and Literature* (New York: Columbia University Press, 1997), 8.

51. David Mitchell and Sharon Snyder, *Narrative Prosthesis: Disability and the Dependencies of Discourse* (Ann Arbor: University of Michigan Press, 2000), 3; Tobin Siebers, *Disability Theory* (Ann Arbor: University of Michigan Press, 2008), 27.

52. See Jeffrey R. Wilson, "The Figure of Stigma in Shakespeare's Drama," *Genre* 51, no. 3 (2018): 237–266.

53. While research on Shakespearean intersectionalities is rapidly developing, landmark early statements include Ania Loomba's *Gender, Race, Renaissance Drama* (Manchester: Manchester University Press, 1989); Margo Hendricks and Patricia Parker, eds., introduction to *Women, "Race" and Writing in the Early Modern Period* (New York: Routledge, 1994), 1–16; and Kim F. Hall's "Epilogue: On 'Race,' Black Feminism, and White Supremacy," in *Things of Darkness: Economies of Race and Gender in Early Modern England* (Ithaca, NY: Cornell University Press, 1995), 254–268.

54. For more detail on the African Grove, see William Over, "New York's African Theatre: The Vicissitudes of the Black Actor," *Afro-Americans in New York Life and History* 3, no. 2 (1979): 7–13; Jonathan Dewberry, "The African Grove Theatre and Company," *Black American Literature Forum* 16, no. 4 (1982): 128–131; George Thompson, *A Documentary History of the African Theatre* (Chicago: Northwestern University Press, 1998); Marvin Edward McAllister, *White People Do Not Know How to Behave at Entertainments Designed for Ladies and Gentlemen of Colour: William Brown's African and American Theater* (Chapel Hill: University of North Carolina Press, 2003); Errol G.

Hill, "The African Theatre to Uncle Tom's Cabin," in *A History of African American Theatre*, ed. Errol G. Hill and James V. Hatch (Cambridge: Cambridge University Press, 2003), 24–60; Shane White, *Stories of Freedom in Black New York* (Cambridge, MA: Harvard University Press, 2009); and Danielle Rosvally, "'Off with His Head! . . . So Much for Hewlett/Brown': The African Grove Theater Presents Richard III," in *Shaping Shakespeare for Performance: The Bear Stage*, ed. Catherine Loomis and Sid Ray (Lanham, MD: Fairleigh Dickinson University Press, 2016), 127–140.

55. *National Advocate* (September 21, 1821), 2, quoted from Thompson, *African Theatre*, 61.

56. Frances Beal, "Double Jeopardy: To Be Black and Female," in *Black Women's Manifesto* (New York: Third World Women's Alliance, 1969), 19–34.

57. Patricia Hill Collins, "Learning from the Outsider within: The Sociological Significance of Black Feminist Thought," *Social Problems* 33, no. 6 (1986): 19.

58. Deborah K. King, "Multiple Jeopardy, Multiple Consciousness: The Context of a Black Feminist Ideology," *Signs* 14, no. 1 (1988): 42–72.

59. Kimberlé Crenshaw, "Mapping the Margins: Intersectionality, Violence Against Women of Color," *Stanford Law Review* 43, no. 6 (1991): 1245.

60. Robert McRuer, *Crip Theory: Cultural Signs of Queerness and Disability* (New York: New York University Press, 2006), 37.

61. Alison Kafer, *Feminist, Queer, Crip* (Bloomington: Indiana University Press, 2013), 13.

62. Sami Schalk, "Coming to Claim Crip: Disidentification with/in Disability Studies," *Disability Studies Quarterly* 33, no. 2 (2013).

63. *National Advocate* (Nov. 19, 1921), 2, quoted from Thompson, *African Theatre*, 78.

64. Nirmala Erevelles and Andrea Minear, "Unspeakable Offenses: Untangling Race and Disability in Discourses of Intersectionality," *Journal of Literary and Cultural Disability Studies* 4, no. 2 (2010): 127–145.

65. *New-York City-Hall Recorder* 6, no. 10 (November 1821): 88, quoted from Thompson, *African Theatre*, 79.

66. Robert McRuer, "Compulsory Able-bodiedness and Queer/Disabled Existence," in *Disability Studies: Enabling the Humanities*, ed. Sharon L. Snyder, Brenda Jo Brueggemann, and Rosemarie Garland-Thomson (New York: Modern Language Association, 2002), 88–99.

67. *National Advocate* (October 27, 1821), 2, quoted from Thompson, *African Theatre*, 72.

68. *National Advocate* (January 9, 1822), 2, quoted from ibid., 85.

69. See Jones, *Richard's Himself Again* (London: J. Davis, nineteenth c.), at the Folger.

70. *Life of Jim Crow* (Philadelphia: James M'Minn, 1835), quoted from W. T. Lhamon Jr., *Jump Jim Crow: Lost Plays, Lyrics, and Street Prose of the First Atlantic Popular Culture* (Cambridge, MA: Harvard University Press, 2003), 388.

71. Dennis Tyler Jr., "Jim Crow's Disabilities: Racial Injury, Immobility, and the 'Terrible Handicap' in the Literature of James Weldon Johnson," *African American Review* 50, no. 2 (2017): 185.

72. See Bernth Lindfors, "'Mislike Me Not for My Complexion . . .': Ira Aldridge in Whiteface," *African American Review* 33, no. 2 (1999): 347–354.

73. Quoted from William J. Simmons, *Men of Mark* (Cleveland: Geo. M. Rewell, 1887), 488.

74. King, "Multiple Jeopardy," 47.

75. Marlis Schweitzer, *Bloody Tyrants and Little Pickles: Stage Roles of Anglo-American Girls in the Nineteenth Century* (Iowa City: University of Iowa Press, 2020), 31.

76. Laurence Hutton, *Curiosities of the American Stage* (New York: Harper and Brothers, 1891), 241.

77. Noah M. Ludlow, *Dramatic Life as I Found It* (St. Louis: G. J. Jones, 1880), 463.

78. Quoted from Jane Woollard, "Hidden Women of History: Eliza Winstanley, Colonial Stage Star and Our First Female Richard III," *The Conversation* (May 1, 2019).

79. Rosemarie Garland-Thomson, "Integrating Disability, Transforming Feminist Theory," *NWSA Journal* 14, no. 3 (2002): 2.

80. Ibid., 4.

81. Kim Q. Hall, ed., "Reimagining Disability and Gender through Feminist Studies," in *Feminist Disability Studies* (Bloomington: Indiana University Press, 2011), 6.

82. Sumi Cho, Kimberlé Williams Crenshaw, and Leslie McCall, "Toward a Field of Intersectionality Studies: Theory, Applications, and Praxis," *Signs* 28, no. 4 (2013): 787.

83. Martin Luther King, "I Have a Dream," speech in Washington, DC (August 28, 1963).

84. Audre Lorde, "The Uses of Anger: Women Responding to Racism" (1981), in *Sister Outsider: Essays and Speeches* (Berkeley: Crossing Press, 2007), 124–133.

85. Carlyle Brown, *The African Company Presents Richard III* (New York: Dramatists Play Service, 1994), 74.

86. Lisa Anderson, "When Race Matters: Reading Race in *Richard III* and *Macbeth*," in *Colorblind Shakespeare: New Perspective on Race and Performance*, ed. Ayanna Thompson (Abingdon: Routledge, 2006), 99.

87. Robert McRuer, "Richard III: Fuck the Disabled: The Prequel," in *Shakesqueer: A Queer Companion to the Complete Works of Shakespeare*, ed. Madhavi Menon (Durham, NC: Duke University Press, 2011), 297.

88. Evan Choate, "Misreading Impotence in *Richard III*," *Modern Philology* 117, no. 1 (2019): 24–47; Lauren Coker, "Masquerading Early Modern Disability: Sexuality, Violence, and the Body (Politic) in *Richard III*," *Screen Bodies* 3, no. 1 (2018).

89. Aya Kanno, *Requiem of the Rose King* (2013–), trans. Jocelyne Allen (San Francisco: Viz, 2019–).

90. Kimberlé Crenshaw, "Demarginalizing the Intersection of Race and Sex: A Black Feminist Critique of Antidiscrimination Doctrine, Feminist Theory and Antiracist Politics," *University of Chicago Legal Forum* 140 (1989): 139.

91. Michael Paulson, "Danai Gurira Will Star as Richard III at Shakespeare in the Park," *New York Times* (February 2, 2022).

92. Several of the examples in the paragraphs that follow come from M. G. Aune, "The Uses of Richard III: From Robert Cecil to Richard Nixon," *Shakespeare Bulletin* 24, no. 3 (2006): 23–47.

93. John Milton, *Eikonoklestes* (London: Matthew Simmons, 1649), 11.

94. "Prologue to Richard the Third," in A. B., *Covent Garden Drolery, or A Colection of All the Choice Songs, Poems, Prologues, and Epilogues* (London: James Magnes, 1672), 13.

95. Donald Wolfit, quoted from Scott Colley, *Richard's Himself Again: A Stage History of* Richard III (Westport, CT: Greenwood, 1992), 168, citing a review of *Richard III* in *New Statesman and Nation* 23 (1942): 205.

96. Mark Sokolyansky, "*Richard III* in Russian Theater at the Twilight of the 'Thaw,'" *Multicultural Shakespeare: Translation, Appropriation, and Performance* 4 (2007): 70.

97. *Richard III* (1920), dir. Leopold Jessner, at the National Theater (Berlin, Germany); see Andreas Höfele, "Leopold Jessner's Shakespeare Productions, 1920–1930," *Theatre History Studies* 12 (1992): 141–144.

98. Bertolt Brecht, *The Resistible Rise of Arturo Ui* (1941), trans. George Tabori and Alistair Beaton (London: Bloomsbury, 2013).

99. *Richard III* (1953), dir. Margaret Webster, at the City Center of Music and Drama (New York); as well as Colley, *Richard's Himself Again*, 184.

100. Colley, *Richard's Himself Again*, 209–216; Aune, "Uses of Richard III," 38–39.

101. *Richard III* (1990), dir. Richard Eyre, at the National Theatre (London, England); *Richard III*, dir. Richard Loncraine (United Artists, 1995).

102. Marcus Cheng Chye Tan, "(Echo)Locating Other Shakespeares: An Aesthetics of Pop and the Ear of the Other," in *Acoustic Interculturalism: Listening to Performance* (New York: Palgrave Macmillan, 2012), 93.

103. Sulayman Al-Bassam, *Richard III: An Arab Tragedy* (2007), in *The Arab Shakespeare Trilogy* (London: Bloomsbury, 2014), 78.

104. Graham Holderness, "From Summit to Tragedy; Sulayman Al-Bassam's *Richard III* and Political Theatre," *Critical Survey* 19, no. 3 (2007): 126.

105. Michael Dobbs, *House of Cards* (London: Harper Collins, 1989), *To Play the King* (London: Harper Collins, 1992), and *The Final Cut* (London: Harper Collins, 1994); Dobbs and Andrew Davies, *House of Cards* (BBC, 1990–1995); Beau Willimon, *House of Cards* (Netflix, 2013–2018).

106. See Marina Gerzić, "Broadcasting the Political Body: Richard III, #Brexit and #Libspill," *Shakespeare Bulletin* 39, no. 1 (2021): 109–129.

107. Ramin Farhadi, "Adapting Shakespeare's *Richard III*: A Political Reading of Hamid-Reza Naeemi's *Richard*," *Cogent Arts and Humanities* 7 (2020): Article 1823599.

108. Scott Anderson, dir., *King Richard III* (unreleased, 2008); Paul Cornell, wr., and Jimmy Broxton, il., *Batman: Knight and Squire* 3 (New York: DC Comics, 2011).

109. Lee Chee Keng, "Performing Cultural Exchange in *Richard III*," in *Shakespeare Beyond English: A Global Experiment*, ed. Susan Bennett and Christie Carson (Cambridge: Cambridge University Press, 2013), 77.

110. Magdalena Cieślak, "Grzegorz Wiśniewski's Production of *Richard III* in Teatr Jaracza in Łódź: Textual Authority, the 'Director's Cut,' and Theatre Status," *Multicultural Shakespeare: Translation, Appropriation, and Performance* 17 (2018): 70.

111. See https://twitter.com/richard_third.

112. See Andrea Peghinelli, "'And Thus I Clothe My Naked Villainy': *Richard III* and the Deformed Body as Rhetorical Camouflage in Thomas Ostermeier's Production," *Shakespeare Bulletin* 39, no. 1 (2021): 93–107.

113. Stephen Greenblatt, "Shakespeare Explains the 2016 Election," *New York Times Sunday Review* (October 8, 2016).

114. Anton Juan and Ricardo Abad, dir., *RD3RD*, at the Fine Arts Black Box (Ateneo de Manila University, 2018).

115. Will Power, *Seize the King* (San Diego: La Jolla Playhouse, 2018).

116. Kai Wiegandt, "Shakespeare and the Present: History and Mediality in *Richard III*," *Shakespeare* 16, no. 4 (2020): 331–339; Richard Ashby, "'Retailed to All Posterity': Post-Truth, Oral Tradition, and the Popular Voice in *Richard III*," *Cahiers Élisabéthains* 103, no. 1 (2020): 6–20.

117. See two articles by Marina Gerzić, "Determined to Prove a Villain? Appropriating Richard III's Disability in Recent Graphic Novels and Comics," in *The Routledge Handbook of Shakespeare and Global Appropriation*, ed. Christy Desmet, Sujata Iyengar, and Miriam Jacobson (Abingdon: Routledge, 2019), 409–419; and "'I Wish the Bastards Dead': Adapting Richard III in Children's Literature," in *Playfulness in Shakespearean Adaptations*, ed. Marina Gerzić and Aidan Norrie (Abingdon: Routledge, 2020), 56–74.

118. Lennard J. Davis, "The End of Identity Politics and the Beginning of Dismodernism: On Disability as an Unstable Category," in *Bending over Backwards: Essays on Disability and the Body* (New York: New York University Press, 2002), 9–32.

119. Williams, "Enabling Richard."

120. Sigmund Freud, "Some Character-Types Met with in Psycho-Analytic Work: The 'Exceptions'" (1916), in *The Standard Edition of the Complete Psychological Works of Sigmund Freud*, ed. James Strachey (London: Hogarth, 1958), 14:314.

121. The Americans with Disabilities Act of 1990, available at http://www.ada.gov/archive/adastat91.htm.

122. See Carrie Sandahl, "Black Man, Blind Man: Disability Identity Politics and Performance," *Theatre Journal* 56, no. 4 (2004): 579–602; and a response in Lennard Davis, "Dismodernism Reconsidered," in *The End of Normal: Identity in a Biocultural Era* (Ann Arbor: University of Michigan Press, 2013), 15–30.

123. Kafer, *Feminist, Queer, Crip*, 13.

124. Alexis Martin and Jean-Pierre Ronfard, dir., *Dave Veut Jouer Richard III*, at Sainte-Justine Children's Hospital (Montreal, 2001).

125. Leanore Lieblein, "*Dave veut jouer Richard III*: Interrogating the Shakespearean Body in Quebec," *Canadian Theatre Review* 111 (2002): 19.

126. See Jim Ferris, "Cripple," in *Encyclopedia of Disability*, ed. Gary L. Albrecht, Sharon L. Snyder, and David T. Mitchell (Thousand Oaks, CA: Sage, 2006), 328.

127. The term "cripping up" is often traced to Jozefina Komporály, "'Cripping Up Is the Twenty-First Century's Answer to Blacking Up': Conversation with Kaite O'Reilly on Theatre, Feminism, and Disability—6 June 2005, British Library, London," *Gender Forum: Illuminating Gender* 12 (2005): 58–67.

128. See Graeae, "Our Artistic Vision," at http://graeae.org/about/our-artistic-vision/.

129. See the Alliance for Inclusion in the Arts, "Mission," at http://inclusioninthearts.org/about/mission/.

130. Petra Kuppers, "Deconstructing Images: Performing Disability," *Contemporary Theatre Review* 11, no. 3–4 (2001): 25.

131. Tobin Siebers, "In/Visible: Disability on the Stage," in *Body Aesthetics*, ed. Sherri Irvin (Oxford: Oxford University Press, 2016), 227.

132. Kirsty Johnston, *Disability Theatre and Modern Drama: Recasting Modernism* (London: Bloomsbury, 2016), 52.

133. Thomas Fahy, introduction to *Peering Behind the Curtain: Disability, Illness, and the Extraordinary Body in Contemporary Theatre*, ed. Thomas Fahy and Kimball King (New York: Routledge, 2002), x.

134. Introduction to *Bodies in Commotion: Disability and Performance*, ed. Carrie Sandahl and Philip Auslander (Ann Arbor: University of Michigan Press, 2005), 1.

135. Petra Kuppers, *Disability and Contemporary Performance: Bodies on Edge* (New York: Routledge, 2004), 12.

136. Carrie Sandhal, "The Tyranny of the Neutral: Disability and Actor Training," in *Bodies in Commotion*, 255.

137. Terry Galloway, Donna Nudd, and Carrie Sandahl, "Actual Lives and the Ethic of Accommodation," in *Community Performance: A Reader*, ed. Petra Kuppers (New York: Routledge, 2007), 229.

138. Carrie Sandhal, "Why Disability Identity Matters: From Dramaturgy to Casting in John Belluso's Pyretown," *Text and Performance Quarterly* 28, no. 1–2 (2008): 227.

139. Leslie C. Dunn, "Shakespearean Disability Theatre," in *Performing Disability in Early Modern English Drama*, ed. Leslie C. Dunn (New York: Palgrave Macmillan, 2020), 297–318.

140. Union of the Physically Impaired Against Segregation, *Policy Statement* (1974), available at www.leeds.ac.uk/disability-studies/archiveuk/UPIAS/UPIAS.pdf.

141. See Mike Oliver, *Social Work with Disabled People* (Basingstoke: Macmillan, 1983).

142. See Chapter 5, note 126.

143. See *Richard III* (1984), dir. Bill Alexander, at the Royal Shakespeare Theatre (Stratford-upon-Avon, England).

144. Antony Sher, *Year of the King: An Actor's Diary and Sketchbook* (London: Methuen, 1985), 13.

145. *Richard III* (2000), dir. Jakub Špalek, by the Divadelní Spolek Kašpar company, at the Divadlo v Celetné (Prague, Czech Republic).

146. Marcela Kostihová, "Richard Recast: Renaissance Disability in a Postcommunist Culture," in *Recovering Disability in Early Modern England*, ed. Allison P. Hobgood and David Houston Wood (Columbus: Ohio State University Press, 2013), 135–149.

147. *Richard III* (2003), dir. Barry Kyle, at the Globe (London, England).

148. Kathryn Hunter, interview with Caroline Woddis, quoted from Elizabeth Klett, "Redressing the Balance: All-Female Shakespeare at the Globe Theatre," in *Shakespeare Re-dressed: Cross-gender Casting in Contemporary Performance*, ed. James C. Bulman (Madison, NJ: Fairleigh Dickinson University Press, 2008), 185n36.

149. Charles Spencer, "Sex-Change Villain Lacks Frisson of Fear," *Telegraph* (June 12, 2003).

150. Klett, "Redressing the Balance," 176–179.

151. *Richard III* (2004), dir. Peter DuBois, at the Public Theatre (New York).

152. Charles McNulty, "The Little King," *Village Voice* (August 31, 2004).

153. Ben Brantley, "A Big Throne to Fill, and the Man to Fill It," *New York Times* (October 12, 2004).

154. Allison P. Hobgood, "Teeth before Eyes: Impairment and Invisibility in Shakespeare's *Richard III*," in *Disability, Health, and Happiness in the Shakespearean Body*, ed. Sujata Iyengar (New York: Routledge, 2015), 33.

155. *Richard III* (2005), dir. Heidi Lauren Duke, at the Spoon Theatre (New York).

156. Rachel Saltz, "This Lame King Has Another Self to Lean On," *New York Times* (July 21, 2007).

157. Henry Holden, "Dispelling Stereotypes, on Stage and Off," *New York Times* (April 27, 2013).

158. Stephanie Barton-Farcas, *Disability and Theatre: A Practical Manual for Inclusion in the Arts* (New York: Routledge, 2017).

159. *Richard III* (2008), dir. Ian Leson, at the Kitchen Dog Theatre (Dallas, TX).

160. Jerome Weeks, "Richard III—Hell on Wheels," *Art and Seek* (April 11, 2008).

161. See *Richard III* (2015), dir. Sally Wood, at the Portland Stage Company (Portland, ME).

162. Bob Keyes, "'I'm in a Wheelchair. I'm not an Actor.' Novice Actor Stephen Madigan Portrays Richard III at Portland Stage," *Main Today* (August 12, 2015); Megan Grumbling, "Madigan on Richard III: A Role That Explores the Idea That 'This Disability May Be Why I'm Killing People,'" *Portland Phoenix* (August 12, 2015).

163. *Richard III* (2016), dir. Christopher Brauer, at the Trappist Monestary Provincial Heritage Park (Winnipeg, Canada).

164. Randall King, "Bent but Not Broken," *Winnipeg Free Press* (May 31, 2016).

165. Tom Power, "How MS Helps Actor Debbie Patterson Understand Richard III," *Q with Tom Power* (May 31, 2016).

166. *Richard III* (2016), dir. Jessica Thebus, at the Garage Theatre at Steppenwolf (Chicago, IL).

167. These two moments are described by Chris Jones, "Remarkably Able Moments in Gift Theatre's 'Richard III,'" *Chicago Tribune* (November 17, 2017).

168. Dominic Cooke, dir., *Richard III*, in *The Hollow Crown* (BBC, 2016).

169. Sonya Freeman Loftis, "Cripping (and Re-Cripping) Richard: Was Richard III Disabled?" in *Shakespeare and Disability Studies* (Oxford: Oxford University Press, 2021), 42.

170. See "Benedict Cumberbatch on *The Hollow Crown*, Bloody Warfare and Discovering He's Richard III's Cousin," *Radio Times* (May 14, 2016).

171. Carol Ann Duffy, "Richard," *Guardian* (March 26, 2015).

172. *Richard III* (2017), dir. Peter Evans, for Bell Shakespeare (Australia).

173. Elissa Blake, "Kate Mulvany Takes on Villainous Richard III for Bell Shakespeare's 2017 Season," *Sydney Morning Herald* (September 22, 2016).

174. Richard Watts, "Shakespeare's Body Shaming Confronts Melbourne," *Arts Hub* (February 24, 2017).

175. Caitlin Mary West, "Resisting Processes of Othering: Implied Stage Directions in Australian Theatre Productions of *Richard III*," *Otherness: Essays and Studies* 8, no. 2 (2021): 73.

176. *Richard III* (2017), dir. Barrie Rutter, at the Hull Truck Theatre (Hull, UK).

177. Daisy Bowie-Sell, "Mat Fraser: 'Theatres Who Don't Employ Disabled People Should Be Ashamed,'" *What's on Stage* (May 8, 2017).

178. Ian Youngs, "Mat Fraser on Playing Richard III and TV's 'Pathetic' Disabled Casting," *BBC News* (May 4, 2017).

179. Mat Fraser, "All Theatres Should Cast at Least One Disabled Actor a Year," *Stage* (May 11, 2017).

180. Alfred Hickling, "Mat Fraser on Playing Richard III: 'I'd Begun to Feel Like Yesterday's Cripple,'" *Guardian* (May 8, 2017).

181. Harriet Sherwood, "'There's a Truth to It': RSC Casts Disabled Actor as Richard III," *Guardian* (February 7, 2022).

182. Lars Romann Engel and Nila Parly, "Casting and Directing Disability in *Richard III* at Kronborg Castle," *Otherness: Essays and Studies* 8, no. 2 (2021): 61.

183. Christopher Kelly, "Are Straight Actors in Gay Roles the New Blackface?" *Salon* (June 12, 2013).

184. Frances Ryan, "We Wouldn't Accept Actors Blacking Up, So Why Applaud 'Cripping Up'?" *Guardian* (January 13, 2015).

185. June Thomas, "Is It Ever OK to Cast a Cisgender Actor in a Transgender Role?" *Slate* (September 1, 2016).

186. Roberta Barker, "Bodies: Gender, Race, Ability, and the Shakespearean Stage," in *The Arden Research Handbook of Shakespeare and Contemporary Performance*, ed. Peter Kirwan and Kathryn Prince (London: Bloomsbury, 2021), 220.

187. Mike Lew, *Teenage Dick* (New York: Dramatists Play Service, 2019).

188. Kaite O'Reilly and Phillip Zarrilli, *richard iii redux* (2018), in *The "d" Monologues* (London: Oberon, 2018), 76.

CONCLUSION

1. Stephen Greenblatt, *Will in the World: How Shakespeare Became Shakespeare* (New York: Norton, 2004).

2. Jack Lynch, *Becoming Shakespeare: The Unlikely Afterlife That Turned a Provincial Playwright into the Bard* (New York: Walker, 2007), 9.

3. Jan Kott, *Shakespeare Our Contemporary*, trans. Boleslaw Taborski (Garden City, NY: Doubleday, 1964); Samuel Schoenbaum, *Shakespeare's Lives* (Oxford: Clarendon Press, 1970); Terence Hawkes, *That Shakespeherian Rag: Essays on a Critical Process* (London: Methuen, 1986); Graham Holderness, ed., *The Shakespeare Myth* (Manchester: Manchester University Press, 1988); Gary Taylor, *Reinventing Shakespeare: A Cultural History from the Restoration to the Present* (Oxford: Oxford University Press, 1989); and Jean Marsden, ed., *The Appropriation of Shakespeare: Post-Renaissance Reconstructions of the Works and the Myth* (New York: Hemel Hempstead, 1991).

4. *Borrowers and Lenders: A Journal of Shakespeare and Appropriation*, ed. Christy Desmet and Sujata Iyengar (2005–), http://www.borrowers.uga.edu.

5. Douglas Lanier, "Shakespeare and Cultural Studies: An Overview," *Shakespeare* 2, no. 2 (2006): 228–248.

6. Douglas Lanier, "Shakespearean Rhizomatics: Adaptation, Ethics, Value," in *Shakespeare and the Ethics of Appropriation*, ed. Alexander Huang and Elizabeth Rivlin (New York: Palgrave, 2014), 28.

7. Valerie M. Fazel and Louise Geddes, eds., "The Shakespeare User," in *The Shakespeare User: Critical and Creative Appropriations in a Networked Culture* (New York: Palgrave Macmillan, 2017), 4.

8. Gorgias of Leontini, *Encomium of Helen* (ca. 400 B.C.E.), trans. Michael Garagin and Paul Woodruff (Cambridge: Cambridge University Press, 1995); Plato, *Republic* (ca. 375), trans. G.M.A. Grube and C.D.C. Reeve (1995), in *Plato: Complete Works*, ed. John M. Cooper (Indianapolis: Hackett Publishing, 1997), Book X.

9. Aristotle, *Poetics* (ca. 335–323 B.C.E.), trans. Richard Janko (1987), in *The Norton Anthology of Theory and Criticism*, ed. Vincent B. Leitch, 2nd ed. (New York: Norton, 2010), 88–115.

10. See M. H. Abrams, "Orientation of Critical Theories," in *The Mirror and the Lamp: Romantic Theory and the Critical Tradition* (Oxford: Oxford University Press, 1953), 3–29.

11. Cleanth Brooks, "My Credo: The Formalist Critics," *Kenyon Review* 13 (1951): 71.

12. Harold Bloom, *A Map of Misreading* (New York: Oxford University Press, 1975), 19.

13. Stanley Fish, "Interpreting the *Variorum*," in *Is There a Text in This Class? The Authority of Interpretive Communities* (Cambridge, MA: Harvard University Press, 1980), 172.

14. Stephen Greenblatt, "The Circulation of Social Energy," in *Shakespearean Negotiations: The Circulation of Social Energy in Renaissance England* (Berkeley: University of California Press, 1988), 12.

15. Citing Martin Heidegger, John Dewey, and Ludwig Wittgenstein, Richard Rorty's *Philosophy and the Mirror of Nature* (Princeton, NJ: Princeton University Press, 1979) is the first to identify this anti-foundationalism. The term "anti-foundationalism" is coined and defined by Fish in such essays as "Consequences" (1985) and "Anti-Foundationalism, Theory Hope, and the Teaching of Composition" (1987), both in *Doing What Comes Naturally: Change Rhetoric, and the Practice of Theory in Literary and Legal Studies* (Durham, NC: Duke University Press, 1989).

16. Roland Barthes, "The Death of the Author," trans. Richard Howard, *Aspen* 5–6 (1967).

17. Michel Foucault, "What Is an Author?" (1969), in *Language, Counter-Memory, Practice: Selected Essays and Interviews*, ed. and trans. Donald F. Bouchard and Sherry Simon (Ithica, NY: Cornell University Press, 1977), 113–138.

18. For the argument audience-oriented theory was positioned against, see William K. Wimsatt and Monroe Beardsley, "The Affective Fallacy," *Sewanee Review* 57 (1949): 31–55.

19. For the major moments in reader-response theory, see Georges Poulet, "Phenomenology of Reading," *New Literary History* 1, no. 1 (1969): 53–68; Stanley Fish, "Discovery as Form in Paradise Lost" (1970), in *New Essays on Milton*, ed. by Thomas Kranidas (Berkeley: University of California Press, 1969), 1–14; Stanley Fish, "Litera-

ture in the Reader: Affective Stylistics," *New Literary History* 2, no. 1 (1970): 123–162; Wolfgang Iser, "Interaction between Text and Reader," in *The Reader in the Text: Essays on Audience and Interpretation*, ed. Susan R. Suleimoan and Inge Crosman (Princeton, NJ: Princeton University Press, 1980), 106–119; and Paul Ricoeur, "What Is a Text? Explanation and Understanding" (1971), in *Hermenentics and the Human Sciences*, ed. and trans. John Thompson (Cambridge: Cambridge University Press, 1981), 148–164.

20. The major statement on interpretive communities is Fish, "Interpreting the *Variorum*."

21. Stephen Booth, "On the Value of *Hamlet*," in *Reinterpretations of Elizabethan Drama*, ed. Norman Rabkin (New York: Columbia University Press, 1969), 138.

22. Norman Rabkin, foreword to *Reinterpretations of Elizabethan Drama*, v–x; Norman Rabkin, *Shakespeare and the Problem of Meaning* (Chicago: University of Chicago Press, 1981), 13.

23. Terence Hawkes, *Meaning by Shakespeare* (London: Routledge, 1992), 147.

24. Wolfgang Iser, "The Dramatization of Double Meaning in Shakespeare's *As You Like It*," *Theatre Journal* 35 (1983): 307–332; Wolfgang Iser, *Prospecting: From Reader Response to Literary Anthropology* (Baltimore: Johns Hopkins University Press, 1989).

25. Hans Robert Jauss, "Literary History as a Challenge to Literary Theory" (1967), trans. Elizabeth Benzinger, *New Literary History* 2, no. 1 (1970): 7–37; Steven Mailloux, "Rhetorical Hermeneutics," *Critical Inquiry* 11 (1985): 631.

26. Steven Mailloux, *Reception Histories: Rhetoric, Pragmatism, and American Cultural Politics* (Ithaca, NY: Cornell University Press, 1998), 55.

27. Steven Mailloux, *Disciplinary Identities: Rhetorical Paths of English, Speech, and Composition* (New York: MLA, 2006), 42.

28. Stuart Hall, *Cultural Studies 1983*, ed. Jennifer Daryl Slack and Lawrence Grossberg (Durham, NC: Duke University Press, 2016).

29. Peter Stallybrass, "Shakespeare, the Individual, and the Text," in *Cultural Studies*, ed. Lawrence Grossberg, Cary Nelson, and Paula Treichler (New York: Routledge, 1992), 593–610.

30. On the dominance of scientific attitudes in the U.S. university in the early twentieth century, see Gerald Graff, *Professing Literature: An Institutional History* (Chicago: University of Chicago Press, 1987), especially 65–80. Formalism rests on some of the "articles of faith" described by Brooks, "The Formalist Critics": e.g., "that literary criticism is a description and an evaluation of its object" and "that form is meaning" (72). Old historicism seeks to relate "how it really was," as called for by Leopold von Ranke, "Preface" to *Histories of the Latin and Teutonic Nations 1494–1514* (1824), trans. P. A. Ashworth (London: Bohn's Standard Library, 1909).

31. Cultural materialism was especially influenced by the politics of the "dialectical materialism" that grew out of Raymond Williams, "Notes on Marxism in Britain since 1945" (1976), in *Problems in Materialism and Culture: Selected Essays* (London: Verso, 1980), 233–251. For the founding texts of cultural materialism, see Jonathon Dollimore, *Radical Tragedy: Religion, Ideology and Power in the Drama of Shakespeare and His Contemporaries* (Chicago: University of Chicago Press, 1984); Jonathan Dollimore and Alan Sinfield, eds., *Political Shakespeare: New Essays in Cultural Materialism* (Manchester:

Manchester University Press, 1985); and Alan Sinfield, *Faultlines: Cultural Materialism and the Politics of Dissident Reading* (Berkeley: University of California Press, 1992).

32. For a more detailed discussion, see Neema Parvini, *Shakespeare and Contemporary Theory: New Historicism and Cultural Materialism* (London: Bloomsbury, 2012).

33. New historicism is especially influenced by Clifford Geertz and his idea of "Thick Description: Toward an Interpretive Theory of Culture," in *The Interpretation of Cultures: Selected Essays* (New York: Basic Books, 1973), 3–30. For the founding texts of new historicism, see Stephen Greenblatt, "Towards a Poetics of Culture" (1987), in *The New Historicism*, ed. H. Aram Veeser (New York: Routledge, 1989), 1–14; and Louis Adrian Montrose, "Professing the Renaissance: The Poetics and Politics of Culture," in *The New Historicism*, 15–36.

34. Stephen Greenblatt, introduction to "The Forms of Power and the Power of Forms in the Renaissance," *Genre* 15 (1982): 3.

35. See Robin Headlam Wells, "'Historicism' and 'Presentism' in Early Modern Studies," *Cambridge Quarterly* 29, no. 1 (2000): 37–60; Hugh Grady, "Shakespeare Studies, 2005: A Situated Overview," *Shakespeare* 1, no. 1 (2005): 102–120; Tracey Sedinger, "Theory Terminable and Interminable: On Presentism, Historicism, and the Problem of *Hamlet*," *Exemplaria* 19, no. 3 (Fall 2007): 455–473; and Ros King, "Dramaturgy: Beyond the Presentism/Historicism Dichotomy," *Shakespearean International Yearbook* 7 (2007): 6–21.

36. David Scott Kastan, *Shakespeare after Theory* (London: Routledge, 1999), 31. See also Jonathan Gil Harris, "The New New Historicism's Wunderkammer of Objects," *European Journal of English Studies* 4, no. 3 (2000): 125–139; Douglass Bruster, "The New Materialism in Renaissance Studies," in *Shakespeare and the Question of Culture: Early Modern Literature and the Cultural Turn* (New York: Palgrave, 2003), 191–206; Andrew Hadfield, "Shakespeare and Republicanism: History and Cultural Materialism," *Textual Practice* 17 (2003): 461–483; Duncan Salkeld, "Shakespeare Studies, Presentism, and Micro-History," *Cahiers Elisabéthains* 76 (2009): 35–43; and Paul Stevens, "The New Presentism and Its Discontents: Listening to *Eastward Ho* and Shakespeare's *Tempest* in Dialogue," in *Rethinking Historicism from Shakespeare to Milton*, ed. Anne Coiro Baynes and Thomas Fulton (Cambridge: Cambridge University Press, 2012), 133–158.

37. Terence Hawkes, *Shakespeare in the Present* (London: Routledge, 2002), 4. See also Hugh Grady, "Terence Hawkes and Presentism," *Critical Survey* 26, no. 3 (2014): 6–14. "Shot through with chips of Messianic time," presentism is grounded in Walter Benjamin's "Theses on the Philosophy of History," in *Illuminations: Essays and Reflections*, ed. Hannah Arendt, trans. Harry Zohn (New York: Schocken, 1968), 263.

38. See Stephen Greenblatt, "The Circulation of Social Energy," in *Shakespearean Negotiations: The Circulation of Social Energy in Renaissance England* (Berkeley: University of California Press, 1988): "I began with the desire to speak with the dead" (1).

39. Hugh Grady and Terence Hawkes, eds., introduction to *Presentist Shakespeares* (London: Routledge, 2007), 4, 2.

40. Donald Hendrick and Bryan Reynolds, eds., "Shakespace and Transversal Power," in *Shakespeare without Class: Misappropriations of Cultural Power* (New York: Palgrave Macmillan, 2000), 3.

41. Julia Reinhard Lupton, "Recent Studies in Tudor and Stuart Drama," *SEL Studies in English Literature 1500–1900* 54, no. 2 (2014): 485.

42. Philip Sidney, *An Apology for Poetry (or the Defence of Poesy)* (ca. 1579–1581), ed. Geofrey Shepherd, rev. R. W. Maslen (Manchester: Manchester University Press, 2002).

43. Milton Nahm, *The Artist as Creator* (Baltimore: Johns Hopkins University Press, 1956), 12.

44. That description of literature is influenced by Kenneth Burke, "Literature as Equipment for Living," in *Philosophy of the Literary Form: Studies in Symbolic Action*, 3rd ed. (Berkeley: University of California Press, 1973), 293–304.

Index

Abad, Ricardo, 173
Abbey, Edwin Austin, 156
Abildgaard, Nicolai, 133
ableism, 16, 23, 27, 160–161, 174
Abrams, M. H., 196
Adamantius the Sophist, 43
Addison, Joseph, 135
Adler, Alfred, 140
African Grove, 2, 161–164, 167–168
Agathyllus, 44
Al-Bassam, Sulayman, 171
Aldridge, Ira, 164
Alliance for Inclusion in the Arts, 176
Americans with Disabilities Act of 1990, 174, 179, 189
Anderson, Lisa, 168
Anderson, Susan, 16, 17
Andry, Nicolas, 136
Anne, Lady and Queen, 27–29, 54, 55, 61, 64, 78–81, 91–94, 97–98, 117, 153, 167
anthropology of audience, 3, 15, 145–146, 176, 194–195, 199–200, 205–207
Antichrist, 32, 92
anti-figural interpretation, 116–119, 129–131, 227n40
Aristotle, 42, 44, 73–74, 195
Arneaux, J. A., 164
Ashby, Richard, 173

Assheton, William, 115
Auerbach, Erich, 46, 56, 135, 137
Augustine, 10–12
Auslander, Philip, 176

Bacon, Francis, 50, 69, 108, 116, 125, 137–138
Baker, Richard, 115
Bannister, John, 148
Barker, Roberta, 189
Barthes, Roland, 197
Barton-Farcas, Stephanie, 181–183
Bate, Jonathan, 199
Bateman, Kate and Ellen, 165–166
Bates, Alan, 3–4
Baumbach, Sibylle, 75
Beal, Frances, 162
Bearden, Elizabeth, 4, 7
Beatles, 22
Beaumont, John, 113
Bedford, Brian, 171
Beer, Sara, 190
Bell, Christopher, 16
Benedetti, Jean, 134
Benjamin, Walter, 7
Ben-Moshe, Liat, 160
Betty, William Henry West, 165
bible, 10–11, 28, 40, 52

Bida, Alexandre, 134
Blake, William, 133
Bloom, Harold, 196
Boaistuau, Pierre, 49
Booth, Edwin, 154–156
Booth, Junius Brutus, 150, 153, 164
Booth, Stephen, 197
Bourne, Randolph, 138
Brecht, Bertolt, 171
Brooke, Christopher, 112
Brooke, Gustavus Vaughan, 154
Brooks, Cleanth, 196
Brown, Carlyle, 167–168
Brown, William Henry, 161, 164, 167
Buck, George, 38, 116, 129
Buckingham, Duke of, 76, 85–90, 93
Burbage, Richard, 1, 3, 111, 178
Burton, William, 32
Byron, George Gordon, Lord, 139

Camden, William, 115
Capell, Edward, 133
Caryll, John, 114
Castiglione, Baldassarre, 43
Catesby, William, 85–86, 89–90
causal paradigm, 50, 55–65, 67, 69, 97–98, 105, 107, 110, 115–132, 134, 137–144
Cecil, Robert, 112–113, 170
Cerberus, 52
Chakravarty, Urvashi, 160
Charles I, King, 170
Charlton, James, 138
Charnes, Linda, 18, 65
Charney, Maurice, 103
Choate, Evan, 168
Chute, Anthony, 42
Cibber, Colley, 121–123, 131–132, 150, 156, 158, 235n38
Clarence, Duke of, 38, 59, 71–72, 76, 82–83, 88
Clarence's son, 82–83
Clifford, Old, 47, 54, 71, 80
Clifford, Young, 47, 54
Clint, George, 150
Clubbe, John, 136
Cobham, Thomas, 150
Cohen, Adam, 51
Coker, Lauren, 168
Coleridge, Samuel Taylor, 129

Collins, Patricia Hill, 162
Comber, Abigail, 49
Connolly, Phillipa Vincent, 36
Cooke, George Frederick, 148–149, 163
Corbalis, Brendan, 168
Corbet, Richard, 111
Cornwallis, William, 116
Couldock, Charles Walter, 154
Crenshaw, Kimberlé, 162, 167, 169
cripping, 176–191
cripping up, 176–178, 240n127
Cromwell, Oliver, 170
Crowne, John, 114
Crump, Casper, 188
Cumberbatch, Benedict, 185, 191

Dalí, Salvador, 20–22
Dance-Holland, Nathaniel, 123
Dante, 52
Daston, Lorraine, 12
Dávidházi, Péter, 199
Davies, John, of Hereford, 111
Davis, Ethel, 137
Davis, Lennard, 135, 140, 174, 178
"Deformity Not Always a Sign of an Ill Man" (1746), 138
De Grazia, Margreta, 199
Dennis, John, 137
Derrick, Samuel, 124
Descartes, René, 108
Desmet, Christy, 194
Dethe, 103–104
Deutsch, Helen, 138
Dighton, Robert, 148
Dinklage, Peter, 181
disability, 3–5, 15–16, 17, 20, 138, 213n55
Disability Discrimination Act of 1995, 179, 189
disability history, 5, 15–18
disability studies, 1, 15–16, 134–144, 178
disability theater, 175–191
disability visibility, 3
Dobson, Michael, 199
Dollimore, Jonathan, 200
Dolman, John, 39
dramatic reality, 97–106, 123–124, 132–134
Drayton, Michael, 111
Drummond, Samuel, 148
Dryden, John, 117
Duffy, Carol Ann, 185

Dunn, Leslie, 178
Dunthorne, Anna, 3
Duterte, Rodrigo, 173

Edward IV, King, 6, 71, 101, 103, 114
Edward V, King, 27, 76, 93
Eidinger, Lars, 172, 191
Elizabeth Woodville, Queen, 71, 76, 82, 84–87, 91–95
Elizabeth I, Queen, 26, 42
Equestri, Alice, 17
Erasmus, 74
Erevelles, Nirmala, 162
etiology, 9, 13, 143–144
evil, 10–13, 15, 19–20

Fahy, Thomas, 176
Fazel, Valerie, 194
Fehling, Jürgen, 156
Ferrer, José, 156, 171
Ferrers, George, 38–39
Fiedler, Leslie, 140
figuralism, 46, 135, 137–138
figural paradigm, 29–57, 60, 63, 65, 69, 78–81, 91, 94, 96, 98–101, 105, 107, 110–124, 127, 129, 135, 140–141, 143–144
figural realism, 46, 98
Fish, Stanley, 5, 7, 13–14, 108, 196–199
Fisher, Clara, 165
Fisher, Jane, 165
FitzGerald, Katherine, Countess of Desmond, 119, 151–152
Fletcher, Giles, 42
Ford, B. J., 164
Forrest, Edwin, 150–154
Foucault, Michel, 16, 135, 197
Fraser, Mat, 186–187, 189
Frazer, James, 53
Freer, Charles, 150
Freud, Sigmund, 53–54, 56–63, 69, 125–126, 174
Fuseli, Henry, 132–133

Gaines, Barbara, 168
Galen, 43
Garland-Thomson, Rosemarie, 66, 135, 140, 160, 166, 178
Garrick, David, 1, 120, 123–126, 134, 136, 147, 178, 191

Geddes, Louise, 194
Gentleman, Francis, 127
Geoffroy Saint-Hilaire, Étienne and Isidore, 136
Gerzić, Marina, 173
Gilbert, John, 154
Godden, Richard, 4–5
Goebbels, Joseph, 156, 170
Goffman, Erving, 45, 67–69, 71, 90, 110, 140
Goltzius, Hendrick, 42
Goodbye Girl, The (1977), 168
Gorgias, 195
Goring, Marius, 156, 178
Grady, Hugh, 199
Graeae Theatre Company, 176
Grafton, Richard, 36
Greenblatt, Stephen, 172–173, 193, 196, 200–201
Griffith, Elizabeth, 126, 128, 132
Gurira, Danai, 169

Hall, Edward, 36, 103
Hall, Joseph, 12
Hall, Kim Q., 166
Haller, Albrecht von, 136
Halls, John James, 148
Halsted, Caroline Amelia, 151
Hamilton, William, 133
Hanson, N. R., 108
Harvey, William, 136
Hastings, William, Lord, 39, 72, 76, 85–88, 93–94
Hawkes, Terence, 194, 197–199, 201–202
Hay, William, 118, 137–140
Hayman, Francis, 123
Hazlitt, William, 129, 133–134
Hegel, Georg Wilhelm Friedrich, 136
Henry VI, King, 12, 54, 98–99, 123, 133
Henry VII, King, 25–26, 30, 34, 41–42, 47, 51, 76, 80, 93–98, 100, 114, 122, 132
Henry VIII, King, 26, 30, 36
hermeneutics, 20, 143–144
Hervey, John, 137
Hewlett, James, 163–164, 167
Heywood, Thomas, 102, 111, 113
Hill, Thomas, 43–44, 69, 73–74
Hippocrates, 42
historical presentism, 202–203

historicism, 193–194, 196, 200–203
Hitler, Adolf, 170
Hobgood, Allison, 8, 16, 17, 50, 66, 77, 181
Hogarth, William, 120, 123, 133, 134, 191
Holden, Henry, 181–182
Holderness, Graham, 171, 194, 199
Holinshed, Raphael, 40, 42, 59, 105
Holloway, James, 150
Hollow Crown, The, 85, 185
Holm, Ian, 156, 178
Holman, George, 148
House of Cards, 2, 172
Howard, Henry, 134
Howard, Jean, 13
Hughes, Arthur, 187
Hugo, Victor, 140
Hume, David, 120, 129, 135
Hunt, Leigh, 148
Hunter, Kathryn, 169, 180–181
Hussein, Saddam, 171

Indagine, Johannes, 43
intersectionality, 16, 160–170, 180
irony, 2–3, 9–10, 19, 142, 175
Irving, Henry, 85, 154–157, 178, 235n35
Iser, Wolfgang, 198–199
Iyengar, Sujata, 194

James, King, 105–106
Jauss, Hans Robert, 198
Jessner, Leopold, 159, 170–171
Jim Crow, 164
Joan of Arc, 99, 101–102
Johns, Geoffrey, 49
Johnson, Samuel, 125–127, 129, 131–132, 136, 139
Johnston, Kirsty, 176
Jonson, Ben, 111
Joshua, Essaka, 135
Juvenal, 138

Kafer, Alison, 162, 174
Kant, Immanuel, 11, 135, 136
Kastan, David Scott, 201
Kean, Charles, 150–151, 159
Kean, Edmund, 1, 133–134, 148–150, 153, 163, 178
Kemble, John Phillip, 133, 147

Kierkegaard, Søren, 129
King, Deborah, 162, 165
King, Henry, 114
King, Martin Luther, Jr., 167
Klett, Elizabeth, 180
Kostihova, Marcela, 144, 180
Kott, Jan, 194
Kuhn, Thomas, 29–39, 41, 45–47, 108–110, 115, 118, 124–127, 140, 142–144
Kuppers, Petra, 176–177

Lamb, Charles, 148
Lanier, Douglas, 194
Lavater, Johann Kaspar, 75, 135–136
Lee, Nathaniel, 117
Le Fevre, Mrs., 146
Legge, Thomas, 41
Leroux, Gaston, 140
Lew, Mike, 189–190
Lichtenberg, Georg Christoph, 75, 136
Lin, Zhaohua, 171
Linton, Simi, 140, 178
Lisbon earthquake of 1755, 10–13, 142
Little, William John, 136
Locrine, The Lamentable Tragedie of, 104
Loftis, Sonya Freeman, 17, 185
Loncraine, Richard, 168, 171
Long, Edwin, 156
Longmore, Paul, 15
Lorde, Audre, 167
Love, Genevieve, 14, 17
Lucifer, 52
Lynch, Jack, 193

Macready, William Charles, 150
Madigan, Stephen, 193–194
magical thinking, 53–54, 62–63, 65, 67
Mailloux, Steven, 198–199
Mansfield, Richard, 156–157
Margaret, Queen, 50–55, 57, 66, 68, 76, 78, 94–106, 114, 119, 123, 128, 142
Marlowe, Christopher, 99, 101, 104
Marsden, Jean, 194, 199
Martial, 44
Master of the Mallet, 133
McCarthy, Grace, 17
McCullough, John, 154
McKellen, Ian, 160, 168, 171, 191

McRuer, Robert, 68, 162–163, 168
meaning, 7, 9, 14, 20, 194–195, 200, 202
Merrick, Joseph, 140
metaphysics of stigma, 10–13, 47, 50–55, 92–106, 121–124, 135, 143
Miller, Donald, 137
Milton, John, 52, 110, 170
Minear, Andrea, 162
Mitchell, David, 16, 83, 140, 160, 178
Mittman, Asa Simon, 4–5
modernization, 13, 134, 142–145
Molyneaux, Paul, 164
monstrosity, 3–7, 12, 18, 40–42, 44–45, 49, 52–53, 77, 87, 104, 111–116, 118, 135–137, 140, 148, 210n14, 218n32
Montagu, Elizabeth, 126–127, 132
Montagu, Mary Wortley, 137
Montaigne, Michel de, 135
Monthly Mirror, 133
More, Thomas, 34–42, 76–77, 87, 89, 116, 127, 152
Moreno, Rene, 183
Moriarty, Michael, 171
Mozgala, Gregg, 189
Mulvany, Kate, 169, 185–186
Muppet Show, The, 22
Myrroure for Magistrates, 38–39, 111–112

Naeemi, Hamid-Reza, 172
narcissistic physiognomic revisionism, 58–60, 82–91
Nashe, Thomas, 100
Neagle, James, 132
Neiman, Susan, 10–13
Nevil, Cecily, the Duchess of York, 25, 30, 35, 51–52, 55–57, 76, 83–84, 88, 91–94
Niccols, Richard, 111–112
Noah, Mordecai, 161
normality, 16, 67, 71, 110, 160
normal science, 45, 109–110
Northcote, James, 148
Nutter, William, 148

Oliver, Mike, 178
Olivier, Laurence, 2, 20–22, 85, 156, 159, 178, 191
O'Reilly, Kaite, 190–191

orthopedics, 135–137
Ostermeier, Thomas, 172
Ovid, 52

Pacino, Al, 171
Paré, Ambroise, 41, 49, 69
Park, Katharine, 12
Parker, Henry, 115
Parly, Nila, 188
Parsons, James, 74, 136
pathognomy, 74–75
Patterson, Debbie, 194
Payntour, John, 32
Phelps, Samuel, 150
physiognomy, 40, 42–46, 59, 73–76, 135–136, 140
Plato, 42, 195
Poel, William, 158
Polanyi, Michael, 45
Pope, Alexander, 118, 137–139
Poppelau, Nicholas von, 216n13
Porta, Giambattista della, 44, 135
Porter, Martin Henry, 43
Potměšil, Jan, 179–180
Power, Will, 173
presentism, 193, 200–203
prodigies, 12–13, 40, 49–51, 78, 81, 114

Quayson, Ato, 140

Rabkin, Norman, 7, 14, 197, 199
Rainolde, Richard, 36–38
reader-response criticism, 5, 7, 13–14, 196–197, 199, 244–245n19
realism, 46, 135
Rees, James, 151–154
Rehnquist, William H., 129
Requiem of the Rose King (2013–), 168
Reynolds, Bryan, 202
Richard, Duke of York, 25, 84–85, 93
Richard III: disability of, 26–29; implicativity of, 9–10, 19–20; multi-temporality of, 2–3, 5, 14, 15, 18–19; portraits of, 32–33, 36–37, 42, 111, 116, 120–123; royal seal of, 39–40, 52, 93–94; skeleton discovered, 1, 26, 140, 144, 184–185, 191
@Richard_Third, 172
Richardson, William, 129

Richer, Dave, 175
Rocca, Bartolomeo della (called Cocles), 43–44
Rodway, Norman, 156
Rossiter, A. P., 40
Rous, John, 30–35, 39, 59, 76–77, 80, 92, 115–116
Roussat, Richard (called Arcandam), 43–44
Rowe, Nicholas, 118, 120–123, 133–134
Row-Heyveld, Lindsey, 4, 17, 64, 81
Rowley, Samuel, 113

Sandahl, Carrie, 174, 176–177, 187
Sandford, Samuel, 114
Satan, 52
Sawyer, Elizabeth, 104
Schalk, Sami, 162
Schlegel, August Wilhelm von, 65, 129, 144
Schoch, Richard, 159
Schoenbaum, Samuel, 194
Schweitzer, Marlis, 165
Schwyzer, Philip, 95
Scot, Reginald, 104
Scratch, Annabel, 148
Scylla, 52
Sellers, Peter, 22
Shakespeare, William, works of: *Coriolanus*, 104; *Cymbeline*, 104; *Hamlet*, 9; *1 Henry IV*, 126; *2 Henry IV*, 104; *Henry V*, 108; *1 Henry VI*, 72, 99–102; *2 Henry VI*, 47, 49, 66, 99, 102–103; *3 Henry VI*, 12, 50–51, 55–56, 58, 62–64, 71–72, 76, 79, 80, 88, 91, 99–101, 103, 118–120, 125; *Julius Caesar*, 10, 11; *King John*, 13, 104; *King Lear*, 13, 106; *Lover's Complaint*, 108; *Lucrece*, 74–75; *Macbeth*, 11, 75, 105–106; *Merchant of Venice*, 83, 104; *Richard III*, 1–2, 5–13, 25, 34, 51–55, 57–62, 64, 71–106, 112, 117–118, 160; *Romeo and Juliet*, 9, 104; *Venus and Adonis*, 104
Sharp, William, 133
Shaw, George Bernard, 158
Sher, Antony, 178–179, 191
Sherbo, Arthur, 199
Show Must Go Online, The, 168
Shrek, 22–23
Sidney, Philip, 203–106
Siebers, Tobin, 1, 15, 66, 140, 160

Siemon, James, 2, 65, 118
Sinfield, Alan, 200
Singleton, Henry, 148
Skinker, Tannakin, 104
Slotkin, Joel, 76
Smee, Dominic, 29
Smith, Samuel Morgan, 164
Snyder, Sharon, 16, 83, 140, 160, 178
Sommers, Will, 36
Speed, John, 115
Spenser, Edmund, 104
Stalin, Joseph, 170
Stallybrass, Peter, 199
Stanley, Thomas, Earl of Derby, 76, 86, 93–94, 95
Steevens, George, 127–128, 132
stigma, 47, 50, 51, 66–68, 98; psychological model of, 55–66; sociological model of, 65–69; spiritual model of, 50–55, 65–66
Stiker, Henri-Jacques, 16, 135, 140, 178
Stothard, Thomas, 133
Stow, John, 38, 116
Stuart, Gilbert, 147
Sullivan, Barry, 154
Sully, Thomas, 148

Taft, Charles, 161–163
Talbot, Thomas, 111
Taylor, Gary, 194, 199
teratology, 135–136, 141
Tey, Josephine, 129
That Most Important Thing: Love (1975), 168
theatrical historicism, 146–160
theatrical intersectionality, 169–170
Theobald, Lewis, 119
Thompson, Ayanna, 160
Thornton, Michael Patrick, 184–185
Tillyard, E.M.W., 25, 65, 144
Torrey, Michael, 73
tragedy, 2–3, 7–10, 19–20, 44–45, 67, 96, 103, 173–174
True Tragedie of Richard the Third, The, 41–42, 50, 100
Trump, Donald, 2, 173–174
Trussell, John, 115
Tudor myth, 25–26, 29, 95–96, 118
Turner, David, 135
Turner, Sharon, 150

Tyler, Dennis, Jr., 164
Tylor, E. B., 53

Union of the Physically Impaired Against Segregation, 15, 66, 178

Vergil, Polydore, 34–35
Vice, the, 63–65, 85
visuality, 3, 78, 81, 91, 108–111, 118
Voltaire, 11, 120

Walpole, Horace, 118–119, 126, 129, 142
Wang, Xiaoying, 172
Warburton, William, 119–120, 132
Warde, James Prescott, 150
Warkany, Josef, 136
Washington, Denzel, 168
Weird Sisters, 105–106
Weldon, Anthony, 115
West, Caitlin Mary, 186
Whately, Thomas, 127

Whitelaw, Archibald, 30, 116
Wiegandt, Kai, 173
Williams, Katherine Schaap, 2, 17, 66, 76–77, 87, 174
Wincoll, Thomas, 113
Winstanley, Eliza, 166
Winstanley, William, 116
Wiśniewski, Grzegorz, 172
Withers, A. J., 160
Wolff, Caspar Friedrich, 136
Wolfit, Donald, 156, 170
Wong, Alice, 3
Wood, David Houston, 5, 16, 65, 77
Woodson, Elizabeth Morton, 166
Wright, Beatrice, 140
Wright, J. A., 154

Yarington, Robert, 104

Zarrilli, Phillip, 190
Zhang, Dongyu, 172

JEFFREY R. WILSON is a teacher-scholar at Harvard University and the author of *Shakespeare and Trump* (Temple).

www.ingramcontent.com/pod-product-compliance
Lightning Source LLC
Chambersburg PA
CBHW030534230426
43665CB00010B/883